H/68

FASHION
IN LITERATURE

FASHION IN LITERATURE

A STUDY OF CHANGING TASTE

BY

E. E. KELLETT

AUTHOR OF "THE STORY OF MYTHS," ETC.

LONDON

GEORGE ROUTLEDGE
& SONS, LTD.

1931

CONTENTS

CONTENTS

FASHION IN LITERATURE

I

ON TASTE IN GENERAL

THIS book will be restricted to the study of literary
taste, and will probably be finished long before even
that bounded theme has been half exhausted. Nevertheless, it may be desirable to halt on the threshold in
order to consider for a moment the general conception
of which literary taste is but one manifestation. Even
the most obvious ideas may put on a certain clearness,
if defined, in the good old fashion, by genus and
differentia : and literary taste is far from an obvious
idea. It belongs, pretty plainly, to the same wide
class as musical taste, artistic taste, the taste for
natural beauty, and æsthetic sensibility generally :
but it is by no means easy to mark the lines which
separate it from these related feelings. Its rules,
if it had any, are not theirs : witness the appalling
opinions often passed on Milton by good judges of
Beethoven : yet these two great men must be similar,
and it is certain that Milton himself would have
appreciated Beethoven, and would have found in him
a kindred spirit. The rules of painting, again, are
like those of poetry, but, as Lessing showed once for
all, they are not the same. Painting gains by being
directly presented to the eye, which, if Horace is

B

right, has a great advantage over the ear as a means
of stirring the imagination ; and its rules are aimed
at making the most of that advantage. But poetry
can describe continuous action, and may thus make
up for its deficiencies in other respects. The laws of
each art tell the art, first, how to make full use of its
best points, and secondly, how it may ' turn its necessity to glorious gain ' : and neither its strong points nor
its necessities are the same as those of any other art.
It is only with some caution, then, that the study of
art in general can be applied to the use of one art in
particular. None the less, as these arts *have* after all
much in common, and as the tastes to which they
appeal have much in common also, we can hardly
speak of one without at least attending to another.
Assuredly no man can be a good judge of any art unless
he has some, however slight, acquaintance with
another to which he may compare it. It may pay us,
then, if we trace all these similar but different tastes
to their common original : for we cannot appreciate
difference till we form some conception of likeness.
And, as so often, we find the original a commonplace,
almost vulgar conception. All these varied sensibilities
are called tastes because they resemble, in a marked
and unmistakable manner, the simple physical sensation which is one of the very first the human being is
capable of. The word, starting with this humble
connotation, has gradually enlarged itself until it
embraces some of the very highest powers of the
human mind. But, airy and delicate as it often is, it
still retains marks of the hole of the pit whence it
was digged. As we can recognise in the most intellectual of men the clear traces of their descent from
arboreal ancestors—as, for example, our upright gait,

though a second nature, still plainly shows that it is not our first—so the most exquisite and refined literary or artistic taste shows by its very name that it has ' poor relations ' ; and, as comparative anatomy is useful to us in studying our own frame, so some light may be thrown upon the most refined of literary experiences by a consideration, however hasty, of the parental germ from which these other phrases are derived.

The word *taste*, the philologists tell us, comes ultimately from *tangere* to touch—it is a frequentative or intensive form of that verb. In this sense, of course, the tangent tastes the circle. But if we imagine the circle, as Canning[1] imagined the triangle, to put on human feelings, if we picture ' circles joining in osculation sweet,' we get an image of what happened later to the word. We came to limit tasting to touching with the tongue or palate, and forgot entirely that it once was used of contact with the tips of the fingers. The gain of this division of labour was, however, great. The word did not lose the sense of resistance, roughness, or smoothness, associated with touch : but it acquired in addition the connotations of sweetness, sourness, and all the other sensations we associate with the tongue or palate : so much so that, as we shall see later, we can talk of tactile tastes without noticing the pleonasm. This is aided, I think, by the fact that some tastes, especially those of the palate, are passive or reflex, whereas in others, though we cannot call them fully active, we are more or less conscious that we are using the tip of the tongue, and that the

---

[1] Or somebody else. The *Antijacobin* is of composite authorship ; and the *Loves of the Triangles* is said to be the joint work of Canning, Ellis, and Hookham Frere.

mind is taking some part in the process. This is certainly the case with those extraordinary people called ' tea-tasters ' : they are assuredly mental workers. In that case, however, in my opinion the word has gone beyond its proper use ; these gentlemen, as I shall indicate in a moment, ought to be called tea-critics or tea-discriminators. But the intervening stages, in which taste is half-way on to criticism, may be well exemplified by Chaucer's description of the Friar :

> ' Somwhat he lipsed, for his wantownesse,
> To make his English swete upon his tonge ' ;

where we see almost the exact point of transition between the physical and the mental applications of the term taste. We see the Friar experiencing a physical sensation, but we also catch him taking mental note of it ; we can all but see the persuasive and eloquent Franciscan *touching* the sounds with his tongue, and feeling their sweetness. Having satisfied himself that they *are* dainty and attractive, he sets out on his circuits in order by means of his *sweet* English, to charm a ' pitaunce ' out of the widows he meets.

This transition is further assisted, I doubt not, by the common confusion, of which Shakespeare himself is guilty, between tasting and testing. The two words have, originally, nothing in common ; but, as with *aby* and *abide*, or *mean* and *demean*, the likeness has led to the annexation of the realm of each by the other. When Sir Toby says to Viola, ' Taste your legs, sir, put them in motion,' there can be no doubt that the two words could be used interchangeably. And so also when *we*, who ought to know better, speak of those ' tea-tasters,' we are really hesitating between the taste and the test—a hesitation which would be dangerous in the case of arsenic or aconite. *Test*, I may say in passing, is from *testa*, a pot,[1] and, like *terra*, the earth, is ultimately derived from a word meaning *dry*. But this quite accidental likeness in the words is a type of what happens with the ideas. Taste passes very rapidly into discrimination : so rapidly indeed that we cannot decide the instant at which it does so. And, as we shall see, literary taste does the same thing. It is not by any means easy to tell when our mere *sense* of the beauty of a poem passes into criticism of it. We shall find, if we look carefully into Reynolds's *Discourses*, that he constantly leaps from one to the other, as if he knew no difference between the two ; and, what is more surprising, Newman, in his essay on Aristotle's *Poetics*, is equally loose, and in one place actually identifies taste with good sense. Nevertheless, I think it exceedingly desirable to keep the two, as far as possible, apart in our minds, as we keep youth apart from maturity, or maturity from age, though we can never draw a clear line between them. Things are well worth distinguishing in thought, though in the outer world they may overlap.

I might draw here a comparison between taste and experimental science. Most of us remember how Bacon traces the various stages of experiment from *mera palpatio*—just a touch—through *inductio per enumerationem simplicem*, to the practical certainty which arises when the instances are numerous and the comparisons and distinctions precise. But there is no clear line marking off these stages from each other : even at the end of the series the certainty is never more than extreme probability, and at the beginning the slight chance is a probability after all. So with taste :

[1] So that *test-tube* is a pleonasm.

it begins with a *mera palpatio*, passes on into comparing, distinguishing, and testing, and terminates in something beyond itself, which is usually called criticism. But there is no marked division between these stages. They shade off gradually into each other, and in the highest criticism there is often to be traced something of the 'just-touching' of its poor and despised ancestor.

Thus, like all expressions for mental modes and processes, the word taste involves a metaphor drawn from a bodily sensation. We *see* a geometrical proof : this is a figure from sight ; and to *see* is itself probably, in origin, merely to follow ; it connotes a chase and finally a capture. We *grasp* an argument ; here the figure is still more obvious. But we *taste* the beauty or simplicity of the demonstration : the image here is from yet another bodily sense. And it is worth noticing that this image is much more powerful and persistent than the others : the metaphor is surely not entirely dead. We feel it, subconsciously or otherwise, to be endlessly appropriate, as we do not with most of the established metaphors. We rarely desert it for another, as we do with seeing and grasping. Not only is the word still very much alive in its literal and primary sense, but even when transferred to the mental sphere it carries, I imagine, as often as not, a conscious apprehension of its material associations. All forms of physical taste have their analogues in literary or artistic appraisals ; and, in judging works of high intellectual rank we have our dinners or lunches before us as a sort of standard of comparison. Mendelssohn, says the musical critic, is too 'sugary' : the style of *Samson Agonistes* is 'austere,' that is, it makes the tongue dry : the humour of Swift leaves a bitter taste in the mouth : Keats is sometimes too ' luscious ' : we ' like ' this, we ' savour ' that : Browning is harsh or ' rough on the palate ' : the *Rehearsal* ' has not wit enough to keep it sweet ' : so and so ' nauseates.' ' Poetry,' said Coleridge, ' ought not always to have its highest relish.' Occasionally the metaphor is drawn out into a formal and recognised simile, as when Macaulay remarks that to read Seneca through is like dining exclusively on anchovy sauce and *pâté de foie gras :* or as when Bacon, in one of the most famous passages in literature, says that some books are to be chewed and digested, some swallowed, and some *tasted*—that is, merely *touched* with the tongue. All of us, in fact, acknowledge a close analogy between the feeling aroused by a work of art, whatever its kind, and the tasting of food.

My tentative account of taste, then, will be this— it is the mental power which enjoys or rejects an external work of art or nature, in a fashion analogous to that in which the palate enjoys or rejects the food that is presented to it. An art of taste is an art of enjoyment : and the training of taste, if such a thing should turn out to be possible, consists in teaching the mental palate to enjoy more keenly, and to discover more refined objects to enjoy. Mark that I call this definition tentative : there will be some points in which we may be inclined to alter it. But we are not likely to get rid of the metaphor of a ' mental palate.'

If then this ' taste,' however high it may soar, remains like Wordsworth's skylark, ' true to the kindred points of heaven and home,' it may be of use to consider briefly what the physiologists have to say about the humble original of this dainty, chastened, and educated mental capacity of ours. There are, we are told, three kinds of physical taste. There are relishes and their opposites, disgusts : these are closely allied with the digestive apparatus, they are large and massive, not acute, they are somewhat rough, and tend to give way, as the palate is educated, to less coarse appreciations. A savage may be said to ' relish ' his animal food, but hardly so clearly to discriminate his feelings as to arrive at taste proper ; and his ' disgust,' if it arises, may take very obvious and violent forms. He would rarely, one fancies, be able to tell us where the pleasure arising from the satisfaction of hunger ceases and the epicurean titillation of the palate begins. Children, again, as a rule, relish sweet things that would revolt their elders ; with time they come to prefer more neutral savours. We instinctively feel that it is un-natural for a child to like the foods that please its parents : and, on the other hand, few things are re-garded as surer marks of vulgarity than the gust of a savage if exhibited by a civilised man.

Such ' relishes ' find their parallel in the literary sphere. Violent effects, sharp contrasts, exaggerations, puns, paradoxes, excessive alliterations, these appeal to the uncultivated taste. The orator addressing a mob has to employ coarser methods than those which are adapted to an assembly of dons : and an essay of Addison's fails utterly when read to those who are accustomed to the captions and startling phrases of a daily newspaper. A figure of speech which earns the admiration of a child, to whom it is new, will not stir the languid pulse of a man who has seen a thousand examples of it, and observed it catalogued and analysed in half a dozen manuals of rhetoric. Münchhausen adventures, hairbreadth escapes, murders and Udolpho mysteries are ' relished ' by the unsophisticated palate :

they cloy with years, and Jane Austen gains the suffrage once given unhesitatingly to the ' big bow-wow style.' St. John's parable, in the Apocalypse, of the book which was in his mouth sweet as honey, but which when swallowed produced bitterness and revolt, might be applied to the change of taste which thus so often shows itself as man passes from youth to maturity.

From ' relish ' we turn to Taste proper. This specially distinguishes not the rich and the neutral but the sweet and the bitter : and it is possible to detect in it some approach to the intellectual. We can mark degrees in it ; it is not ' massive ' but ' acute ' ; and we can recall afterwards certain manifestations of it almost as readily and distinctly as sensations of smell. In Taste proper (it is a pity there is no simple name for it) the mind can almost construct a measuring-table, and compare one degree with another. Similarly with its opposite Distaste : here also we can mark degrees of repulsion, and recall with considerable accuracy distasteful feelings which this or that food has aroused in us. A sweet taste, though falling far short of an over-sugared relish, can give pleasure long after the actual sensation has passed away : and a bitter taste, in like manner, can give us a distinctly realised posthumous pain.

It is this Taste proper that provides the real analogue to artistic and literary taste—the analogue of which we are most often conscious, and to which we most often refer as a kind of standard. In artistic and literary taste, also, the pleasures and pains admit of being registered, recalled in memory, compared, and analysed; it, too, is ' acute,' balancing, and even discriminating ; the emotions connected with it are regulated and controlled ; and in it a mild intellectual element is clearly to be discerned. For it will, I think, be conceded that there is no ' taste,' in this restricted sense, to be detected in the frenzied zest with which the Red Indian attacks his hard-earned and precarious meal, any more than in the greed with which the child devours its supper. I wish to avoid showing any idea of *reflection* to intrude into the idea conveyed by ' taste ' ; but I imagine—though I am far from wishing my opinion to be accepted without consideration—that in taste in this proper sense the element of *memory* is largely predominant. Such taste is something *added* to relish, or at least it is a relish with something added. And that element the memory provides, thus allowing the comparing powers to come into play. *So far*, but no farther, the intellect may be said to exert itself. True taste, in Wordsworthian language, is thus ' an emotion recollected in tranquillity.' However short the interval between the enjoyment and the recollection, *some* recollection there must be before taste proper can arise. You must not merely like your meal ; you must be able to *say* you like it. It is here as with the two fools in Lear :

> That Lord, which counselled thee
> To give away thy land,
> Come place him here by me,
> Do thou for him stand :
> The sweet and bitter fool
> Will presently appear,
> The one in motley here,
> The other found out there.

But you cannot place the sweet and the bitter in this opposition without the exertion of memory. And it is this exertion, almost imperceptible though it be, which marks off true taste from mere relish.

That the case is the same with literary and artistic taste will, I think, be generally admitted. You enjoy the Venus of Milo : the moment you begin to *realise* your enjoyment, but not before, you are exercising taste. And the word ' exercise ' is part of the definition.

Finally, the physiologist draws attention to those tastes which, being closely allied with the sense of touch, may be called for convenience the Tactile. These all contain an element of pungency, and the pleasure they involve arises from a slight irritation. Such tastes are the saline, the alkaline, the sour, the astringent, the fiery, the acrid. It is doubtful whether any of these give immediate pleasure to the ' natural man.' As a rule, they are sought by the elderly, whose senses have been to some extent sophisticated, or by others as a variation on the relishes or saccharine tastes which have preceded them and require some contrast. Often they are ' acquired ' tastes : they demand considerable use before the initial repulsion is first overcome and then transformed into liking. But the victory is sometimes singularly complete : there are many people who are almost incapable of receiving pleasure from any other kind of taste. The mental analogue to this it is hardly necessary to point out. Many will recall, for example, the repulsion they felt on first approaching the style of Sterne, Carlyle, Meredith, or any other ' astringent,' difficult, or eccentric author. Some of the older generation will perhaps recall their introduction to Browning, the taste for whom is certainly ' acquired.' Some Mentor, perhaps, told them the taste was worth the trouble of ' acquisition,' and they took the trouble. A few hours of annoyance, or even of exasperation, followed : but the trouble

did prove worth while. With some authors the induce-
ment was of a different kind. It was like the taste for
smoking, reached ' through peril, toil, and pain,'
because the ' enjoyment ' is forbidden, or because it
is imagined that it is manly to seek it. What the elder
brother of nineteen may do, you at fourteen will not
be deterred from attempting.

Notice once more that, as in the physical world so
in the mental, we can speak of ' cloying ' tastes. A
style, or an author, can satiate the appetite or cloy the
palate, just as a food can. And what more than anything else marks the superiority of Taste proper and
of the Acquired Taste over the Relishes is that they
cloy much later and more rarely. We are far sooner
cloyed with Seneca than with Cæsar : an epigrammatic
or paradoxical style nauseates much sooner than a
simple and straightforward one. I do not deny that
we like the epigrams *as a change* ; but we speedily
return to the plain and more nutritious fare.

It is needless to draw out the parallel farther ; and
there is always the risk, in pursuing parallels, of landing
ourselves in the contradictions and quagmires of infinity.
But, ere I pass on, I might point out that, as the necessary condition of physical taste is solubility, so the
necessary condition of its mental analogue is that the
material given should be intelligible. Otherwise, taste
does not enter at all, even as its own contrary. There
are certain works of art which are so far outside our
experience that we are not even disgusted by them. To
bite on granite may hurt, but it causes no nausea :
and a child set to read *Sartor Resartus* or *Sordello* does
not dislike the book ; he merely rejects it : if he dislikes anything at all, it is the useless toil. A boy who

says he hates Virgil hates him only at second-hand : it is the slavery of construing that he really loathes.

When a mental emotion vastly enlarges its range, it is obvious that the analogies which have been hitherto sufficient and satisfying must often be found inadequate. Thus a mathematician may sometimes cease to speak of doing a problem, and speak of wrestling with it or digging at it. He may renounce it for a while, and let it ' simmer.' But no mental emotion has enlarged its range, or deepened its intension, more enormously than artistic and literary taste. Starting from mere enjoyment or repulsion, it has grown with our growth, extended through all extent, spread undivided, and operated without exhausting itself. We may well, therefore, expect to find that analogies have constantly to be drawn from other senses : and in particular from those of hearing and sight. As, for example, our feeling for poetry deepens, we realise the inadequacy of such metaphors as sweet and bitter, pleasant and unpleasant, nice and nasty. We call on such images as sublimity, profundity, the distant, the near, the thunderous, the still and small, the great, the little, the weighty, the light. And finally, as other arts and sciences obtain their own special character and vocabulary, we draw on *them* to illustrate our own, and speak of the breadth of a musical composition, the tone of a painting, the balance of an essay, the rhythm of a landscape. And yet, amid all this wealth of metaphor, it will, I think, be found that the ultimate reference, the deciding factor, is our own *personal* enjoyment or distaste : the poem, the statue, the sonata is judged by a faculty for which, we instinctively feel, the appropriate analogy is to be found in the palate which appreciates our food. Taste

may be, as some say, the lowest of our senses : but there
is something so ultimate about it that though we may
at times seek something wider, we can rarely discover
anything higher, to express our judgment of the lof-
tiest, the most ethereal, the daintiest, the most solid
and permanent, the most transient and vaporous, of
all the emotions that an intellectual exercise can arouse
in us.

Little is altered if we substitute the phrase
' æsthetic appreciation ' for ' taste ' in this sense.
' Æsthetic ' is, of course, a metaphor derived not from
the palate but from our powers of perception, and
specially from those of seeing and hearing. It may
seem, therefore, more generally suitable than what
some may regard as a ' lower but loving likelihood.'
On the other hand, if I am not mistaken, it has some
disadvantages. It appears, for instance, at least at
times, to presume the *objective* existence of beauty,
independently of the percipient. As, for example,
when we say ' We perceive a house,' we are tempted to
believe that the house is there whether we perceive
it or not, so when we say we perceive beauty, we are
tempted to assume that the beauty is there quite apart
from us the perceivers. On this tremendous question
I do not intend to pronounce an opinion : it is one
of those best left to the metaphysicians. It is pretty
certain that they alone can deal with it : and it is
equally certain that a question handed over to them
will, like the woman in the Gospel, suffer many things
from many metaphysicians, and be no better but rather
the worse for their ministrations. What one meta-
physician says about it another will deny : and Greek
will meet Greek in endless logomachy. Is the Ode to
a Nightingale *really* beautiful apart altogether from

the reader ? Is sugar really sweet, or is the sweetness but a gift to it from us ? This leads to another question, Does sugar itself exist, or is it a mere projection of our minds ? And this later question, if ever solved, will probably be solved only at the expense of yet another interrogation. Coleridge, who derived the senses from the mind, might give our answer : ' O Lady, we receive but what we give, and in our life alone does Nature live ' : but Coleridge is not the only philosopher, and his view is not the only one. I purpose to leave all such enigmas on one side : allowing myself, however, one touch of the dogmatism which makes the whole world kin. Matter has been cautiously defined as the permanent possibility of sensation. I will venture—provided that I am not asked to defend the position—to define beauty as the permanent possibility of enjoyment. When you have found a ' beautiful ' thing you can recur to it with a reasonable hope of enjoying it again. You may not always enjoy it as much as before, or in the same way, but the *chance* of enjoyment is there.

One more enigma may perhaps implore the passing tribute of a mention. Is there any criterion by which we can decide whether one taste is higher or lower than another ? Some even to-day may have read Coventry Patmore's *Angel in the House*, and may recall the question he put to himself, ' How has your Beloved surpassed, so much, all others ? ' The answer was simple—' She is mine.' But though mere possession may thus decide the superiority of one girl to all others, we require more than this to prove the superiority of our tastes. We all know the contempt always felt, and not invariably dissembled, by certain wine-drinkers for the wretched creatures who cannot tell the difference between a superior and an inferior brand. It is something which, once experienced, is likely to teach the sufferer a lifelong humility, and is in fact almost enough to account for all the ' inferiority complexes ' with which Freud has ever been called to deal. But after all, is the thing so certain ? Is there more in it than in Sir Willoughby Patterne's mere *sense* of his unassailable position above everybody else ? Is there any *rational* ground, admitting of proof, why we should concede to these connoisseurs the eminence they somewhat arrogantly claim ? Can they *prove* that champagne is better than lemonade, and if so, can they convince us that they feel the difference ? The proverb gives the answer of the experience of the whole human race, ' *Chacun à son goût.*' To each man his own taste is the only standard. In fact, the proverb is a truism : ' What I like best tastes best.'

When we turn from the material to the mental, we meet the same difficulty. ' It is better to be Socrates dissatisfied than a pig satisfied,' said John Stuart Mill ; and his admission was taken as a renunciation of the whole case for hedonism, and for the quantitative measurement of happiness. It does, indeed, appear to involve a reliance upon some intuitive sense of values, totally independent of reason, and as dogmatic, in effect, as Johnson's ' We know, and there's an end on't.' With literature the same question at once arises. After we have catalogued a few very simple and almost trifling indications of what all will recognise as good points, we are left to face endless disputes, eternal readjustments, innumerable personal equations, multitudinous mere prejudices, against which no amount of argument avails anything. If a man does not *like* Dickens, you cannot reason him into liking. If he likes Edgar Wallace, there is no ' computatio sive logica ' to demonstrate that he is doing what he ought not to do. As well try by syllogism to make a man who detests marmalade revel in it, as seek by argument to convert a man of a certain literary taste to another.

Attempts have often been made to get over this difficulty, and by none more ably than by Mr. Stace in his recent book on the *Meaning of Beauty*. He draws a distinction between Æsthetics and Taste, the one being in his opinion scientific and solid, the other unstable and personal. Those who have been puzzled by the varieties of ethical doctrine existing in different times and places have sometimes, to save ethics from total destruction, recalled to us the fact that though conscience may lay down different precepts in different cases, she is still conscience. She may say sometimes this is right, and sometimes the same thing is wrong : but she always recognises *a* right and *a* wrong. Similarly, if I understand Mr. Stace, he would maintain that though one man may like a poem and another dislike it, both have somewhere a standard of excellence, an æsthetic conscience, the possession of which is an indication that there is in us all *an* Idea of Beauty, though we may apply it variously. A man may prefer the *Grecian Urn* to the *Nightingale ;* but he sees beauty in both. If, says Mr. Stace, he thinks them ugly, we have a right to say he is a man who either has not yet gained an æsthetic conscience, or has seared it with a hot iron.

It will be plain as we proceed that I am no believer in an *innate* æsthetic conscience of the kind Mr. Stace and so many others believe to exist. Or, at any rate, if it be so deeply rooted in *us* to-day, the heirs of

c

all the ages, that it may not unfairly be called innate,
I see no reason for believing that it was so in the beginning. I shall try to show later that it has in all probability developed, by a natural evolution, from very
simple feelings : that the sense of beauty or ugliness,
which now seems so instantaneous, is a growth from
something much more primitive than itself, which has
in the first instance little apparent relation to beauty
or ugliness, and which might conceivably, had circumstances been different, have evolved into something
quite other than what we now see. At least, I am
pretty sure of this, that *individual* appearances we now
call beautiful might quite easily have been to-day
thought ugly and *vice versa*. Nay, we can see this very
thing happening before our very eyes. We need but
look around, or in ourselves, and we see taste, or the
æsthetic faculty—call it what you will—constantly
changing both in individuals and in communities.
The causes are by no means always obvious ; but the
effects are very visible, and in the midst of much
obscurity and irregularity we can, if only with difficulty, detect certain laws. A man grows older, and
his tastes change by the mere process of the years.
They are a function of the whole man, and vary as he
varies. He becomes satiated with an old style and
demands a new ; or he grows fixed in the capacity to
enjoy an old style and rejects the new with disgust.
Especially is this the case when middle age is past.
Some men rest in memory, and want no further experience. I have known people who, having heard
Liszt play, would never listen to another pianist, and
others, in a different sphere, who, having seen W. G.
Grace bat, would never watch a cricket-match. A
great change in external circumstances, again, as from

poverty to wealth or *vice versa*, may alter a man's whole outlook on life, and with it his susceptibility to certain forms of literature or art : as the War altered the taste of a whole generation. There may be changes in the taste of the circle in which he moves, and these changes will act on him according to his temperament. If he is easily influenced by others, he will, like Mr. Pickwick, shout with the crowd, and, should there be two crowds, he will shout with the larger. If he is stubborn and independent, the movement of the crowd will probably drive him further in the opposite direction than he would otherwise have gone. As an old lady of my acquaintance once observed, ' I pay not the slightest attention to the opinions of other people. If they tell me they think one thing, I think the opposite harder than ever.'

It is a mistake to press far the likeness between a community and an individual. Yet there are certain similarities. A community, like a man, may take to the new simply from satiety with the old ; or it may cling to a fashion simply because a neighbouring community has rejected it ; or again it may, for no assignable reason, imitate its neighbour. A crowd may be stubborn, conservative, radical, vacillating, as an inexplicable whim may take it. And it will stick to its tastes, or take up new ones, in the same inexplicable way. The historical analyst, coming solemnly to the study of these unreasoned rebellions or equally unreasoned loyalties, is perplexed to account for them. He is like Pope when he began to contemplate the ' mighty maze ' of mankind as a whole : or like the father in Wordsworth's poem when his boy preferred Kilve to Liswyn Farm. He is lucky if he reaches as satisfactory a solution as that supplied by the pestered child. He finds dubious causes in great upheavals, in victories, in defeats, in national triumphs or humiliations ; sometimes, but rarely, in the influence of a great man : but as a rule he is guessing, and knows he is guessing. Men, like the ship of the Ancient Mariner, are often driven by winds, and of the wind we know not whence it cometh nor whither it goeth. And often their ideas are held becalmed by a spirit that works nine fathom below the surface of the sea, invisible, and to be detected only in dreams. Of one point, however, we can be sure, that the taste for one kind of literary excitement or another is due less to the literature itself than to its association with something else.

And, as these associations are necessarily different in any one man from what they are in every other, we must not be surprised if there are great differences in our appreciations of what, for the sake of convenience, we call the ' same ' work. Nay, as no man is the same for a day together, *his* judgments of the ' same ' work must alter. ' Beauty,' says Walter Pater, ' like all other qualities presented to human experience, is relative : and the definition of it becomes unmeaning and useless in proportion to its abstractness. The aim of all true criticism,' he goes on, is to inquire ' what is this song or picture, this engaging personality, to *me* ? Does it give me pleasure, and if so, what sort or degree of pleasure ? How is *my* nature modified by its presence, and under its influence ? He who experiences those impressions strongly has no need to trouble himself with the abstract question what beauty is in itself—a metaphysical question as unprofitable as metaphysical questions elsewhere.'

If this be so, and so I think it to be, a full analysis

of taste would involve a full, and therefore impossible, analysis of the lives, circumstances, and characters of all the persons to whom the particular work comes— an obviously impossible task. And, on the other hand, the acquisition, or the bestowal, of a sound taste might seem equally impossible, for it might appear that we should have to alter, by main force, the whole circumstances, ancestry, and character of any person we met whose taste we thought bad but wanted to improve. But the difficulty is, as usual in such cases, solved *ambulando*. As the theologians speak of religion as a life, and not as a mere science of living, a life of which the vitalising elements are supplied to you as you go along, so with taste. If you want to live a good life, do not go seeking for another than what you have—just live as well as you can the life that you have to live every day—it will give you plenty of means of living well. So, if you want a good taste, do not go making violent changes in your reading. Only try to read as well as you can the books you like. It will soon appear, with regard to some of them, that if you *do* read them carefully and well, they will themselves provide you with the judgment that will reject them. If a schoolboy reads *thoughtfully* a bad novel, putting his best self into it, he will soon begin to care for higher literature. To quote a despised Victorian author, he will rise on stepping-stones of his dead self to higher things.

And here, as with other kinds of goodness, lies the consolatory aspect of a truth which I venture to enunciate—though with trepidation. Religion, we are told, has primarily nothing to do with the intellect, though plenty of religious men have intellect enough. And so with the subject of our inquiry. Primarily,

and in essence, matters of taste, being matters of
living, have little to do with the intellect ; nor is
there any reason why an artist, *as such*, or an appreciator
of art, as such, should be a highly intellectual person—
though the intellect comes in to aid them both. When
Opie said that he mixed his colours with brains, he
showed that he had even less mental capacity than
artistic genius. Real brains, downright hard thinking,
are not necessarily characteristic of the artist pure
and simple : they are the mark of the mathematician,
the physicist, the chess-player. It is true that many
artists are also men of brains ; but that is an accident.
It is also true, conversely, that many mathematical
theorems and chess-games are full of beauty. I know
no poem more beautiful than the exponential
series, and no painting more beautiful than some of
Morphy's chess-games. But beauty is not the essence
of mathematics, and Morphy did not win his games
by the beauty of his combinations—it was their
accuracy that confounded his antagonists. So, on
the other hand, it may be possible to compare Burke
and Milton, as intellectual giants, with Newton and
Faraday : but the *artistic* beauty of their works is a
function not of their intellect but of their taste. In
Paradise Lost the intellect is clearly there, and it is
obviously immense : but it is quite subsidiary. The
same intellectual power, without the taste, would have
produced the ' Chaos Restored ' of which Pope speaks
in the *Dunciad*.

In a lesser degree, the same thing is true of the
appreciation of art. So far as we appreciate, we are
artists, and by no means necessarily people of brains.
At first hearing, this may discourage or exasperate my
readers ; but let us look on the bright side. As I said

a moment ago, this truth *has* a cheerful aspect: and, as Job said to his friends, ' Hear diligently my speech, and let this be your consolations.' Many of us are uneasily conscious of inferiority as we compare ourselves with certain highly-endowed acquaintances of ours, to whom the integral calculus is no mystery, and who sport with Relativity in the shade. Let us take comfort. We have access to realms of beauty which provide full compensation. The Senior Wrangler who said that poetry proved nothing had *his* reward. He could sit down and prove the provable. We can, humbly and modestly, sit down and enjoy the enjoyable : and that enjoyment sometimes reaches an intensity and an exaltation which hardly anything else on earth is capable of giving : and which, unlike most other pleasures, does not wear out by use, but intensifies with every exercise of it, and can be renewed at will.

I cannot, indeed, better express my meaning than by applying to this exaltation, arising from literary study, the words which John Smith, one of the glories of seventeenth-century Cambridge, applied to the study of theology :

' Were I to define divinity, I should rather call it a divine life than a divine science. To seek our divinity merely among books and writings (that is, in the intellect) is to seek the living among the dead : we do but in vain seek God many times in these, where His truth too often is not so much inshrined as entombed : no, seek for God within thine own soul ; he is best discerned, as Plotinus phraseth it, by an intellectual *touch*. The soul itself hath its sense as well as the body ; and therefore David, when he would teach us to know what the divine goodness is, calls not for speculation but sensation : *Taste*, saith he, and see how good the Lord is. That is not the best and truest knowledge of God which is wrought out by the labour and sweat of the brain, but that which is kindled in us by a heavenly warmth in our hearts. When the tree of knowledge is not planted by the tree of life, and sucks not up sap from thence, it may as well be fruitful with evil as with good. Such as men are, such will God himself seem to be.'

Similarly with the lower but equally true delights of literature. Literature, too, is not a science but a life. To gain these delights to the full, we must touch and taste : the taste may indeed be intellectual, but high intellect is not necessary to it. We need no *understanding* equal or superior to that of the poet to taste and see how good the poem is, or to attain the winged souls which may appreciate the highest heaven of invention, and gaze like Beatrice at the sun of genius. We need not so much the intellect of a Newton as the capacity to feel. Such as we are in ourselves and in our daily lives, such will Shakespeare, Milton, and Dante seem to be.

II

THE EVOLUTION OF TASTE

LITERATURE, to dress a platitude in the garb of paradox, began before letters existed. It may seem unnecessary to emphasise so obvious a point : and yet so great a scholar as Gaston Paris thought it desirable to dwell upon it in the beginning of his history of early French literature. Nor is it a mere fact without a meaning. I shall have many opportunities of noting how frequently fashions, once living and needful, tend to survive when the cause that brought them into existence has ceased to operate : and there are many features in written literature which have thus survived from the oral stage. Many, for example, of Homer's devices for helping his memory—his repetitions, his tags, his prayers to the Muses—which once had a real importance, have descended as fashions not merely to Virgil and Milton, but to Glover and Blackmore, and end—or rather do *not* end—in the mocking mimicries of Pope or Byron.

We tend to forget the obvious : yet we shall be wise to keep in remembrance the simple fact that there is no *vital* difference between prose or poetry spoken and prose or poetry written—vast as the unessential differences have come to be : and to employ the word literature is to seize upon an accident, instead of an essential, as the ground of definition. The word, however, is now established and irremovable.

and we must stick to it. I imagine that if we ever
discovered that ants or bees had some sort of story-
telling or other intellectual enjoyment, as distinct
from mere business-messages, which they passed on to
their neighbours by means of their antennæ, we
should still have to call it literature. At any rate we
must always remember that, as a manuscript never
printed may yet be the highest form of literature, so
a poem never reduced even to manuscript may be
literature too. The poems of Homer, the sagas of
Iceland, were literature none the less because for
hundreds of years they remained unwritten; and
conversely an inscription or a Bradshaw's Guide is
not literature because it uses letters to convey its
information.

To discover the beginnings of literature, then, we
must investigate not writing but speech : and here I
know no book better worth study than Jespersen's
Language—though I do not imagine that some of the
books of our schooldays are altogether superseded ;
and in particular I retain a fondness for Darmesteter's
La Vie des Mots. There is some truth, amid much
that has been shown to be mistaken, in Max Müller's
Science of Language ; but in all sciences the later works
either are, or ought to be, better than the earlier, and
no science has advanced more rapidly than philology
and semantics. It may be that even Jespersen is now
out of date. Whether this is the case or not, he is
worth consulting. He holds, apparently, that the
power of *communication* arises in us somewhat later
than we might suppose. A child's screaming, he thinks,
though it draws the mother to his side, does not
summon her ; it is not the child's way of *saying* ' I am
in pain ' or ' I want food,' any more than the kicking

of its feet means ' I feel happy.' These are but more or less reflex actions, limited to the child's own world, and involve no attempt to explain his emotions to others. We have to start a little later. True speech, according to the best authorities, would begin with some sort of musical intonation, or possibly with a semi-musical lilt. ' The progenitors of man,' says Darwin, ' probably uttered musical tones before they had acquired the power of articulate speech '; and we may imagine that they contrived, by this musical means, to effect some rough communication with their neighbours. But this, I think, would be from the very first combined with imitation, both vocal and ' actional ' : the hands, the head, the feet, nay the whole body, would come to the aid of the tongue, and the play of the features would unconsciously add force to the sounds. Darwin notices that children, when using scissors, move their mouths in scissor-fashion. Can we doubt that our ancestors, in *describing* the throwing of a stone, or the rush of a tiger, would *act* the incidents ? An animal would be represented, possibly, by a mimicry of its roar, its death by a mimic death. Nay, there are some who believe that the simple mathematics of early man were done by imitations : *one* was expressed by a rounded mouth, *two* by showing both rows of teeth, and *three* by the teeth with the tongue between them. There, in all likelihood, numerical science stopped for centuries : it was long before *five* was shown by the fingers of the hand, and longer still before *ten* was seen to be the fingers of both hands.[1]

[1] The evolution of mathematics has been closely studied of late years, and the counting-powers of savages have been investigated with precision. It is enough to refer to Galton's *Tropical South Africa*

The power of expression attained by these simple means would probably be very great : much greater than we, who have so largely superseded action by words, can easily conceive. I doubt not that whole narratives of furious encounters, of wounds, of hair-breadth escapes, of moving accidents by flood and field, would be conveyed by primitive Othellos to primeval Desdemonas, and that to hear, and *see*, them, Desdemona would seriously and literally incline. That a practically full conception may thus be communicated could be shown by many instances. One will do for a thousand. A missionary told me that, in a wild part of India, he came upon a crowd listening to a professional tale-teller. He joined the throng, and *watched ;* for the tale was being told in a language of which he did not understand a single word. But so vivid, so ferocious was the acting of the man, that he followed the story without difficulty, and, on repeating his idea of it to a friend who had *heard* it, found that he had lost nothing but a few insignificant details. Much more would this be the case in still more savage communities.

Now imagine that in the tribe there was one man who stood out from the rest in this art of narrative. He would please by a variety of powers. First, the mere *sounds* might be what his fellows would regard as attractive : his intonations might be clear and musical, and his rhythms distinct and easily caught by his audience. Secondly, we cannot doubt that his

and Rae's *Eskimos*. But something was known long since. Condamine, the author of the *Account of a Savage Girl*, met a tribe that could not count beyond four. ' This,' said Dr. Johnson, ' should be told to Monboddo, and would help him to prove his favourite theory '— that men are descended from monkeys. *Tour to the Hebrides*, September 23, 1773.

imitations of the rustling of trees, the rippling of waters, the voices of animals, the whistling of winds, the hissing of rain, would be so exact as to convey to his hearers instantaneously the wished ideas. Possibly he had a certain power of parody or comic imitation ; this would give added pleasure. Without quite knowing why, the tribe would prefer such a man to a weaker performer. They would have a *taste*, or rather a relish, for his stories and, in comparison, a *distaste*, or rather a disgust, for those of others. They would, we imagine, not *criticise* overtly ; but they would do what the Elizabethan audiences did with *Julius Cæsar* and with *Catiline* ; they would throng to the one and stay away from the other—or possibly show their likes and dislikes in a still more drastic manner.

When sounds were combined into something resembling sentences, and the tunes into something resembling airs, the old associations would remain. The words *describing* ugly things would be ugly at second-hand, and what *described* beautiful things would similarly be beautiful ; for there would still remain the vivid associations with terror or delight, and, what is equally important, the very sounds that had so exactly imitated the things which had roused those emotions. These sounds, *recalling* pleasure or fear, would come in time to be, in themselves, pleasurable or terrible, even when used without direct reference to the things which had been called up by those sounds. A literary sense would thus be gradually created, and there would arise a perception of literary beauty, as words were employed which, by association with pleasurable things, had come to be thought, or rather felt, beautiful in themselves. A habit would be formed, which could not be distinguished from an intuition. But it is not difficult to see that it was but habit after all. If a cobra had happened to sing, and a nightingale to hiss, the song, being associated with fear and horror, would have sounded ugly, and the mimic hiss would at least have been neutral, associated as it would have been with something quite harmless. If men knew nothing of laughter but as the cry of a hyæna, and nothing of the *word* but as the mimicry of the cry made by narrators of encounters with that loathsome beast, the word 'laughter' would itself be hideous. The test can easily be applied. There are words in English which are pleasant or unpleasant. Exactly the same sounds in other languages, being associated with different things, are often the exact reverse.

It is easy, however, also, to perceive how these associations might in some cases be corrected. As men conquered their terrors, it would be possible to snatch a fearful joy out of terror itself ; and primitive poets might anticipate Aristotle's tragedians by ' purging the mind of pity and fear ' through the operation of those very emotions. If a man, describing how he had succeeded in killing a tiger, was a good narrator, he would learn that there is a delight in *remembering* the roars and growls which, though fearful at the time, had proved harmless in the end. ' Haec olim meminisse iuvabit ' is a saying that will apply to anxieties and dangers overcome long before the time of Æneas : and such a narrator would soon learn how to increase the final satisfaction of his hearers by piling up the preliminary horrors. Every time he did so, the taste of the hearers would be enlarged, so as to include the pleasure to be derived from pain : a new set of associations, both verbal and ' actional,' would be formed and unconsciously handed on. Among the hearers, of course, would be future narrators, at the most susceptible period of their lives, catching tones, gestures, and collocations of words which they perceived to be effective, and storing them up for use when the opportunity should arise. A literary language would thus, in a few generations, be formed : the orators would use it, and the audiences would expect it.

On such points as these, of course, certainty is unattainable ; but we have good authority for believing that even the song the sirens sang, or the name of Hecuba's mother, is not beyond all conjecture. Something like what I have been suggesting may have happened, and, viewing the results, we may say that something not very dissimilar *must* have happened. We can dimly perceive how, at a very early stage, certain words or collocations of words were believed to have a magical efficacy—a belief which is by no means dead even yet—and as soon as this happened, those words or collocations would put on a beauty or an ugliness according as the magic in them was supposed to be protective or destructive. If the pronunciation of a word would bring you food or kill a wild animal, that word would be beautiful ; if it was used to bring down a curse on your head, it would be ugly. We can trace, further, in some cases the nature of these powerful collocations. To judge by the almost universal delight in puns and assonances at certain stages in the historical evolution of literature, one may be tolerably certain that ' in the beginning ' the delight was still greater. If Samson could celebrate his triumph over the Philistines with a threefold pun, if the Philistines, when their turn came, could retort on him

with a fivefold rhyme,[1] we may presume that long
before Samson, our ancestors, discovering that the
same sound might have two meanings, or that two or
three sounds coming near one another might happen
to jingle, would ascribe to such coincidences a magical
force, and would gain pleasure from the discovery.
We need not go far in search of illustrations. Even
Shakespeare found a pleasure, like that of stout Cortes,
when he hit on a word like ' will,' ' light ' or ' gilt,'
which could do multiple service : much more the
Palæolithic man. The Book of Genesis, especially
in its earliest parts, is full of puns : it is not hard to
picture the glee of the first teller who saw that one
could play nicely with ' Babel ' and ' balbal.' And
the glee would deepen as the hidden *force* of the as-
sonance was revealed. If a man's name turned out to
be capable of two applications, it would be pleasant
to realise its magic power. ' Gad,' for instance, was
perhaps originally the name of a god ; but use it to
mean ' happy,' and you secured the prosperity of the
tribe : use it for ' troop,' and you gave a further
impulse to the tribal fortunes, while giving yourself
the delight of conscious power. Beyond reasonable
doubt, such accidents would be even more significant
and pleasing in still earlier times. When it was noticed,
further, that lilts could be measured, and that one
rhythm could be matched with another, the charm
would gain an added potency. It was with this sort
of thing that what we may tentatively call poetry
first began. It was a union of the measured stress,
marked by the feet (whence perhaps the name *foot*

---

[1] ' Chamór chamór chamórathāim.' The Philistine retort may be
represented thus : ' And so our foe that laid us low, and wrought us
woe, is made a show.'

for the unit of metre) with words, that started the enormous output of poetry which has since staggered the world. And it was magical, or religious, call it which you will. For those who desire further information, I cannot do better than refer them to Professor Gilbert Murray's chapter on the " Molpë " in his *Classical Tradition in Poetry*. He there shows how Greek poetry (and here it is more or less a type of all poetry) began with the ' dance-and-song,' the origin of which was ascribed to Apollo and the Muses. The bard started the music ; his chorus beat the floor with their feet ; and then he began his song. The floor, when thus used, became ' divine,' for the Molpë was a divine service, a piece of magic. If a threshing-floor, it produced fruitfulness, as the tug-of-war does in many countries even to-day. If it was by a fountain, it ensured that the fountain would not run dry. It was from such crude beginnings that the highly elaborated Odes of Pindar ultimately sprang ; and it would seem that Pindar himself knew it. The First Pythian gives us an almost archæological account of this development. But even those who do not know Greek need not go outside our own literature to learn much about it. Gray, in his *Progress of Poetry*, imitating that very Ode, tells us nearly all we can wish to learn. He shows how the Golden Lyre is the gift of Apollo and the Muses, how the voice and dance obey the lyre, and how the rosy-crownëd Loves are seen

> With antic Sport and blue-eyed Pleasures,
> Frisking light in frolic measures,
> Now pursuing, now retreating,
>   Now in circling troops they meet ;
> To brisk notes in cadence beating,
>   Glance their many-twinkling feet.

D

But not merely the choric Ode had this original. From a like beginning sprang the epic—it was thus that Demodocus sang his lay to Alcinous—and from this beginning sprang the drama.

For ere long, or perhaps after centuries, it was perceived that the dance and the words might be separated. Even Apollo was not always accompanied by his Muses. The Delphian oracle, it is true, was said to have uttered the first hexameter verse, but these verses were spoken or chanted by one person, without the necessity of a chorus. From this recognition would proceed, by gradual steps, the narrative poem, and the metrical speech, which later became the dialogue. It may have been the desire to use the magic of verse against an enemy that led to the Fescennine verses of which Horace speaks, or to the ' gephurism ' of the Greek women—the insults hurled at each other when crossing a bridge—or to the composition of ' runes ' to bring down disaster upon someone's head. Sometimes this versified ' flyting ' had another aim ; it was, by exhausting the power of the curse during sacred periods in which it would be harmless, to make it harmless at other times also. We know, of course, that it lost its religious character, degenerated into mere abuse, and had to be stopped ' formidine fustis ' : much as the consecrated libels of the Attic comedy had to be checked by law : but its religious *origin* was never quite forgotten. In some countries even the gods were represented as thus ' flyting,' or engaging in abusing-matches : the *Lokasenna*, or Loki's Abuse of the Gods, is well known, and there is something like it in *Bandamanna saga*. Even so late as the fifteenth century the custom was kept up : the set-to between Dunbar and Kennedy, though tolerably vigorous, has a peculiar underlying tone which seems to show that it was meant to be taken, if not in a sacred, yet in a Pickwickian sense : this was because the old religious atmosphere still clung to the mimic warfare.

It is impossible to believe that in the hearers of early poetry, taste ever advanced further than the most rudimentary ' criticism.' They knew, of course, that they ' preferred' one bard to another : the magic of the one was the more powerful, his incantations more compelling. But they might ' prefer' him only in the sense that they were more afraid of him : that they dreaded his pronunciation of some rune or spell which would bring disaster, and which had in the past prevailed over the protective rune of the other. Or, in the tribal gathering, they might find themselves carried away by the rhythm of his words and the vigour of his performances on his rude musical instrument. Again, when going to battle against their enemies, under the inspiration of their own bard, they might if victorious, dully compare him favourably with the poet of their opponents. Beyond this, I do not think they would ever go. Nor do I think there was much self-criticism done by the bards themselves. Accustomed to sing under an excitement which they regarded as divine, they would ascribe an occasional failure not so much to a weakness of their own as to the anger of the god, who, we may be sure, would oftener be smiting their hearers with stupidity than themselves with incapacity. As their songs were usually, if not always, improvisations, they would show all the characteristics of extempore performances, in which literary defects are covered up by force in the delivery or magnificence in the accessories.

A sort of criticism, I think, was more likely to grow up alongside of the short gnomes and couplets which passed from mouth to mouth, and became part and parcel of the wisdom of whole communities.[1] All languages, of course, show plenty of these. Everyone's own studies will have brought to his notice the Anglo-Saxon specimens, which bear evident traces that they are but settings of old sayings : just as the Proverbs of Solomon must in many cases be much more ancient than Solomon. 'Wind is in air swiftest, thunder at times loudest, weird strongest, winter coldest, Lent most rainy, summer sunniest'; these, though summing-up ordinary experience, are not very striking or elegant in expression. Passing as they did from man to man, they allowed time for reflection, and would inevitably be criticised, either as inaccurate in their statement of fact, or as poor in diction. The reader will recall examples from his own childhood. I remember, for instance, hearing the rhyme, 'Rainbow at morning is the shepherd's warning : rainbow at night is the shepherd's delight.' Young as I was, I compared this with the facts, and found it not true. It was therefore with some pleasure that I heard another boy say that the correct version was 'Red sky,' not 'rainbow' : and this I found to be more nearly representative of natural laws. Who can doubt that similar 'material' criticisms were passed on much earlier maxims ? What is said about everyday things *can* be thus criticised : what is said about your ancestors is not open to such tests. And the criticism

[1] These seem to show an advance, or at least a change, in the poet's habits. In Greece, and probably also elsewhere, they were spoken, rather than chanted or sung : and we hear of the reciters as actually sitting, like Deborah under her palm tree. (See the *Theatre of the Greeks*, pp. 32, 33.)

would be not only material but formal. A clumsy line would be, sooner or later, amended into smoothness ; and every improvement that made such a line more tuneful, and therefore more easy to remember, would be the work of an untutored criticism, resting on a rudimentary taste. For example, it may be observed that some of the Anglo-Saxon gnomes alliterate very poorly. It would be the work of this untutored criticism to complete the alliteration. Thus in the later gnomes we find

> Life strives with death, light with darkness,
> Fyrd with fyrd, foe with foe,
> Loathed one with loathed one on the land striveth ;
> After death-day doom we must abide
> In the Father's face : the future lieth
> Dark and dismal :

whereas in those I quoted above the alliteration is feeble.

With the growth of a poetical vocabulary, and the accumulation of a set of stock phrases, we may imagine that the eternal conflict between the older generation and the younger would find new material : the old resenting any change and the young demanding it : the old relying on the wisdom of the ages, and the young protesting, like Sydney Smith in his dispute with Toryism, that the further back you went the chubbier the children you found, and that the wisdom of the ages was but infantile folly. In this conflict, unless it were summarily settled by the simple method of clubbing the weaker party, something like reasons would be found for preferring one style to the other : often, doubtless, irrelevant, but one can detect much irrelevance in the most apparently profound and philosophical criticism even in the present day. As now, so then : minds were made up beforehand, and reasons were invented afterwards. I dare say that the Athenians, who fined Phrynichus for reminding them of their failure to save Miletus from the Persians, did not own to themselves that they were really venting their own remorse on the dramatist. They would say that the play was *artistically* bad. Criticism, in this case, was an excuse or a pretext ; and often enough in later times it has been the same thing. What we do not like to hear, even if we know it to be the truth, we choose to find badly expressed. Exactly the same style, if conveying pleasing matter, would be warmly praised. The messenger, bringing good tidings to the Sultan, is rewarded : a week later, bringing evil, he is condemned to the bowstring—on the ground that he is losing his oratorical powers.

Gradually, of course, as a few men here and there gain the capacity of discrimination, and learn to distinguish between matter and manner, we find a judgment of style in itself. But even to-day this is rarer than we are inclined to imagine. It is certain that when a critic believes he is censuring a style he is often moved by dislike of the substance. I remember once remarking to a scientific friend of mine how strange it was that in *Sordello*, harsh and crabbed as so much of it is, should occur two such lovely lines as these :

> ' New pollen on the lily-petal blows,
> And still more labyrinthine buds the rose.'

But my friend, though not destitute of literary feeling, would or could see no beauty in them. They were ugly ; and he then proceeded to show why they were ugly : the botany was, it appeared, all wrong. The majority of novel-readers, I am sure, judge the style of a novel, if they think of it at all, by the plot : and indeed it is not easy to be sure they are mistaken. Even so profound and minute a student of words and phrases as Henry James[1]—even this perhaps over-precious stylist, exquisite both in French and in English, found some of the greatest masters of French style unreadable because of the subjects on which they chose to write, and actually went so far as to say that style and matter were inseparably one. On similar grounds Cardinal Newman refused to allow the name of poetry to Byron's so-called immoral writings, and asserted—in direct contradiction to the opinion of Dr. Johnson—that revealed religion was essentially poetical. This was because, so soon as poetry ceased to be religious, it ceased to engage Newman's sympathy. But I am straying beyond the bounds of my immediate subject, and must leave my reader for the present to make his own reflections on this subject. It will come up again.

Let us now take a very wide leap, and arrive at the time when one of the greatest of all inventions, writing and its correlative reading, have pretty firmly established themselves. The likelihood has not, I think, been sufficiently emphasised that writing and reading would alter taste, and alter it enormously. Scores of poems, which had pleased when recited, would be found wanting when read. For one reason, when *you* read a poem, *you* are the reciter, and your recitation is and must be different from that of the poet or the rhapsode. The gestures that have attracted you are no longer there ; the tricks that have deceived you are but matters of feeble memory. I suppose that

[1] See Morris Roberts, *Henry James's Criticism*, p. 37 *et al.*

some of the most effective speeches made since Demosthenes were Gladstone's in the Midlothian campaign. Of them a good judge said, 'I have heard all the greatest orators of my time, and the greatest actors : but if I had not heard the Midlothian speeches I should not have had the faintest idea of what can be achieved by the human voice.' But read them now, and where is their power? The flashing eyes of the orator are dim, the gestures are still, the withering scorn in the tone is inaudible, and, more than all, the passions of the time are silent and the hypnotism of the idolising crowds is not there. Your taste for them can never be like that of your grandfathers. The whole tremendous struggle has sunk, like the Crusades, to silence, and one says of it, as of the old knight, 'Dead the warrior, dead his glory, dead the cause in which he died.'

On the other hand, the fact that so many of Burke's speeches failed when spoken is a matter of historical fact, and of vast historical importance. Had they been as impressive in Parliament as they were and are in the study, the whole history of the world might have been changed : America might have remained in the Empire, and our Indian troubles might not have been. To the immortal speech on the Nabob of Arcot's Debts Pitt, looking at the empty benches, thought it needless to reply : it was published, and it shook the educated country. The House of Commons, which was not educated, it did not shake.

In a lesser degree the same thing is constantly seen. In my youth I heard John Bright : and I shall have occasion to refer to his speeches again. One of those speeches I well remember. I did indeed admire it when spoken—who could help admiring it?—but I admired it far more when I read it verbatim in the paper next day. There was a beauty born of the unmurmuring sound of silent mental reading, which exceeded even the beauty of that melodious voice and the added inpressiveness of one of the most striking personalities I ever saw : and the extraordinarily exquisite choice of words, rich with all the associations of Milton and the Bible, was more easily perceptible to the reader than to the hearer. If anyone wishes to *see* the English language, at its simplest and best, I know no place when he is more likely to find it than in some of the *printed* speeches of John Bright.

Thus the spoken and the read are never *quite* the same : one may be now better than the other; now worse, or their merits may be nearly equal—but they are different. Even when nearly equal, they are *magis pares quam similes :* and we have to consider literature, in these aspects, as not one thing but two things. Every book, every page, is one thing, spoken, and another, read.

Again, you can read a poem twice or thrice or many times. Who feels the tenth time quite as he felt the first ? One recalls the story of Lysias, which Macaulay liked to repeat. Lysias made a speech for a man who had a case coming on in the Law Courts. After a week the man returned, and demanded another—the speech was bad. 'When I read it through the first time, I thought it magnificent; but now I know it by heart it seems so poor I do not dare to speak it.' 'Just so,' said Lysias, 'but remember the judges will hear it only once.' There is a world of wisdom in that anecdote.

But further, there is a second stage in reading perhaps even more important than the first—the stage at which we cease to read aloud, even to ourselves, but carry through the whole process in the mind. Many of us can remember the date of this change in our own reading, and the immense revolution it caused in our whole mental outlook. One might almost date from that point the realisation of the distinction between the outer and the inner world, the ' ego ' and the ' non-ego.' But we do not realise how long it took before this change took place in the world at large. As that great scholar S. H. Butcher remarks in his 'Harvard Lectures,' the whole Græco-Roman world read, when it read at all, aloud : and the very idea of mental reading had scarcely arisen. He refers, by way of illustration, to the curious passage in which Augustine describes his wonder when he saw Ambrose reading without even moving his lips. Had Ambrose been a Manichee, Augustine would have called it a trick of the devil ; but in the case of so good a man as Ambrose, he decided, there would be nothing wrong about it.

Now when reading reaches this Ambrosian stage, which it now has done through the whole civilised world, it sets up a style and taste of its own, quite distinct from those appropriate to a literature which is an affair of the voice only. It is impossible to exaggerate the importance of this advance : it marks the difference, to a very great degree, between ancient and modern criticism—the ancients troubling so much about sounds, and we so much about thoughts. We can make the experiment for ourselves. We shall find that a poem silently read has a metrical beauty or ugliness strangely remote from the beauty or ugliness it would show if it were read aloud. We hear it, but we hear it with the ears of the mind ; and these mental sounds are not by any means exact reproductions of those the outer world would hear. A first-rate musician may, in reading a score, hear in his mind exactly, or nearly exactly, what he is about to hear when the score is rendered in the concert-hall : though even he, I believe, finds *some* addition to what he has heard. But when we read a poem of Tennyson or Keats there is little or nothing of the kind. There is a *sight-audition*, and the mere appearance of the page has much to do with it. A harshness or a smoothness that is *invisible* the mind neglects to notice. Many of us must often have *seen* a beauty in a page of poetry, which, when the verses are read aloud, is discovered to be no longer there.

It may be interesting here to give incidentally another example. All will know that Wordsworth was constantly observed to be wildly excited as he conned over some of the prosiest lines of the *Excursion*. This was partly vanity, from which, with all his great-ness, Wordsworth was by no means free. But it was, I think, largely due to something else. Wordsworth read, or declaimed, his poems *aloud*, and thought of them as recitations rather than as signs on paper. He often recited them to himself, out of doors, with such furor that the villagers used to remark how old William had broken out again. Now I have tried the experiment, and I think if the reader tries it also he will be astonished at the result. Let him take one of those prosy passages, try to get up a little excitement about it (even, if humble enough, fancy it is his own) and read it with as much force as he can muster, out of doors for preference. He will, if I am not mistaken, discover that the prose has put on poetry. This is because Wordsworth wrote, or composed, to hear himself : he made his poems, often without pencil or paper, *aloud* ; and he fails, again and again, to be duly appreciated because he is tested by silent reading. He did not realise the effect of his verses on people who never read aloud : and that is one of the reasons why so much of his poetry is flat and unprofitable to-day. On the other hand, the worship which Coleridge paid to him is largely explained by the fact that he *heard* so much of the poetry, recited on those long and open-air West of England walks.

Conversely, many of the verses which Robert Bridges thought inharmonious, he thought so because he *looked* at them. He saw consonants crowded together, and fancied they would not pronounce easily. Had he tried, he would have found that many of them, so heavy in appearance, ran lightly and easily from the tongue. There are lines in the *Sensitive Plant* which *seem* open to censure ; but it is only seeming after all.

With prose the case is the same. By a pleasant illusion we *imagine* a series of sounds, and enjoy them, though they correspond to nothing in reality ; and many a writer has gained credit for a harmonious style simply because, as things are now, reading aloud is uncommon, and the hearing eye slides easily over roughnesses which become instantly apparent when the test of recitation is applied. The mind-voice runs gently along the page : the outward ear speedily brings clumsiness to light. And as writers write for the inner ear, this kind of harmony will be more and more cultivated, and the old more and more neglected.[1]

[1] Let the reader, by way of experiment, read a few pages of eighteenth-century writing, which were composed before the art of *paragraphing* had been studied as it has been since. He will notice how this mechanical device has become a stylistic aid. The same thing will be

Some idea of the immense change of taste which the introduction of writing must have brought about may be obtained by considering facts which are before our own eyes. We constantly observe that the same passage appears altogether different in writing, in typescript, and in print. Each of these systems of communication, having established its own standard of taste, constrains the same piece of literature to arouse varying degrees of pleasure or aversion in our minds. As a letter, for instance, in typescript, carrying business-associations, and being so obviously destined for speedy consignment to the waste-paper basket, only with difficulty stirs feelings of friendship and intimacy, so a story or an essay read in typescript starts suggestions which have to be vigorously checked if we are to appreciate it duly. We read writing in one way, typing in another, and print in a third. How much more strongly marked must have been the revolution when the voice was first transferred to vellum or papyrus, or when, as Macaulay imagined, the poet-laureate of Babylon, instead of mouthing his panegyrics of the King, published a bridge and four walls in his praise! It may be said that we can still recite a poem as well as read it, and thus compare the two effects. But recitation as an *alternative* to reading can never be what recitation was when it was the *sole* means of publishing it to the world. For of old the hearers could compare one recitation with another : we, to-day, compare the

seen, in exaggerated fashion, if he considers other mechanical devices, such as footnotes, appendices, and genealogical tables. All these are incorporated in the *text* of ancient writers, and spoil their *style*. For instance, there can be no doubt that had the appendix or the footnote existed in the time of Thucydides, he would have thrown the episode of Pisistratus and his sons, which now so gravely disturbs the balance of Book VI, into small print, and relegated it to the bottom of the page.

recitation with the *ideal* recitation which the reading has given us or will give us ; and the effect is often disastrous. It was Charles Lamb's private reading of *King Lear*, and all the endless reverberations of that mental voice, which made it impossible for him to endure seeing and hearing it on the stage. A modern work has thus to pass several tests of different kinds, whereas the early bards had to face but one. Even when Æschylus and Euripides published the tragedies that had been heard, they took a great risk, worse even than that taken by a writer of articles in the weekly press who collects them in a volume. Would the play that had taken the thronging audience with beauty capture the solitary student ? Sometimes, we know, the play that had failed at the Dionysia succeeded in private ; sometimes the converse happened. A Xenocles might defeat Euripides in the theatre ; but he has not done so in the study.

Taste, then, evolves not only as men themselves change, but as the media of communication vary ; and if ever some method be discovered by which thoughts may be conveyed directly from mind to mind, taste will assuredly change again. Suppose some future Shakespeare or Dante to be able to think, and by mere thinking make us think his thoughts, it is tolerably certain that many old works of genius will pass out of fashion, and will fail to hit the new taste thus generated. The old immortals will die, and new immortals will arise to flourish their little season, knowing as little as their predecessors how much of their glory had been due to circumstances and accidents entirely outside themselves.

III

LITERARY TASTE IN GENERAL

IT may seem unnecessary to remark that tasting, as applied to literature, is a mere metaphor. Yet it may well be remembered that metaphors are deceptive, and that half the mistakes in thinking are due to yielding to their deceits. Nothing, for instance, has done more harm to the science of politics than the habit of carrying too far the analogy between the State and a person : and the errors due to the analogy between the education of children and the tending of plants have been almost equally numerous. The fact is that metaphors, like other good liars, tell the truth till they have induced us to trust them, and then come out with the lie.

In the case we are considering the figure tells, or implies, a good many of these preliminary truths. As in our physical aspect we do not live by tasting but by eating and digesting, so in our mental we do not live— in plain words we do not learn—by taste. The pleasure derived from eating may indeed *induce* us to eat and so keep up our strength ; and the pleasure derived from a book may induce us to read and so to learn. But it is not itself learning, and is at best—to use another deceptive metaphor—the handmaid to learning. And when we talk of literature as such, we are not thinking of the instruction it may give, but of

47

the more or less pleasant way in which it gives it. This is what Charles Lamb meant when he talked of books that were no books : a parcel of pages stitched together that gave him no enjoyment was to him not a piece of literature at all. And this was what I meant when I said above, taste, in itself, was not an affair of brains.

But, having told the truth so far, the metaphor proceeds, as so often, to deceive. The next feature to be pointed out is one in which the likeness fails, and in which the use of the word taste may, unless we are on our guard, lead us astray.

In physical taste, at least in its elementary stages, the pleasure or revulsion is felt directly and almost, if not quite, instantaneously. We like or dislike the thing itself, without reference to anything else. We never say, ' I like this because it reminds me of that ' : we like it in itself. With literary taste, the case may often appear the same : but no one, as I have already pointed out, can carry his analysis far without perceiving that the sense of beauty or ugliness we derive from literary works is always, or almost always, a matter of association and suggestion. If we put aside the plain *satisfaction* which we feel when, by an orderly arrangement of sentences, or by the use of the appropriate words, the author has made reading easy to us, it would I think be no exaggeration to say that our pleasure in ' good ' writing, as our annoyance with ' bad,' is *always* a matter of association. Where it may seem to be otherwise, this is because, by habit, the association is made so swiftly as to seem instantaneous. This is why books, passages of poetry or prose, even the complete works of an author, which once pleased or displeased us, are found later to act on us in the opposite way. New associations have gradually and unconsciously arisen, and the same words now suggest different images. There is, in fact, no sound, word, or combination of words, which is beautiful in itself, or which cannot become ugly by association with something we dislike. Examples gross as earth will instruct us. We have only to consider the simplest of consonants to be convinced. It is well known, for one instance, that Milton disliked the hissing palatal *sh*, and substituted *s* for it whenever he could. The Semitic languages, on the other hand, indulge freely in it : and hence Milton, drawing so largely on Hebrew names, behaved like the Ephraimites at the ford, and was often hard put to it to avoid the objectionable sibilant. Tennyson went still further. He was delighted when he heard that Archbishop Trench had been acute enough to notice how dexterously he shunned the sound of *s* : Pope, on the other hand, most certainly did not shun it. These differences were plainly due to differences in the associations these consonants stirred in the minds of the different poets. And so with words. Some years ago, as Mr Spender tells us, the *Westminster Gazette* set a prize-competition for the most beautiful word in the English language. The word fixed upon was ' swallow.' ' Do you mean a bird or a gulp ? ' said Mr. Spender : and the prize was not given. But where is the difference in the *sound ?* Is it not plain that among the things which go to making the so-called beauty of a word the strong association of its *meaning* is one of the most powerful? To turn to accent. An Irish brogue is often sufficient to induce an Englishman to empty his pockets: Bernard Shaw, a competent authority, has told us there is nothing in it. I knew a Scots boy whose accent could get round the sternest of his English

E

schoolmasters : but his Scottish mother had sent him to school in order that he might get rid of the horrible tone, and acquire the charming English one. Matthew Arnold imagined there was an absolute beauty in Greek proper names as compared with our English ones, and poured cultured scorn on our surname 'Wragge.' He did not pause to consider that familiarity had bred contempt. The English names came to him associated with the sordid surroundings which nauseated his Oxonian soul ; whereas the Attic names came to him linked with a thousand memories of pleasure derived from Greek poetry, and with the deceptive glamour of Greek myth. Time has washed away the squalor of the Athenian slum, and left the Parthenon to delude our historic sense. I have little doubt that, if the Greeks had come two thousand years after us, and studied our literature as we study theirs, some Matthew Arnold of Athens or Alexandria, mocked by the magic of Shakespeare or by the charm of the ruins of Westminster Abbey, would have fancied a beauty and a glamour in Dickens's 'Mr. Grewgious' or 'Mr. Snodgrass' which he sought in vain in the 'Socrates' or 'Themistocles' that he heard every day. This is not to deny that there is often an ugliness in the merely strange. The law of association moves in mysterious ways. We cannot rouse much enthusiasm at first for Tiglath-pileser or Hatshepsut : and our interest in Utnapishtim is usually no more than interest in the grotesque. But let a man be once 'bitten' with the splendour of the ancient monarchies, let him be carried away with the sense of immemorial age, and these names acquire a beauty which is not at first to be perceived in them. On the other hand, all sorts of impulses, patriotism, family feeling, clannishness, mere perversity, may lead men to fancy a beauty in their own language which is quite imperceptible to the callous outsider. The Kalmucks, according to De Quincey, are quite convinced that their own tongue is the most exquisite in the world ; and the Germans love the gutturals which annoy some foreigners. A dialect charms its native speakers, as a Yorkshireman uses his broad patois in his home, refusing to talk standard English in surroundings that arouse tender associations, and reserves the affected and mincing style for business hours : or as a Hanoverian will stoutly maintain that his pronunciation of German is the only wear, while it annoys the Rhinelander or Swabian. Yet it is the same sound—with different associations to different people. But we need not cross the North Sea to find proofs that when we talk of beauty in words we are really, consciously or subconsciously, having regard to something else. It is enough to look at recent baptismal registers. Thirty years ago, what middle-class mother called her daughter Elizabeth, Anne, or Jane ? These were associated with the kitchen. Later, as the kitchen began to poach on the drawing-room, the aristocratic names were dropped, and the ' good old-fashioned ' ones returned. They are, and must be, in themselves as beautiful, or as ugly, as ever : the suggestions they carry have altered. And so it is with the appellatives : it is certain that words now hateful, and hardly to be pronounced at all, were once absolutely harmless. Does the reader see any difference between *tishshagalnah* and *tishshachabnah?* Yet, if he were to pronounce the one in a Hebrew synagogue all the audience would hiss him from the lectern : if the other, he would cause no excitement.

One main element, then, in a ' good ' book is that
it contains a series of words and sentences which call
up pleasing associations ; and a writer who does this
continuously is said to have a good style. But it is
plain that the associations must vary from practically
nil with one reader to almost infinity with another.
To the beginner in Latin, Virgil's style is non-existent :
his arrangement of words appears arbitrary and
stupid : the words themselves have a meaning, to be
found out from a dictionary, but nothing else : his
rhythms, and his variations of rhythm, cannot be felt.
So far, he can appeal to the reader merely through
his story ; and that unravels itself so slowly that he
knows no more of it than a pedestrian learns of England in a day's walk. The ' taste ' for Virgil of such
a reader is not very delicate or discriminating.

But now let us imagine that he acquires a little more
knowledge. He learns, let us say, to scan. He thus
gains the power of perceiving that the lines run with
a swing. His ideas are crude : he probably recites the
lines with a sing-song like that with which a child recites
a nursery-rhyme. But he has made *some* progress,
however slight : he can admire the mere fact that
without destroying the sense, Virgil has contrived to
keep to one metre. Possibly this metre has English
associations for him : he can compare it with that of
Evangeline or the *Bothie*. His taste is growing.

Now take him half a dozen years later, when he can
sense, to some extent, the use of words in a certain
order, the elaboration of the sentences, the repetitions
which never fail to add something, the dignity and
stateliness of the diction. He may, further, learn that
Virgil borrows, and yet always puts himself into his
borrowings ; that passages from Ennius or Lucretius

are always appropriate to their changed setting, and always new however old. He may be able to feel the rhythmical beauty of the *Georgics,* or the tender grace of many paragraphs of the *Æneid.* It is plain that all this growth of taste is due, in the main, to an enlarged acquaintance with the Latin language and literature, as well as with other languages and literatures. Nothing is as it was, to *him :* the words once dead are now alive with associations, some conscious, more subconscious ; the rhythms, once mechanical, perhaps even beaten out with the fingers, are now musical, and their subtlest variations are ' felt in the blood, and felt along the heart ' ; the phrases, once but accumulations of words, ' disturb him with the joy ' of innumerable suggestions ; until at last he tastes, with Newman, those ' pathetic half-lines, giving utterance, as the voice of Nature herself, to that pain and weariness, yet hope of better things, which is the experience of her children in every time.' A perfect Latin—and Greek—scholar, if such a man could be found, would be the perfect appreciator of Virgil : and even to-day, with all the hindrances of two thousand years, some men come not far off the ideal.

Or, to take an example from our own literature, a student of Milton, who in many respects appears to resemble Virgil, may easily apply the test by his own memories. Let him recall his first reading of *Paradise Lost,* perhaps in early youth. He may remember how much in that poem passed by him quite unnoticed, how he was conscious but of a strange narrative, not always pleasing, and of a roll of majestic sound. He may even have been fretted by the blank verse, and may, like Johnson, have wished the poem had been in rhyme ; or, more probably, the long paragraphs, the inversions and involutions of the style, may have given him some annoyance. Gradually, however, if he is one of those on whom Milton makes an insistent inscrutable demand, he sees the enormous power of the ' planetary ' style, and the vast range of possibilities open to the poet who has discarded the ' unnecessary adjunct ' of rhyme, and the ' jingling sound of like endings.' Or he may have been at first totally blind to the associations of the mere words, which in Milton, as is well known, are packed with varied suggestion, and are meant to call up every image that can be drawn from their ultimate derivations. How different is it all when he learns to weigh and analyse these words, and wring from them their full meaning : when, for instance, *idea* comes to him with the whole burden of the Platonic philosophy, and without the enfeebling associations of to-day ! Or, again, he may have been deaf to the multitude of classical allusions or reminiscences sometimes hidden in the slightest turn of phrase. As these loom on him, one by one, what added beauty do they bring ! To feel these things is but a fragment of the vast potentiality of enjoyment open to the diligent reader of Milton. To a man totally destitute of the capacity to feel them, *Paradise Lost*, though it has a strange power of stirring the dormant poetry even of the ignorant, must yet often appear weary, flat, and if not stale yet unprofitable. He will be in the painful position of seeing that something is aimed at that he cannot perceive : he will ' behold a great tumult, but wit not what it is.' Contrast such a man with the ' consummated scholar ' of whom Mark Pattison speaks, whose ' last reward is the due appreciation of Milton.' To him the poem comes with an appeal derived from ten thousand associations, slight, strong, verbal, stylistic, phraseological, rhythmical : and when once this mastery has been attained, the man has a ' possession for ever,' not merely in his knowledge of the poem itself, but in the trained taste which will thenceforward enable him, like the child of prophetic promise, to ' know the evil and to choose the good.' However many standards he is able to acquire later, he will now have at any rate one standard. Not the least of his acquisitions will be a new and almost unlimited store of noble associations, by which he will be able to judge other poems and assign to them their proper places. To take but one example out of hundreds, he will no longer be content with verse that merely scans. He will weigh in Milton's balances the blank verse of *Festus*, of the *Seasons*, of the *Night Thoughts*, and find it wanting : while, with a due sense of originality in imitation, he will weigh that of Tennyson, Keats, or Shelley, and note that it does not kick the beam.

It was a man like this that Milton had in mind when he prayed for an audience fit though few. And this once more leads us to the perception of the relativity of taste. No poet's repute is more firmly established than Milton's : it stands, amid all changes, ' like Teneriffe or Atlas, unremoved,' and perhaps the more securely because, like Teneriffe, Milton stands alone. He is not, like Shakespeare, the Everest among a thousand lesser peaks : he rises solitary from a plain. You cannot miss his grandeur. And yet it is clear that hardly two people can read him in the same way. He makes one appeal to the ignorant, another to the fairly well-read, another to the profoundly learned : one to the student of Homer, another to the Dante-enthusiast, another to the ' correct ' Frenchman who is steeped in

Racine : yet another, may I add, to Mr. T. S. Eliot ? For even Mr. Eliot, amid all his depreciation of Milton, reveals that he is somehow conscious of the poet's greatness : and his very depreciation, so far as it goes but proves my point. To quote once more Coleridge's familiar saying, ' We receive from Nature but what we give her ' ; and in this respect Milton, like every other poet, resembles Nature. We receive from him not what we give exclusively, but nothing that is not tinged with what we give. We cannot bring to the reading of *Paradise Lost* ' an understanding equal or superior ' to the poet's : but unless we bring something like it, in whatever degree, we shall fail to gain from it. If from ignorance, prejudice, or obstinacy, we do not bring this element of our own, the poem will not speak to us. It is this union, or fusion, of the poet with the reader that provides the sphere in which taste works. No writer lives for himself alone ; his book is for reader and writer. Nay, in a very true sense it is written *by* the reader, who must collaborate with the writer if the book is to achieve any sort of real existence. Even if the writer finds no one else to read it, he has been two persons in producing it. He has made it and he has read it ; he has prepared the meal and he has tasted it.

No mistake is more far-reaching than that which conceives of a book as something merely written. Unless it is read it is a maimed thing, or rather nothing at all. It exists, if it exists, in that mysterious region of which the metaphysicians speak, where the object is without a subject to perceive it : it is an abstraction totally without interest to the ordinary human being. And, as there are millions of readers—at least for those books which live long, and for those books which have a short life but an ignoble one—every book is many books. It is a phenomenon seen by a million eyes, absorbed into a million consciousnesses. To talk of a *Buch an sich* is to talk of an impossibility. A book is the impression it makes on this reader, another reader, and yet another : all that, but nothing else. To the wrong reader *Paradise Lost* is but a perform- ance : to the right one it stands among the greatest achievements of the mind ; precisely as a symphony of Beethoven makes every sort of appeal, from the agony it gives to the tone-deaf, through all grades of annoyance and pleasure, to the trance-like ecstasy it affords to the man who, by nature and nurture, is worthy to hear it.

Every book, and every paragraph, that we read, supplies in its measure—sometimes insignificant, some- times great—a standard for later books ; and this reference to a standard, consciously realised or not, is what we mean by taste. A child may have read but one book ; it appreciates the next by a comparison or contrast with the first. I do not mean that it measures it *solely* by this comparison ; but this previous book is one, and often the chief, element in the child's experiences which are brought to bear in the apprecia- tion of the book. As he reads more, his reading becomes a more and more important element, for this purpose, among his experiences. He gradually learns, feebly and inexactly, to isolate the pleasure he derives from books, and mark it off as a *literary* pleasure. This we call forming a *literary* taste. The process is astonish- ingly varied and complicated. It may work by con- trast. Previous books, of apparently the same class, have been liked or detested ; this one may repel him or attract him by a clear dissimilarity which appears

to him as a superiority or inferiority. Thus, to take
a familiar example. He may read *Tom Brown's Schooldays*. This—a certain previous experience in *mere*
reading being assumed—will be tasted according to the
boy's own school-life : it will seem probable or improbable, good or bad, by comparison with that life.
The descriptions of football and cricket will be appraised by his own knowledge of those games. He will
think the book mawkish or manly according to the
effect his own upbringing has had upon himself.
Finally, perhaps without knowing he does so, he sums
up the innumerable impressions and feelings he has
had during the perusal, and appraises the book as a
whole. ' It is,' he may say to himself or others, in his
own vernacular, ' not such a rotten affair after all.'
But what I would wish to emphasise is that this is
a decisive experience for him. Its results cannot be
lost, except by some great mental catastrophe, if
entirely even then. His reading of his next book is,
by the very fact that it is a next book, a vastly different
thing from what it would have been had it been the
first. He has now not merely his own life, but a *book*,
as a mental sphere conditioning his reception of another
book. Suppose that he continues his course of school-
stories. Should he choose *Eric*, or *The Fifth Form at
St. Dominic's*, while of course his own school-life will
still set its mark on his appreciation, he will inevitably
feel the new book with a mind of which *Tom Brown*
is now a part. He will contrast or compare the new
book with his remembered feelings as to *Tom Brown*,
and by means of new powers communicated by *Tom
Brown* : and, with the majority of boys, it is to be
hoped, the resultant impression will be that the later
book is somewhat inferior. It is less true to life, less

satisfying to his nascent literary taste. It will be read against a background of something dimly perceived to be higher, and will in all probability be vigorously condemned in consequence. Had the books been read in another order, however, the effect must have been different, for the standard would have been different. A bout of *Eric* might well, to many boys, have made the sentimental parts of *Tom Brown* appear even crudely robust ; while, if the boy had learnt to distinguish between the honest and straightforward style on the one hand and the turgid and over-rhetorical on the other, the revolt against Farrar's flamboyance would be much stronger if he came to it after the simplicity of Hughes.

It is, of course, impossible to enumerate even a tithe of the influences which combine in the strange jumble of feelings that go to the tasting of a book. In early days we accept any or all of them without question. A boy likes or dislikes, in either case violently, but usually without asking why. It cannot well be, until a considerable number of books have engendered in a youth a more or less fixed taste, that all these influences will fail to sway him in disproportionate degrees, or that he can taste—I do not yet say ' judge '—a book in any but a very crude fashion. Though, as I said above, he may have become able to discriminate *literary* emotions from others, he has not yet learnt to use this discriminating power with any regularity or precision. He is still prone to like or dislike a book because it does, or does not, give him an accurate picture of scenes or persons familiar to him in daily life. I have known boys who could not endure *Stalky and Co.* because the slang employed by Kipling's heroes is strange to them : and others, of the public-

school type, to whom Talbot Baines Reed's stories
are annoying because the author has not caught the
peculiar public-school tone. Our youth, in fact, cannot—and, to tell the truth, few of his seniors can—
quite like an author whose opinions he detests. He
cannot read ' objectively,' and distinguish between the
manner of a writer and his matter, or keep irrelevant
prejudices from intruding into what ought to be a
closed compartment of his mind. As a sailor cannot
endure a sea-story, however ' well ' written, in which
the author betrays ignorance of navigation, so with
him. What seems impossible in his own experience
will destroy all appreciation of stylistic merit. Or,
as too often happens, he may associate certain books,
and in consequence their authors, or perhaps even all
books, with the idea of a school-task, or of an examina-
tion in which they were set. A thousand other influences may affect him, and distort his powers of
appreciation, as a thousand may go to the development
of his literary feelings. But in any case, so long as these
irrelevancies *do* affect him, we say that his taste is as
yet ' unformed.'

If we consider the enormous variety, alike in general
experience of life, in mental acquirement, and in special
literary capacity, which is to be observed in readers,
variety in language, in nationality, in nurture, in
heredity, in daily occupation, and in a thousand other
points, we shall once again perceive how impossible
it is for the same book, the ' Buch an sich ' which we
may assume for the moment to have a real existence,
to produce the same impression on them all. It would
indeed be a miracle if it produced the same impression
on any two, though those two were twins brought up
in one house, and never separated for a day. And, as

the ' Buch an sich ' has in fact no existence ; as a book
is—to repeat what can scarcely be too often repeated—
the result of a chemical combination between author
and reader, it is still more improbable that this combination can in any two cases be the same. There are
in truth more *Iliads* than there are transcripts of the
Iliad, more ' best-sellers ' by far than there are copies
sold. It would seem, then, as if there could be no
satisfactory standard of taste : and in one sense this is
unfortunately the fact.

Things, however, are not quite as bad as that : and
what I have already said about standards may provide
some comforting suggestions. As, in medicine, the
doctor has to deal with human bodies, and minds, no
two of which are exactly alike, and occasionally makes
some appalling mistakes, yet is recognised to be a better
judge of the human frame and its peculiarities than
the layman, so in the world of literature. There are
men who have read more books, or have read fewer
books with more care and better comparing powers,
than others. Their minds are enriched with more
various associations, alike of words, of phrases, and of
whole works, than are the minds of others. They can
therefore come more closely into contact with the
minds of the writers than the majority. We recognise,
for example, that a man who is steeped in medieval
lore is a better judge of Dante than we are ourselves,
or that a man who knows Chaucer, his sources, and his
contemporaries, is more likely to understand him than
a mere beginner. If to this equipment he adds the
power of being able to interpret his author clearly to us,
to bring out easily and vigorously his strong and weak
points, to draw our attention to characteristics we
might otherwise have missed, then we are ready to

give him the same sort of confidence we give to a doctor. He is human : he sometimes makes horrible blunders, and, as with doctors, his colleagues are by no means always in agreement with him : but he is none the less, compared with ordinary men, an expert and an authority. He is in our common phrase a ' critic.' In a later chapter I shall attempt the difficult task of showing wherein criticism differs from the ' taste ' about which I have so far been speaking.

IV

ON CHANGES OF TASTE IN GENERAL

A FRIEND of mine once asked me whether I did not think that a fashion in literary taste might be closely associated with fashions in other things. Might we not, he asked, be able, by a little exercise of imagination, to guess at the history of literature by looking at the history of costumes ? The Elizabethans and Jacobeans, he said, wore stiff ruffs and wrote stiff paragraphs. The Victorians wore crinolines, and indulged in flowing periods. The beaver hat and the heavy stock of the Reform period were, he thought, remarkably parallel to the rather heavy language of the novels of the same time : and he went so far as to throw out the suggestion that short skirts and short sentences went together.

I did not quite agree with him. I asked him how he reconciled Addison's portentous wig with his light essays, or what likeness there was between the style of Cowper's John Gilpin and the nightcap so dear to all familiar with Cowper's illustrated works. Again, if short skirts go with short sentences, what about the present time, when—so we are told—short skirts are worn by day and long in the evening ? Is a novel written in the morning more snappy than one written by the same lady at night ? Or could we tell, by inspecting a poem, whether the man who wrote it was still in his plus-fours, or had donned the evening-dress and dinner-jacket before sitting down to work at his *vers-libres* ?

Nevertheless, my friend's theory does call attention to the fact that literary taste, like so many other tastes, is to a very great extent the creature of mere fashion. It is ever varying, not merely among masses of men, but in the individual man. The wind of taste bloweth where it listeth : you can no more tell why it changes, or what will be its next manifestation, than you can say why the crinoline came in or why it went out. So variable is it in fact that, as the reader must have observed, I have not been able to keep myself from talking about its changes even when discussing it in the abstract. So marked a feature of literary taste is this tendency, that I defy anyone to describe it without alluding to its fickleness, however eager he may be to discover some permanent principle on which to base it. It may be that variety is not of the essence of the thing ; in any case it is what the old schoolmen called an inseparable accident of it. It is like liability to error, which does not form part of the definition of humanity, but without which no human being is known to exist. A taste appears, and often runs through the world like a prairie fire : the matter that has kindled it is too small to be detected, and when it ceases to blaze you cannot tell what has put it out.

But sometimes you need not wait for it to go out. You cross a room, and find the fire cold. Later generations do not agree with earlier ; but contemporaries differ equally. No examples are necessary ; but as a mere matter of interest we may glance at Tacitus's *Dialogue on Orators*. There we learn how Cicero thought Calvus, the ' salaputium disertum ' of Catullus, bloodless and chilly, while Calvus called

Cicero loose and without sinew : to Cicero Brutus
was bare and disjointed, to Brutus Cicero seemed
' fractum atque elumbem,' feeble and without back-
bone. ' If you ask me,' says Aper, the speaker, who
lived a hundred years later than these famous orators,
' all these men were right ' : and he goes on to say
why he prefers the men of his own time to the heroes
of the past. It is mainly on that ' why ' that the other
interlocutors do not agree with Aper : Tacitus does
not appear to agree with any of them ; and modern
students, while disagreeing with Tacitus, do not
agree with any of his puppets. This is a type of what
happens whenever two or three critics meet together
—except that Tacitus's characters talk politely and
kiss each other at parting. A change of fashion has
rendered such tokens of urbanity impossible to-day :
but we may endeavour here to discuss the question as
amicably as modern manners permit.

In one sense, and that a not unimportant one, it
would seem that if taste did not change, we should not
have any. All taste, it is obvious, involves comparison,
and comparison involves difference. If all notes in
the scale were reduced to one, we should, apart from
mere numerical distinctions, have no means of telling
one from another, and music would, at best, become
a mere Morse code or clog-dance. One note might
precede, or follow, another, or be longer or shorter
than another ; and that would be all. Time itself,
if not but a name for change, has to be measured by it.
With taste, and things which we tell by taste, whether
physical or mental, the case is the same, ' only more so ' :
for we have nothing outside the ' palate ' by which to
judge them ; whereas with other things we have sometimes the advantage of being able to use more senses

F

than one. Thus space, which in the first instance is
certainly an affair of tactual sensation, is very early in
our lives measured by sight : and even smell and hearing, which in many respects approximate to taste,
may often be corrected by other senses.

I am speaking here, of course, about changes, or
varieties, which we experience when we taste *different*
things. Even when we do not realise that we are comparing tastes, we are in actual fact comparing the taste
of the thing with the neutral taste of the palate itself ;
and not seldom we compare one thing with another
either as present or as remembered. When we taste
sugar, we taste it as sweet compared with other foods.
If all foods were as sweet as sugar, and all sugars equally
sweet, we should have no recognisable feeling, and
should be unable to mark off anything from anything
else. Our only motive for eating—it might perhaps
be to our advantage—would be to abate the pains of
hunger. As things are, comparison is a necessary
element in taste, though it is usually, to all intents
and purposes, instinctive. When we pass to literary
taste, the comparing impulse is much more easily
detected. As we read a poem, and note that it has
pleased or fretted us, a host of comparisons are inevitably made ; and, though most of these are sub-
conscious, we are certain that they are there, and we
can often trace their history. The versification may jar
—that, we know, is because we have, by long practice,
accustomed ourselves to a certain standard of smooth
rhythm. The words may charm—this is because
certain words, in certain collocations, recall past
feelings of pleasure, or subtly avoid feelings of annoyance. The only difference between these mental
tastes and the physical is that the latter, in the main,

are instinctive : they are born with us : while the former have been acquired. Even the pleasure derived from rhyme and lilt is probably not the gift of pure 'nature' : there are tribes, apparently, that are without it. But be this so or not, these literary influences have been so thoroughly assimilated that, to all intents and purposes, they move us as spontaneously as if they were innate. Innate, indeed, they are held by some to be.

But—and here I pass to my main subject—it is impossible that these tastes, though aroused by the same things, can remain the same. A long process of eating sweetmeats, as is well known, produces first indifference, and then disgust. Similarly, a constant process is going on, of the reception and assimilation of new ideas, every one of which makes some change in the receiving mind—if indeed the mind is anything but this very succession of ideas. Repetition of impressions tends to produce, in many cases, satiety, and the desire for something new. The old wine ceases to please. In other cases it produces a dull, flat, unadventurous taste, which is inclined to reject anything not experienced before : but even here there is change, in the direction of greater stubbornness and unreceptiveness. This is very frequently to be observed in men, otherwise of great power, whose studies have been confined to a certain range : their tastes become hardened within that range, and they cannot welcome anything markedly foreign. The classical instance is, of course, that of Darwin, who, after long years of scientific work, found it impossible to recapture the delight which in his youth he had found in Shakespeare. But it is almost equally noticeable in men of more literary turn than Darwin. Few men have read

more, or more widely, than Macaulay : yet his reading
had distinct limitations, and had gradually ossified
his mind. As Trevelyan tells us, he scarcely read
anything, except novels, written after 1840. Ruskin,
Carlyle, were sealed to him. In Buckle he found little
but some of the faults of Warburton ; and of the period
between 1842 and 1850, one of the richest in the whole
poetical history of England, he remarked how barren
it was. He was one of the most modest of men, and yet,
years after the appearance of his *Lays*, he set down in
his journal that he was not aware of any better poetry
that had been published since. Much reading of
earlier poems—though those were assuredly among the
very greatest ever written—had left him dulled to
later harmonies. The change, in men of this kind, is
shown by a growing disinclination to change. Whereas
in youth one had been willing to test almost anything,
now one finds the chief pleasure in retracing old paths.

But there is another way in which reading may
produce change—change to a flat level of undiscrimi-
nating acceptance of anything whatever, good, bad,
or indifferent. Sir William Hamilton was accused
by John Stuart Mill of reading so many works of
philosophy as to have lost the power of seeing whether
the philosophers he studied agreed with him, with each
other, or with themselves. True or not of Hamilton,
it is certainly true of some people that they read so
much of every kind as to welcome anything whatever
with complete impartiality. This was, I believe, the
case with Magliabecchi, who is said to have been the
most voracious reader of all time. He was the shark of
libraries, and devoured everything on paper and in
print, till he did not know the difference between
Ariosto and a poetaster. It was certainly the case with

Joshua Barnes, who, according to Bentley, loaded his mind till the *Iliad* seemed no better than his own *Polemo-middinia*. And it is the case with these ceaseless readers of novels, who as soon as one is finished begin another. A novel, to them, is a novel, yellow or brown, and it is nothing more. There has been here a change, slow but certain, from more or less of daintiness to an extreme of gluttony.

If, then, we find constant variation, gradual or sudden, slight or great, in an individual, so much so that we can never be sure he will like next month a book over which he is enthusiastic to-day, or will not be obstinately liking it still more vigorously, it is plain that we must expect change from generation to generation. We should expect mighty changes in Methuselah or the Wandering Jew as the centuries passed over his head ; but each generation is not only later than its predecessor ; it is made up of different people, who start from a different point, pass through different experiences, and view them with different eyes. A thousand causes, not literary, necessitate this advance or retrogression ; and a thousand literary causes add their weight. Long before Sir Bedivere is old, he finds himself nothing but a voice, among new men, strange faces, other minds. A war, a political or social upheaval, a French Revolution, or an era of repression, a new mechanical invention, and literature responds to it as face answers to face in a mirror. The men of Marathon could not be expected to approve of the drama that sprang up after Salamis : and the young men threw the ancient plays impatiently aside. The change, in fact, is often but the natural antagonism of age and youth, which, as was observed long before the Passionate Pilgrim set out on his progress, cannot live together. Probably, ever since Jubal smote his lyre, the parents have disliked the frivolous fugues the children have pursued, and the children have rejected the stodgy stuff that suits the parents, and laughed at the 'rumores senum severiorum.' We know how the ' vetus poeta ' strove, first by persuasion and then by malediction, to withdraw Terence from the writing of his ' thin and empty ' plays, and how the youthful poet retorted on his elderly enemy. So it was in the beginning, so it certainly is now, and so, in all likelihood, it will be till the final conflagration destroys old and new together. Thus it is that we find literary reigns short, and the poetic dynasty constantly overturned by a revolution. It is rarely that an Amurath an Amurath succeeds : it is an Arician monarchy in which the ruler is ever being deposed by a pretender who is himself always liable to deposition. The king lives within the shadow, like the priest who slew the slayer and shall himself be slain.

No illustration of this truth is necessary. A score of illustrations, all probably different, will start up in the minds of a score of readers. But I cannot refrain from quoting here the words of one of the best poets that even Ireland has ever had. He is talking of the changes that may be expected in the next generation in his own country. ' No doubt that generation will formulate its own ideas. Quite possibly there will be a reaction to romanticism and Sinn Fein. Every generation reacts from the generation that has gone before, just as in Europe the Classical movement was followed by the Symbolist. Years ago, Yeats and O'Grady and Hyde and myself tried to produce the most mystical literature in Europe, and the reaction has been Joyce, O'Casey, O'Flaherty, and MacNamara,

who are among the most realistic of European
writers.

'The next generation will probably get tired of
realism ; but no one can say what it will turn to.
Literature is not like geometry, which advances from
point to point, and the next step in which can be more
or less accurately predicted. But we *can* say, with
great likelihood, that realism will *not* be followed by
realism.'

These, as has perhaps been guessed, are the words
of Æ, Mr. George Russell, who has seen in his life
as many inexplicable changes, both political and
poetical, as most men : and they are true and wise
words, as might be expected of their author. Change,
if not decay, in all around we see.

This is not to say that the new dynasty, however
violent its methods of accession, and however brief
its tenure, is less legitimate than any other. It rests
on a plebiscite, and as long as it can retain the favour
of its public its rule is lawful. There is no test of right-
ful kingship, in this region, save capacity to hold the
allegiance of the ruled. It may appear, to after ages,
that the Napoleon of the realms of rhyme gained his
domination merely by sounding phrases, or that the
Bourbon dynasty, though less showy, was more lasting :
but the true judges, after all, are the contemporaries.
Poetry that suits its time *must*, so far, be true poetry.
That it does not suit a later time is no more against
it than the fact that Marlborough never saw an aero-
plane is against his true reputation as a general. Every
man, whether warrior, statesman, or writer, must use
the means available in his time and country for working
upon the understanding and emotions of his fellows ;
and the fact that these means often go out of date is

no fault of his. ' Who art thou that judgest another man's servant ? To his own master he standeth or falleth ' : and the master of the author is his public. It is common for Englishmen to wonder at the French worship of Racine. But Racine wrote for Frenchmen, and by their judgment he abides. With very short intervals he has carried their suffrages for three hundred years ; long enough to prove that the mass of associations conveyed by his rhythms and phrases awakes a pleasurable response in a vast number of French minds. To millions, then, he is and must be, a great poet : for of great poetry there is no other definition than this, that it stirs deep thought and elevated feeling in multitudes of people. On the other hand, those in whom these feelings are not stirred have a perfect right to say that he is not a great poet—to *them* : although the confession may really be but a confession of their own limitations. For the most universal of poets can appeal only to those who have something in common with him : and such a thing as a poem absolute does not exist. It is a thing to be heard or read, and is a function of the sympathy between the author and his audience. Where there is no such sympathy, *there* the poetry vanishes ; and it is a mere accident of language that we are compelled to say that, on a certain occasion, the *poetry*, as if there were such a thing apart from the hearers, failed to move those hearers. The hearers are as essential to the poetry as the author himself. This was what Milton meant when he prayed for a fit audience : he knew that to the unfit *Paradise Lost* itself would be a thing of no value ; it would be the music of the spheres to a population grossly clothed in with a muddy vesture of decay.

To pass to a variation of taste due not to space but

to time. There are many who deny the title of poet
to Pope ; to whom his monotonous and epigrammatic
couplets are like much study to Ecclesiastes. To such,
then, he is no poet. But he was assuredly a poet, and
a supreme one, to the men of his own generation, and
for fifty years after his death. Even the ' malice '
which, in his own day, ' denied his page its own celestial
fire,' admired in its heart while it refused open admiration. He made, in fact, precisely the impression on his
contemporaries which he wished to make, and it was
to them a poetical impression. Within that world he
sat unquestionably as chief, and like Job he received
in the gate the homage of old and young. The time
came when this homage was denied him : this was
because the world had changed, the ears of the new
age were deaf to him. He ceased, therefore, to be a
poet. And yet a little effort on the part of his detractors, a zealous study of his times, of his language,
of the end he aimed at, and a vigorous endeavour to
cast aside later associations and to live into those of his
time, would have changed their taste again, and made
them appreciate him almost as fully as the men of
1740. Greatness, littleness, mediocrity, are but names
for the impression a writer makes upon his readers,
and will vary with those readers. Gulliver has but to
leave Lilliput and visit Brobdingnag, and the proportions are reversed. Man, to use Voltaire's title for
him, is Micromegas. Nothing is more certain than
that man is the measure of himself and everything
else, and yet nothing seems harder to keep steadily
in mind.

When a change of taste thus occurs, through
process of time, distance of place, mere satiety, or
any other great or trivial cause, directly literary or

quite unliterary, we have to beware of that 'criticism' which, as we shall see later, always comes in to justify it, and tries to dignify mere excuses with the name of philosophical principles. The surest sign of inadequacy in criticism is that it shows itself parochial, and cannot recognise merit beyond certain narrow bounds. When we observe men not content with simply saying that they have ceased to like what pleased their fathers, but presenting us with a vast parade of philosophical and psychological reasons in order to prove that we *ought* to dislike it, then is the time to distrust those men. If the principles of criticism are of such far-reaching and binding character, it is a miracle that our fathers did not perceive them. They are not, like the principles of natural science, matters of gradual and asymptotic approach, involving constant small corrections of previous results. They demand but slight knowledge of human nature, and a very few examples of literary fame and the loss of it are enough to provide a basis for all the reasoning that is necessary. You need, in fact, to know little more than that mankind is *varium et mutabile semper* if you want to explain why the great writer of yesterday is the little one of to-day. Yet each successive generation, with a comical air of profundity, produces its apparatus of critical theory, which, like Kant's somewhat arrogant *Prolegomena to all Future Metaphysics*, is first to demolish all previous structures, and then to lay the foundations for an everlasting and indestructible erection. Unfortunately, this new Tower of Babel never rises very high : and it is soon obvious that every one of the builders is speaking a language unintelligible to his fellow. Ere long they leave off their toil ; but another equally sanguine band is straightway ready to take their place.

Such criticism might as well be ignored from the first : it is an attempt to prove a foregone conclusion, and to demonstrate that what one man now likes all men should always like. Wesley said the world was his parish : these people want to make out that their parish is the world.

If the beauty of a work of art is an absolute entity, inherent in the work itself, and in no way dependent on the percipient, it is plain that no change of taste can make it more or less beautiful. What it was, it is, and what it is, it will be. But if so, it is strange that the passage of a few years, or the distance of a few miles, should mar this wonderful perfection, and blind people to a charm which was so visible to others. If, as Spenser says, ' all men adore perfect beauty,' what is the veil that so often hides it from their eyes? According to the same authority, who himself is building upon the authority of Plato, there is somewhere a wondrous Pattern, to whose mould all beautiful things have been fashioned,

> That now so faire and seemely they appeare,
> As nought may be amended anywhere :

and, as earthly things partake of it more or less, they are able to gain a vision of it. Unfortunately, even Spenser is unable to tell us with precision where this Pattern resides. It may be on earth laid up in secret store, in which case it must be hard to catch sight of it ; or it may be in heaven, that ' no man may it see ' at all. This being so, men have to put up with what poor imitations they can find ; for a pattern that cannot be seen might as well not exist. The fact is that this theory, whether expounded by Plato or by Spenser, is merely poetry—and, for the sake of argument, I am

willing to admit that, as poetry, it is very ' beautiful ' :
but I refuse to go further and to assert, with Keats's
urn, that it is therefore truth. As soon as we try to
reduce it to prose, we are involved in endless confusions
and contradictions. Nay, even in the lovely Hymn
in which Spenser proclaims the doctrine, we cannot
read far without seeing that the poet contradicts
himself, both verbally and substantially, with a
naïveté which, to me at least, adds to the charm of
his verses, but which utterly fails to convince my
understanding.

An illustration may be drawn from a region not
usually considered very poetical. Einstein, if I understand him aright, has shown that if a man, in a moving
train, walks an exact yard in a second, that distance will
not be an exact yard to a man measuring it from the
relatively stationary embankment, whatever precautions he may take to secure accuracy. The ' absolute '
yard may perhaps be ' laid up in secret store ' in the
heavens, but there is no way of getting at it. Now in
studying a work of art, every human being is in a
separate train ; and the trains are moving not merely
with different but with constantly varying velocities, in
all sorts of curves, and in all directions. Every ' yard
per second ' will therefore be different. The arrogant
critic thinks he is standing on the embankment. He is
not ; and if he were the platform also is a moving one.
And *his* measured yard is but relative to himself.

Beauty, then, changes and must change, as the individual man and the race of men, move on their separate
and erratic paths. It is, to repeat, but a function of
the sympathy between the painting and a changing
spectator, between the poem and the altering reader,
between the sonata and the inconstant hearer. Unless

the artist can appeal to a set of associations in the spectator's mind, more or less similar to those which induced him to make the painting or the sculpture, it will be viewed with indifference or even with disgust ; in two words, it will be nothing or it will be ugly. Unless the words, the rhythm, the structure of a poem start a train of suggestions in the reader more or less similar to those in the poet's mind, it will be read with a similar indifference or disgust : it will be ugly, or it will be a thing of naught. The brazen serpent could cure when it made its miraculous call upon the trusting multitude : when it was to them a thing of brass it left them in their pain. As I have said, we can at times, by labour, put ourselves into something like the poet's frame of mind : we can gain some sympathy with him : and then, if there has been some force or energy in him, our minds will answer to his. We shall be able to say, ' That is beauty ' : but we must not be so modest as to deny our own share in the process. With contemporary authors, our labour will usually be less ; and with contemporaries whose experiences have been like our own there will be practically no labour at all ; our minds will unite with the author's instantaneously, and—if we pause to reflect—we say *at once* ' That is beauty.' But give the same work to another, whose experiences have been different, and see how feeble the effect !

Some words once, it is said, spoken by Mr. Sean O'Casey may be here in point. ' An artist,' he said, ' always knows what is his best work.' This is true, in the somewhat platitudinous sense that he knows what is best *for him*. He knows what suggestions he has intended to arouse, and can see, better than anyone else, how far he has succeeded in arousing them in his own mind. But it is not true that he must always think the same work better than others, or even good at all. In the course of a few years he will have become different, and the old work may not suit the new man. It is probable that when Swift finished *Gulliver's Travels* he felt that here was his best work. In his later days his mind changed, and he went back to the *Tale of a Tub*. Still less can Mr. Sean O'Casey be sure that the work he now prefers will seem the best, that is *be* the best, to others. He is right, however, when he goes on, 'Of course, I want people to like my plays, that is, to comprehend them. No audience can get exactly the same vision as the artist, but an audience can get its own vision helped by the artist.' When we say, then, that a work of art is good, we mean, first, that the author's idea is satisfying, secondly, that to a greater or less degree he has realised it, and thirdly that, so far as we understand it, it satisfies *us*. But by no means whatever can we drain ' goodness ' of its relativity : we shall *always* decide merit by reference to ourselves. And, as everybody else must do the same thing, to say a work is good in the abstract is simply to use words without meaning.

There are many people who imagine that it is a mark of superiority to be severe in the rejection of forms or styles that have gone out of fashion. It is certain that the younger generation, when it pours scorn on the works that pleased its fathers, imagines that in doing so it is showing how much better it is than the old. The exact contrary is the case. Inability to appreciate a style once regarded as great is simply a proof of ignorance and narrowness of mind. If we say we cannot endure Pope, Tennyson, or any other of the gods of the past, that simply means that we are hopelessly limited in our outlook : that we cannot take in more than a very little at once. It is the stupid insular arrogance that says all foreigners are fools. It may be that we have not the opportunity of learning the foreign language or the means to go abroad. In that case the *ignorance* may be excusable, but the arrogance is not. It must always be remembered that Pope, having satisfied the Augustan age, *must* have been a great man, unless we are to be guilty of the inexpiable crime of bringing an indictment against a whole century : that Tennyson, having been the idol of the Victorians, *must* have been great, unless we are to claim that the age of Darwin, Huxley, Browning, Clerk Maxwell, and a thousand other names, was an age of imbeciles. That *we* do not like him shows that we do not understand the age in which he lived. It may be that we have not the time to put ourselves, by hard study, into the position to understand that age. So far, we are pardonable : but we are not pardonable if we make a boast of our incapacity. The first thing we have to recognise is that our fathers were *not* stupid, that when they admired they admired with reason. Nothing is more ridiculous than the swaggering vanity which goes about saying, ' Doubtless we are the people, and wisdom *was born* with us.'

If, amid all the uncertainties and vacillations of criticism, there be anything indubitable, it is this, that catholicity of taste is superior to fastidious narrowness, that the man who can find pleasure in the works of a dozen periods and many languages is so far of a higher rank than the man who has to confine himself to one. As I hope to show more fully in a later chapter, nothing is more certain amid uncertainty than that the inability to appreciate, in due fashion and measure, what others appreciate—in fact, to enter sympathetically into the minds of our fellows—is a *disability*, something to be ashamed of rather than to be boasted about. A blind man is to be pitied : but if he begins to howl ' I see,' his sin remaineth.

The acquisition of this catholicity is, of course, no easy matter. We find it hard enough to understand our nearest neighbours : to understand, even partially, those far removed from us is a task of deliberate toil, long continued and intense. Fortunately, it brings its own reward. The enlargement of mind is in itself sufficient recompense ; but when it carries with it the power of appreciating some great work which before was dumb to us, the payment is doubled. The labour of acquiring Greek is great, but the mere labour strengthens the mind, and when it has succeeded so far that in some measure we can hear the ' surge and thunder of the Odyssey,' who would call it wasted ? Nor is our time misspent if it merely teaches us our ignorance, and makes us see that we can never hear that surge as it once was heard. To have learnt modesty is in itself an education.

There is a sense in which even the gradual *refinement* of taste is sometimes to be carefully watched and checked. If we find that books which are to us obviously crude and bad are yet popular, there is a danger, here also, of an arrogant superiority. The right attitude is not that of contempt, but that of humble inquiry into the causes of the sympathy between the ' bad ' author and his public. It may be desirable to study whether a writer with this wide appeal can be altogether bad : whether he has not some quality of humanness which perhaps the more ' high-brow ' author might not cultivate with advantage.

'There is one person,' said Talleyrand, 'wiser than Napoleon ; c'est tout le monde ':[1] and the great world may not be so stupid after all. In any case, the study of the bad author throws light upon the character of the public that likes him : and, if the proper study of mankind is man, one of the best ways of studying him is to study the books he reads.

It will be my endeavour, in later chapters, to illustrate these positions more or less in detail : but before starting on these chapters I should wish to remind the reader that men are never simple. It may be desirable to isolate their motives and likings, and to consider them separately, but in actual fact these motives and likings are inextricably entangled. Ricardo and his followers considered man as an exclusively money-seeking animal, which he never is ; and other philosophers considered him as a merely sentimental animal, which he never is. What an individual man would do, seeking money one hour and sentimentalising the next, remained undetermined. Similarly, I shall isolate certain tastes of man, and for the moment pretend that they dominate him. In real life they scarcely ever do dominate him : he is Habakkuk, *capable de tout*. But there are advantages in considering the tastes separately, provided always that we do not, like King Lear, 'take the indisposed and sickly fit for the sound man,' nor, on the other hand, imagine that even the ' sound man ' is the whole of humanity. Man is never either wholly sound or wholly sick. The instant he is either, he dies.

[1] Canning remarked that the taste of the House of Commons was better than that of the most tasteful man in it : and Canning was neither the first nor the last to make the observation.

G

V

CRITICISM

If Taste always involves a reference to something else, it may appear always to include a judgment : indeed such reference would seem to be the very definition of Judgment. The old philosophers used to say that an Object was ' presented ' to the Subject, and that the Subject ' judged ' it to be so-and-so : that is, compared it with previously presented objects, and concluded that it was either similar or different. If, for instance, an object was presented which we judged to be sufficiently like our concept of Man to be included in the category of Man, we decided that it was a man : if it differed, we decided that it was not a man. It might seem that when we like a verse or a poem because it raises certain pleasant associations, we are exercising a similar activity.

But when we look more closely we see that taste, pure and simple, is not thus active. It is passive : the pleasing or unpleasing associations are roused in us without any effort on our part : whereas the decision that an object is a man, however rapid it may now have become through habit, is none the less an *exertion* of our powers, precisely as a practised musician is exerting his fingers, though his skill may be such that he is quite unconscious of the slightest strain. But no one exerts himself, even unconsciously, to like or dislike sugar : the feeling simply *occurs*. And similarly, though you like or dislike a verse or a sentence not in itself but because of its associations, these associations are not collected with any effort, however small : they arise spontaneously, or rather they usually do not *arise* at all : more often than not they never reach the surface of consciousness. Take, for instance, a line of Chaucer, which I imagine is as likely as any in the language to be generally called ' beautiful ' :

And she was fair, as is the rose in May.

It may be safely asserted that ninety-nine out of every hundred readers of that line simply *taste* its beauty. They do not pause to ask, ' That runs smoothly. Yet it consists of ten monosyllables, and ten monosyllables rarely run smoothly. How has Chaucer managed that ? ' or a score of other questions. Below the surface it is true, but not realised, lie a number of suggestions : those aroused by the poet's previous pictures of Emily, her spring-like youth, the freshness of the early year, the sunlit dew upon the rose on a summer morning. All these things lie beneath the surface of our minds. When we call them forth, when we begin to reflect on them, we have criticism, that is, more or less deliberate comparison and judgment. I said in an earlier chapter that taste, as such, had nothing to do with the intellect. But we may recall the pregnant words of Keats, ' Touch has a memory.' Still more reminiscent is touch when it advances to taste. And when that taste-memory is duly employed to compare and to judge, the intellect comes into play. Add this intellect to taste, and we have criticism.

True criticism will never lose sight of its parent and original. While constantly weighing and appraising, it will, if it is to have its perfect work, be tasting also.

Nothing is less satisfactory than an arid, mechanical, and merely measuring criticism. Reason alone is as feeble an instrument in literature as it is in life, or as a dull calculation of averages is in deciding the grace or skill of a cricketer. The aim of poetry is to give pleasure, and the temptation of a critic is to forget that he, too, is to get this pleasure. He often contents himself with the *enumeration* of faults or virtues, and tends to become a statistician.

This suggests that before advancing further it may be desirable to defecate the word of those evil associations which, in common talk, it carries with it. Criticism does not, or at least should not, mean fault-finding—which itself is an inaccurate word for fault-seeking. It may have to point out faults, as it may have to point out merits : but it does not pry for the faults. When Iago said, ' I am nothing if not critical,' he meant, I believe, to say, ' I am naturally of a judging, discriminating turn : one not to be taken in by casual and superficial likenesses.' He was, of course, speaking ironically ; and, as his real character was that of a cynical, Mephistophelean denier of good, we are apt to fancy that he was using the word in its present-day bad signification ; but we are mistaken in so thinking. He called himself a judge, not a fault-finder. I desire like him to use the word without any of these connotations ; but otherwise I desire to keep it as wide as possible. When Pater (at least in his title-page) avoided it, and used ' appreciation ' instead, he was making the same attempt, and trying to deter his readers from thinking there would be anything carping in his ' weighings of values.' Something of the same motive, amid obvious differences, may have swayed Oscar Wilde when, somewhat fantastically, he talked of his ' Intentions.' But Matthew Arnold's essays in *Criticism*—though I think there *was* some carping in them—were *intended* to be free from it : and the title was not in the least meant to indicate that the chief features in the book would be the detection of flaws. You will find much subtle analysis, but very little sleuth-like tracking of literary crimes, in Pater's studies of Wordsworth, Coleridge, or Charles Lamb : and you will find plenty—often more than plenty—of recognition of good, alongside of some depreciation, in Arnold's essays. My list of critics will include both Arnold and Pater.

Another word, also adopted to avoid the suspicion of fault-finding, is Interpretation. The critic, says Mr. P. P. Howe, is the literary middleman. To the Interpretation school he is rather the literary showman or advertiser. Mr. Wilson Knight, for example, in his recent book on *Shakespeare's Sombre Tragedies*, speaks as follows : ' Criticism to me suggests a process of objectifying the work under consideration—to show in what respects it falls short of or surpasses other similar works : the dividing its good from its bad : and a formal judgment as to its lasting validity. Interpretation, on the contrary, tends to merge into the work it analyses ; it attempts to understand its subject in the light of the subject's own nature, employing external reference, if at all, only as a preliminary to understanding : it avoids discussion of merits, and, since its existence depends entirely on an original acceptance of the validity of the poetic unit which it claims to translate into discursive reasoning, it can recognise no division of good from bad.' It may well seem that the interpreter needs interpretation. I will therefore turn these words into plain English. Interpretation tries to *understand* the work : it assumes the work has some sense in it. If some knowledge of the author or of his sources is necessary, it tries to get that knowledge : after that, it troubles no more but endeavours to make the sense of the work clear. Whether here and there the author fails in putting his case, is of no importance.—Now I regard this 'interpretation' as the first duty of the critic : unlike Mr. Knight, I would include this interpretation in my definition of criticism : and I shall notice it later.

But I have already pretty clearly indicated that I desire to keep criticism, even in this wide sense, as distinctly as possible, marked off from taste : and I have shown how difficult it is to do so. To refer once more to Reynolds. In what is perhaps his most famous discourse, the Seventh, Reynolds declares that 'we apply the term taste to that *act* of the mind by which we like or dislike anything.' If he means here to stress the word *act*, I have shown already that I disagree with him ; and certainly, in the later pages of that discourse, he seems to assign to taste the same active powers which belong to Reason, to Genius, to Calculation, even to Philosophy herself : and he leaps casually from such phrases as ' relishing ' works of art to ' weighing ' and ' balancing.' I pointed out some time ago that the subtle mind of Newman seemed to me to make the same leaps : and we shall find, I think, that Burke and others make similar assumptions. I have no desire to haggle about words, which, as Lewis Carroll remarked, will, if well paid, consent to mean anything whatever. But I think that this confusion, though sanctioned by such distinguished names, is at times productive of mischief, and I shall try to avoid it, as a rule, myself. Criticism comes in later to *justify* taste : but it is not itself taste. Some help in avoiding the confusion may, as so often, be gained from philology : for, though words do not always follow the path indicated by their derivations, yet, as with children, we can sometimes find out the way they were intended to go, and from which in their age they do better not to depart. A glance, then, at the history of the crucial terms shows that the distinction was indistinctly felt from the beginning. Taste, as we have seen, meant touch. The figure of speech involved in the word ' criticism ' is quite other. Unless I am deceived, *krino*, the Greek word from which it is derived, originally meant to separate : it is ultimately the same as the Latin *cribro*, to sieve, and as our word *riddle* in the same sense : a relative of the German *rein* and of our *rinse*. In criticism, then, there is always a conscious or implied Distinguo : we sieve out the good earth and reject the stony, we mark off the bounds between one style and another. This is a mental strain : it implies effort, whereas taste—I speak here generally —arises spontaneously. As, when you touch you feel resistance, but only later judge that the resisting thing is wood or iron, so with taste. It is true that criticism may *affect* taste, as a knowledge of what you are eating may affect, or prejudice, the palate. But the two *are* two : and—if I may be allowed to use for the moment a dubious psychological term—they belong to different ' faculties.' None the less, criticism often precedes taste, and often follows it, in such close neighbourhood that we often do not know which is which. When Leontes drinks without seeing the spider, and likes the potion, that is undoubtedly taste : but when someone ' presents the abhorred ingredient to

his eye,' and he loathes what he had liked, is this taste
or is it criticism ?

When reflection and knowledge thus come in, it by
no means follows that taste is lost, any more than a
trained musician ceases to enjoy a sonata because he
knows all about its form, and can recognise every
chord the pianist is playing. It may well be, and fortunately often is, that the criticism reinforces the
enjoyment, and makes it keener than before. And if
the hearer's knowledge is so thorough that it is part
and parcel of himself—that the mental picture of the
music rises without effort—then the judgment comes
so instantaneously as to blend with the taste, and to
appear practically, if not logically, one with it. It is
for this reason that Reynolds, Newman, and so
many others, pass insensibly from one to the other :
they had lived so long in theory that theory and
practice were one in their minds. But, such is the
weakness and instability of human nature that criticism,
which is essentially an affair of reason, often follows
the lead of taste, instead of guiding or correcting it.
It is no rare thing, as we have seen and shall see, for
a man to find reasons, not always unprejudiced, for
what has been entirely unreasoned. As Macaulay
said of Burke, he adopts his principles like a partisan,
and defends them like a philosopher. If we are candid
with ourselves, we shall, I think, confess that more than
once or twice, we have liked one passage, or disliked
another, in the casual way common to such feelings,
have stuck to our choice from sheer obstinacy, and
have defended it on *ex-post-facto* grounds. We have
a dim suspicion that the taste may be a mere prejudice,
but we will not own it, and we call on all our powers
of sophistication to convince ourselves that we are

right after all. But usually, of course, it is the other man who is prejudiced : as is shown by the fact that he does not agree with *us*. His taste is obviously bad ; but as it is a matter of personality, and springs from millions of associations which cannot possibly be shared, we have to *argue*, to appeal to something which we fondly hope is possessed in common by ourselves and our opponent, and that is, reason. We search for reasons which we imagine may have influenced our own taste, and endeavour, by enumerating them, to rouse the same taste in the other person. If, for example, we find a man to whom a certain series of words, a certain metrical scheme, or the plot of a certain novel, which we dislike is pleasing, or vice versa, we cannot alter his taste by a direct frontal attack, but—until experience has shown us the futility of most such attempts—we hope to do so indirectly. We reason, we lay down general rules, we call in the weight of authority, we point out the monotony or irregularity of the lines ; we draw attention to the associations roused by them in our own minds, as if they were somehow in duty bound to rouse the same associations in others. It was, as the reader will remember, in this way that Matthew Arnold dealt with the metrical scheme of Frank Newman's Homer. The original, he said, among other things, roused in him noble suggestions ; Newman's version reminded him of vulgar ballads like Johnny Armstrong. He was proceeding on the assumption, a right one, that the merit or demerit of a style consists in its *suggestive* power ; but he did not sufficiently realise that until you can take complete charge of a man's life from babyhood to age, and even arrange for his ancestry to be correct, you cannot secure that he will receive the suggestions that you think desirable. He was, however, right in this, that you may hope, by your own personality, to rouse the requisite feelings in your own fit audience, and to guide *their* taste in the ' right ' direction. There are many to whom Arnold's criticism of Newman makes this strong appeal. Prepared by a long series of causes, by natural bent, by education, by previous sympathetic study of Arnold's mind, they are willing to yield themselves to his guidance, and even, in some cases, to welcome his views as a mere affair of authority. They have come to regard him as a sound critic, and what he says carries weight because it is his, and passes muster in their minds just as the view of a doctor, whose advice has proved sound in the past, gains our trust for the future. He did not convince Newman, for obvious reasons : Newman was no ' fit audience.' But to those who held, from experience, that Arnold had a larger number of true and high literary associations, and that these were relevant to the case in point, it would be natural to agree with him. Those, on the other hand—they were probably less numerous—who, on similar grounds trusted Newman, would so far tend to agree with *him.*

This example will help to show, in a rough and tentative manner, what constitutes a critic. He is a man accustomed to weighing and balancing the emotional effects that literature exerts upon himself. Every book we read produces an effect upon us all ; but we are not critics until we have learnt to pause and consider these influences. We must, first, *classify* them. How does the emotion stirred by a play of Shakespeare differ from that stirred by a book of Milton ? Both alike, in any competent mind, stir admiration ; but the critic distinguishes the two kinds of admiration. To do this, he must have a clear idea of the effects aimed at by the two authors : the one writes plays, the other epics. He must therefore have studied plays as a class, and epics as a class, until he has formed a clear generalisation as to the ends of both ; and he will, on the one hand, watch how each ' answers the great idea,' and, on the other, refrain from expecting from either what it never pretended to give. This is one of the first duties of a critic ; and this is why many authors give the critic a hint which may save him initial trouble. When Scott styles *Ivanhoe* a Romance, he is gently warning the critic not to judge it as an ordinary novel : when Mr. Arnold Bennett puts ' Fantasy ' on his title-page, he marks the book clearly off from *Clayhanger* or *The Old Wives' Tale :* if Meredith speaks of one of his works as a ' comedy,' the critic, remembering Meredith's ideas as to what comedy is, knows what class of emotions he is expected to experience. That is, if he is a true critic. A recent well-known case shows how desirable these hints are. Mr. Bernard Shaw, not having defined the nature of *The Apple-cart,* had to put up with a criticism which, according to his own statement, entirely ignored the purpose of the play, and was as utterly beside the point as if *A Midsummer Night's Dream* had been treated like *Every Man in his Humour.* But the incident shows clearly enough what the duty of a critic, on this side, is : it is to inform us to what class the book belongs, and thus to guide us as to the right attitude in which we are to approach it. Not that the author is not sometimes to blame. It is to-day—whether it always was so is another question—a defect in the *Merchant of Venice* that what we rightly expect to be a comedy should turn out to run perilously near to tragedy :

and a similar flaw mars the perfection of *Richard Feverel*. If such defects occur in a book, it is the critic's function to point them out, and if he points them out before we see the play or read the book, so much the better.

The uninstructed reader clearly requires such information. How often, for instance, do we hear men complain of 'improbabilities' in stories which make no profession to be 'probable'! A careless assumption that they were reading an ordinary novel has misled them. 'This couldn't happen,' they say repeatedly. Not till the critic tells them in the *genre* which the author has chosen 'improbability' is by no means ruled out, does the annoyance cease. The critic first of all informs them, either in his own words or in those which Aristotle quoted from Agathon, that it is probable many things should happen contrary to probability; and then points out that this likelihood of the unlikely should be borne specially in mind while they are reading this particular book. The author has tacitly required of them that 'willing suspension of disbelief' which Coleridge claimed for the *Ancient Mariner*; and, says the critic, if we are to enjoy the book we must humour the author. Anyone who seriously expects from *Tristram Shandy* a regular and continuous narrative will be fretted, and deservedly so. The aim of Sterne is to tickle the reader by constantly pretending to give him such a narrative, and constantly disappointing him. A reader worthy of the author will enter into the jest.

For there are works which aim at their effects by *deliberately* disappointing an expectation we have reasonably held as to their character. A score of other examples could be given. *Don Juan* will serve for one

among many. This constantly pretends to be poetry.
Its mere verse-form demands, at first sight, that it
should be so judged : and every now and then there
are passages which, if not poetry, are nothing. Yet
we are continually brought back to prose. Pegasus
has hardly touched the clouds when he suddenly
begins to crawl. The *Isles of Greece* may not be a
perfect poem, but it has many of the elements of true
poetry, and Byron certainly meant us to take it
seriously. But in the very next lines he throws aside
all the romance, with a gesture of contempt :

> Thus sang, or would, or could, or should, have sung
> The modern Greek, in tolerable verse.

So, in the midst of the 'wild farewells' of the ship-
wreck, we are suddenly soused in sarcastic comedy :
and there is never, in all *Don Juan*, a touch of pathos
but is succeeded by, or crossed with, a dash of cynicism : and scarcely a verse of good satisfying sound that
does not close with a Hudibrastic rhyme. This frets
many readers, and is one reason, apart from the general
tone of the poem, why few women can endure it. The
same effect, amid differences, is produced when Bernard
Shaw ironically calls the *Doctor's Dilemma* a tragedy,
and the hearer or reader discovers gradually that it is a
tragedy in a peculiar sense. Here again many of Shaw's
audience are annoyed by what they regard as a deception : and here again it is the function of the 'critic' to
enlighten them. In order to gain an effect by contrast
and surprise, Byron and Shaw have taken advantage
of the ordinary man's limited powers of classification,
of his tendency to separate books too simply into sheep
and goats ; in a word, to believe what he is told. A
critic, then, must classify his classifications, and sub-

divide his divisions. Unless we are ready to accept the author's point of view, and sympathise to some extent with his intention, we shall unavoidably and deservedly fail to gain from his work the kind of pleasure which, rightly viewed, it is capable of giving. Revulsion may, under the spell of a magic criticism of this kind, give way to enjoyment, and we may see in *Don Juan* a masterpiece of modern epic, in the *Doctor's Dilemma* a satire of a high order.

But classification, even when thus sub-classified, is only one part of the functions of a critic. As may be seen from the case of Arnold and Newman referred to above, he must, if he is worthy of the name, be alive himself, and endeavour to make us alive, to a whole series of associations, *in detail*, which the author wishes to arouse. In order that our mind may be in the duly receptive condition, he prepares us, by relevant instruction, not merely for recognising the author's *general* aim, but for viewing aright the means he has chosen to accomplish it. Thus, if he is criticising Gray's *Elegy*, he dwells on the choice of a metre, and points out its appropriateness—whether that appropriateness is really ' natural ' or whether it has come by long habit is an interesting question, but here beside the point. He draws attention to Gray's theory of poetry, to his love of veiled quotations, to his rhythmical suggestiveness, to any other characteristic of Gray's mind which may throw light on the poem. It may be that we have read the *Elegy* before : if the critic does not make us see much that we have not seen already, he is not a good critic, or at least he is no better than ourselves. If we have not read it before, it is for him to prepare us to read it more intelligently, and with a fuller intellectual emotion, than we should

have done without his help. In a word, he is to add
so largely to our mental equipment that we *taste* the
work more keenly and adequately than we otherwise
could do.

It is this, among other things, that makes Sainte
Beuve[1] so great a critic. In dealing with his authors,
he gives us just the amount and kind of information
which enable us to understand their environment and
point of view ; and then proceeds to guide us in studying their works in the light of the knowledge he has thus
imparted. I have in fact such men—alas ! too few—
as Sainte Beuve before my mind as I draw up my tentative list of the qualities of a critic.

Let me pause here for a moment to recall once more
the analogy with which I began these chapters. Dr.
Johnson knew all kinds of meals, from those provided
by the tripe-shop to the banquets of Mrs. Thrale and
the collations of Beauclerk. He had known what it
was to go without food altogether for two days, and
what it was to gorge himself like a Red Indian. And
this is what he said : ' I, Madam, who live at a variety
of tables, am a much better judge of cookery than any
person who has a very tolerable cook, but lives much
at home ; for his palate is adapted to the taste of his
cook ; whereas, Madam, in trying by a wider range,
I can more exquisitely judge.' Whether Johnson was
right in his opinion of his gastronomic acumen may
be doubted ; but there can be little hesitation in

[1] If I may be allowed to mention the name of a living critic, I
should like to add here that of Professor Oliver Elton. In his *Modern
Studies*, for example, he gives precisely that *explanatory* criticism of
Henry James's *Wings of a Dove* which seems to me almost ideal. A
reader of James who prepares himself for his task by first mastering
this article, will have doubled his chance of enjoying the novel, and
will have been saved a great deal of preliminary trouble.

accepting this view if it be applied to literary judgments. The critic must be a man of wide and very varied experience in reading—almost, if not quite, as wide as that of Johnson in eating. Otherwise he will not have sufficient materials in which to base a judgment. His must be no ' inductio per enumerationem simplicem.' He must be thoroughly acquainted with the great authors in several languages, or he will have no standard at all. But he must also have read many inferior authors, or he will put his candidate too low. As an examiner must know the whole range of his subject, or he cannot examine, but must also know the average abilities of men of twenty-two, or his standard will be absurdly high, so with the examiner of a book.

Next, he must not only have read, but must have reflected on his reading, and accustomed himself to analyse the impressions the reading has made on his own mind. In fact, he must be a self-critic, as well as a critic of books, and must be more severe with himself than with them. When he finds himself liking or disliking a book, he must consider whether this or that feeling may not be due to certain features of his own character, and whether these features are accidental or general. Like an astronomer, he will try to correct his personal equation, and detach his own preferences as far as possible from his judgments. It should be his aim to give a fair criticism of something that he may personally dislike. This implies *sympathy*.

Allied with this is a capacity which, of late years, has been more visible, and more strongly insisted on, than before—a psychological gift, both natural and trained : a power to discover, to some extent, the mind of the author behind the book. For the critic realises that the book is part of the man who wrote it, and that, as it throws light on the man, so, when you attain some idea of the man, you understand the book better. This is the secret of the attempts that have so often been made to discover the *real* Shakespeare, the *real* Shelley, the *real* Byron. As an illustration, I need do no more than refer to certain recent works on Milton, both French and English. The writers of these books, by a close chronological study of Milton's works, prose, poetry, Latin, Italian, English, endeavour to reach an idea of the character of the man, and the changes that it underwent as years and circumstances set their mark on it. Thus equipped, they have come back to the poems, and have not only understood them better themselves, but have made *us* understand them better. They are aided, of course, by the fact that we know a good deal, apart from the poems, about Milton. But those who have read Andrew Bradley's essay on ' Shakes- speare the Man ' will see that even in the case of the poet who does not ' abide our question,' much may be learned : and I am convinced that the merit of Bradley's criticism of *Lear* and *Macbeth* is largely due to this attempt, incompletely successful as it neces- sarily was, to get at the mind of their author.

And the complete critic must also have the teaching power. He must not only have the trained taste, and the psychological gift, but he must have the com- municating capacity as well. We do not call a man a critic who can merely criticise in silence : he must be able to give words to his ideas. It may be true— I will consider this in a moment—that critics are men who have failed as writers ; but at any rate they must know how to write. In this respect literary criticism differs from criticism in all other arts ; it is a branch, often a humble branch, of the art it criticises : and

H

sometimes, as in the case of Taine, Sainte Beuve, De Quincey, or Hazlitt, it is not humble, but very lofty. Pope said of the critic Longinus that he was himself the great sublime he drew. We cannot expect all critics to win such praise ; but if who drives fat oxen should himself be fat, who criticises authors must be something of an author himself. In striving to guide our taste, he must not provide a horrid example of tastelessness.

Another very desirable gift of the critic—though some good critics manage to do without it—is the philosophical mind—the mind, to put it crudely and briefly, which is accustomed to distinguish between appearance and reality, and knows from experience how terribly difficult the task of drawing that distinction is. It is largely this which makes Andrew Bradley such a good critic : and is this which makes De Quincey, in my opinion, as great a critic—when he turns his attention that way—as any in our language. We notice, as we read him, the constant ' Distinguo ' of which I spoke just now : he is never content to assume that things which seem the same are anything but similar. As he has also an unsurpassed command of language to mark these distinctions, he is scarcely to be left out of any list of great critics. Something of the same training is to be seen in Lessing, perfectly simple as is the language he chooses to express his thoughts. And it is the absence of this gift which explains Macaulay's weakness on this side of his comprehensive mind—a weakness which, with his usual modesty and self-knowledge, he confessed without reserve. He had taste, but not the critical power. He writes to Napier—' Hazlitt used to say of himself, I am nothing if not critical. The case with me is directly the reverse. I have a strong and acute enjoyment of works of the imagination ; but I have never habituated myself to dissect them. Perhaps I enjoy them the more keenly for that very reason. Such books as Lessing's *Laocoon*, such passages as the criticism on Hamlet in *Wilhelm Meister*, fill me with wonder and despair. I have never written a page of criticism on poetry, or the fine arts, which I would not burn if I had the power.'

This is true ; and it is allied with the fact that Macaulay could not read Kant, and read Plato not for his philosophy but for the style and setting of his dialogues. Consider his treatment of Robert Mont-gomery. Macaulay *felt* the *Omnipresence of the Deity* to be bad ; but he could prove it only by pointing out little slips of grammar and unimportant plagiarisms from better poets. There would have been something very different if De Quincey had handled the poem.

If the saying that a critic is a man who has failed in original work was in the first instance uttered in scorn, it may, I think, be taken quite seriously. No one can criticise fairly who does not know the difficulties of the art ; and he cannot really know them unless he has himself made the attempt. The man who did not know whether he could play the violin or not, because he had never tried, would be a very bad critic of Kreisler or Elman. I have often watched the watchers at a billiard-match, when the hundreds are reeled off so easily that the ignorant do not cheer. It looks so simple that the ordinary man thinks he could do it himself. But the man who can make fifty—*he* praises, and praises unstintedly. It is the same with literature, especially with poetry. I would have every critic of poetry a man who has failed as a poet, and *knows* he has failed. Let me give an instance from my own experience. I have written one or two novels. They have never been published—I never even sent them up to a publisher. But I learnt much from them as to the difficulties of a novelist's art—difficulties often so triumphantly surmounted. Particularly have I noticed the difficulty of the padding—that part of the novel which at first sight seems superfluous, but which is really so necessary for giving the book due balance and proportion. I found this terribly hard to do. And ever since then I have been far more merciful even to some of the worst novelists I know, who have yet contrived, with apparent ease, to pad out their plots neatly and harmoniously. I would then have, as critics of novels, those who have themselves failed as novelists. But they must also be aware of their failure : and this is why good novel-critics are so few.

But a critic must not have failed too completely : he must not be a total incompetent. And this brings me to the one indispensable qualification of the true critic, which I have left to the last because it includes all the rest. Though he may be a poor executant, though he may be incapable of giving due expression to the thoughts which burn within him, he must have a share, and a large share, of the creative imagination which is the mark of the writer whom he undertakes to criticise. He must, in no inconsiderable measure, see what the poet sees and hear what he hears. If, through a defect in his vision or audition, he cannot enter into his author's world, he will obviously be unable to judge fairly the way in which the author has presented it. It is true that the author's own intensity of feeling may render *him* a bad judge *because* of its very intensity. He may be like a good mathematician, who leaps intuitively to conclusions, and is unable to see that his explanations are obscure to the duller perceptions of his hearers. Thus the comparative dullness of the critic's senses may actually help him more calmly to judge the work—it leaves more of his mind at leisure for the exercise of judgment—but unless he has *some* imagination, some spark of the Promethean fire, he will fail utterly. This is why Hazlitt, Leigh Hunt, and De Quincey are such good critics : they are all imaginative writers. And this is why Shelley, Arnold, and Coleridge, in their tranquil moments of recollection, when their highest powers are in abeyance but yet alive, are such good critics also.

The perfect critic, then, was never born, and never will be born. ' Enough,' said Rasselas to Imlac, ' you have convinced me that no man will ever be a poet.' ' Enough,' the reader will say : ' you have convinced us that it is as difficult to judge a book as to make one, and more especially so as one has to make one book while judging another.' The poet soars to heaven ; the critic only climbs a short pole ; but the pole is well greased. Nevertheless the critic, even the imperfect one, has his utility : and all those who have benefited by criticism will admit it. He corrects our tastes, he justifies them, he even in some cases gives birth to them where, in the strict sense, they have hardly existed before.

But to revert. No one can be truly said to taste a literary pleasure, or to feel a literary distaste, unless he does so all but instantaneously. A laborious study, even with critical help, of the beauties or defects of a work, ending perhaps in a wearied appreciation of what is in it, may sometimes be necessary, but is not the joy and crown of intellectual emotion. That we attain only when the criticism has become to all intents and purposes intuitive. What is worse than a pun whose point is toilsomely unearthed, explained, and analysed ? We have, in the early stages of our Greek, or possibly in the later also, to work out the puns of Aristophanes : this does not tend to the due enjoyment of the *Clouds* or the *Wasps*. Such flashes must be seen at once like lightning in the collied night ; the two ideas must combine with the speed of Oliver and Celia : they must be like the fight of two rams or Cæsar's thrasonical brag, and there must be no ' asking the reason.' Similarly, in a different sphere, of a higher order than that of a ' paronomasia or play po' words.' We cannot savour a verse of Gray, or of any other poet, until the measure of our intellectual equipment is sufficient, and our command of it ready. The words must convey their meaning, but they must also carry their associations, before the mind has time to say ' Behold.' We must need no dictionary to interpret them, no turning over leaves to verify them. That addition which the poet makes must attach itself, without conscious effort on our part, to the store we already possess : or, to put the same thing from the other side, our mind, prepared by a long process of ' criticism,' must instantly and naturally leap to the new ideas presented by the poet. If we have to count feet on the fingers, we cannot appreciate a variation in scansion introduced by the poet to convey some idea. If we have difficulty with ordinary language, we cannot appreciate an inversion or a subtle *avoidance* of the ordinary such as is so marked a feature in Tennyson or Virgil. A good critic prepares us for all this, and for more.

It is pretty plain, then, that the secret of true enjoyment is that the reader should himself be a critic :

in fact, all that I have said so far should be read with
the recognition that the two are one, or ought to be.
Little benefit will be gained from the reading of any
book, however ' good ' it may be, unless the reader
brings ' criticism ' to bear upon it. The author is one
human being, using sounds, words, phrases, paragraphs, each with a purpose determined by a set of
associations in his own mind, and those associations
have been built up by gradual, conscious and unconscious, accumulation, during the whole of his life
down to the very moment he had put the last sentence
on paper. It is obviously impossible for anyone else,
even for the author's twin-brother, to appreciate all
these : the book, like the one in the Apocalypse, is
sealed with seven seals. But it is possible, by study
and thought, to open two or three of the seven, and
to obtain some insight into the meaning. Nor is this
study to begin with the book itself, with the author,
or with his age. To this reading must be brought all
the accumulations of our former reading, and of our
external experience, gathered through our own lives.
At times this study will lead, by one set of associations,
to the discarding of others. Thus, for instance, if we
choose Chaucer for our study, we must acquaint ourselves with his language and manner until we are at
peace with them ; until they have entirely lost their
initial quaintness and air of antiquity, and we read him
as naturally as Tennyson : till we have rid ourselves,
for the purpose of studying him, of all modern associations. Within the Chaucerian world, we must be
Chaucer's London contemporaries. It is a hard saying,
but only those who have done this are competent
critics of Chaucer ; and the mere *taste* of others is
worthless in comparison. Yet here, as so often, we

have to qualify—there are so many universal virtues in Chaucer, appealing to all humanity, that it is safe to say the merest beginner must feel them. He will feel them, however, more acutely the more he regulates his taste by criticism. I cannot deny myself or my readers the pleasure of quoting in illustration a passage from Professor Trevelyan's *Clio a Muse*. ' One day, as I was walking along the side of Great Gable, thinking of history and forgetting the mountains which I trod, I chanced to look up and see the top of a long green ridge outline in the blue horizon. For half a minute I stood in thoughtless enjoyment of this new range, noting upon it forms of beauty and qualities of romance, until suddenly I remembered that I was looking at the top of Helvellyn. Instantly, as by magic, its shape seemed to change under my eyes, and the qualities with which I had endowed the unknown mountain to fade away, because I now knew what its hidden base and its averted side were like, what names and memories clung around it.' This is an allegory of what happens when criticism—that is knowledge and thought—begin to play on passages or books hitherto known only to untutored taste. Some loss there may be, but the gain far more than compensates : the passage or the poem comes to us, like the mountain when recognised as what it is, linked with a hundred perceived memories, a thousand things forgotten, and the combined force of a million varied experiences. Or, to burden the reader with yet another analogy. The unhistorical man walks over a field, and sees a mound here, a hill yonder, a patch of grass, a clump of trees, a winding stream. The historian stops, ' for his tread is on an empire's dust ' ; upon his mind surge visions of tramping infantry, of charging cavalry, of triumph and disaster, of desperate valour and pusillanimous retreat. He all but sees wounds, and death, 'rider and horse, friend, foe, in one red burial blent.' To the one the field is but a field ; to the other it is Blenheim or Malplaquet. This is the difference between the man who reads but words, and the man to whom the words are winged messengers, bringing news from far countries and from distant ages.

To this second man, and to him only, 'criticism,' in the sense in which I use the word, comes so instantaneously that it is scarcely to be distinguished from that intuitive feeling which is taste. He will often be hard put to it himself to discriminate the elements of his enjoyment ; and in common speech we call such a man a man of taste without troubling further. But to the true critic there comes that later stage, in which he reflects upon his enjoyment, and to the best of his ability analyses the causes of it, tracing those qualities in the writer which have met with such a response in himself, and marking where the author's success has been more or less conspicuous. If he is of an introspective bent, he turns his eye also inward, and notes what there is in his own mind which thus responds. The complete critic is he who satisfactorily performs both these tasks. It does not necessarily follow that he will impose his opinions on others, or succeed in arousing in them the same emotions as he has himself experienced. He will recognise that after all his emotions are personal, and that every book, and every passage in every book, *must* appeal differently to different people. Nevertheless his experience is of value to others. It is a guide and an example. This, we say, is what can be, and has been, felt by a man of taste and judgment : and if we put ourselves through the same discipline we may feel something of the same exalted kind. And, on a lower plane, the *explanations* of his author which he gives, put us in a position to understand, and understanding is a degree to feeling. Similarly, if the man of taste uncompromisingly *rejects* something that we are tempted to admire, that rejection may induce us to start a ' criticism ' of our own, and it is by no means impossible that the criticism may, with windlasses and indirect assays of bias, so work our taste that in time we too reject it as instantaneously as he. Our enjoyment may be recognised as contrary to reason, and there are times, fortunately for humanity, when, as with Cæsar, reason sways more than the affections. Every time, again, that we prove our mentor right, will increase the likelihood that we shall trust his judgment on the next occasion : and it may even be that we shall need to be on our guard lest we follow him too slavishly.

If things were as they ought to be in the literary world, taste would be oftener ruled by criticism than criticism by taste. That it is not so is due to the weakness of human nature, which prefers prejudice to reason, and fancy to truth. But it likes to *seem* reasonable, and therefore disguises its prejudices under a mask of argument. From a mere love of the old, we try to demonstrate that the old is intrinsically preferable to the new ; or from a mere turn for novelty we prove that the new fashion not only is, but ought to be, like the fool's motley, the only wear. Thus every change in taste is followed by a mass of ' criticism,' proving that this last manifestation is the very final Avatar of the poetic Vishnu. Yet it is as certain that there will be new fashions in the future as that there have been in the past fashions that once were new, each of which was in its time hailed as the ultimate revelation.

Taste being thus variable, and ' criticism,' so called, thus following it as its slave, the only sound method for one who desires to free himself as far as possible from the bonds of time and place is to consider not so much taste itself as tastes, and not so much criticism in itself as types of criticism. But the *sententiae* being almost as many as the *homines*, it will be obviously impossible for me to give the minutest fragment of this history, or to venture more than a few plausible conjectures as to the causes which have influenced the thousand vagaries of which the history is full. Every vagary has innumerable causes, most of them so subtle as to elude the most microscopic search. As to the future I can foretell but one thing. I spoke of criticism as a slave. My own position will be that of the slave in the Roman triumph, whispering in the ear of the haughty conqueror that he is mortal after all, and that the same mob-voice which now exalts him may shortly curse him. Otherwise I can no more foresee the future than I can foresee next year's weather. I cannot even, like a meteorologist, give a plausible guess as to what will come next : and, the majority of mankind being inarticulate, I cannot even tell what is the prevailing taste at the present moment. There are many people who read ' best-sellers,' detesting them all the while, the reason being that one must read what others read. It would be an error to assume that, because they ask for such books at the libraries, that kind of thing is what they like. Nor are reviews— even when they agree—a safe guide as to the opinions of the presumably less cultured world at large. If my readers have watched, as I have more than once

watched with some interest, an author—who probably
knows a good deal about his own book—reading a
critique upon it, they must have perceived very clearly
that there are usually at least two widely-differing
views as to the merits of the work : and, if the work
succeeds so far as to sell a single copy, there is certainly
a third view. Yet author, reviewer, and reader are in
this case contemporaries, and have at least one bond
in common : what endless varieties must we not find
as we pass from generation to generation !

A man of wide reading and great mental power once
did venture a prophecy as to the future of style and
taste. The telegraph, he said, would in his opinion,
produce a staccato and truncated style, with no articles,
scarcely any adjectives, pronouns conspicuous by their
absence, and participles taking the place of whole
sentences. There were, I think, signs that such a
consummation was not by any means impossible. The
prediction has been falsified, not by the precautions of
writers, but by the prevalence of other mechanical
inventions. The telephone and the wireless have
largely counteracted the influence of the telegraph ;
and it may be that *they* will have their own influence.
Or it may be that other inventions will supersede them
in their turn. That whatever does so supersede them
will have *some* literary effect, however, I do not think
at all unlikely. In any case, changes *will* occur, to
whatever cause they may be due ; and as such changes
in our own style come, they will inevitably modify
our judgment of the style of our predecessors. All
things are eternally moving, and nothing, least of all
thought, continues in one stay.

The poet Gray, in his sanguine youth, conceived the
idea of writing a Latin poem *De Principiis Cogitandi*,

a title which, for my present purpose, I may paraphrase
' How men come to think as they do think.' It was an
ambitious scheme, no less than to discover

> Unde Animus scire incipiat ; quibus inchoet orsa
> Principiis seriem rerum, tenuemque catenam
> Mnemosyne ; Ratio unde rudi sub pectore tardum
> Augeat imperium.

He never finished even the first book, and though, after
two or three hundred lines, he boldly leapt to the
fourth, even so he did not manage to put together
an approximately rounded whole. I am essaying a
hardly less difficult task, and one in which it is not
unlikely I shall have to make jumps as huge as Gray's.
Lacunae will certainly be detected : nor will this
confession ward off the inevitable censure. But I
shall endeavour to point out some common varieties of
taste, and to indicate some of their causes. For the
rest, I borrow the language of Homer when he came to
cataloguing the ships that went to Troy : a list which,
as is well known, has given all epic poets, if not their
readers, a taste for catalogues :

> To count them all demands a thousand tongues,
> A throat of brass, and adamantine lungs :
> Daughters of Jove, assist ; inspired by you,
> The mighty labour dauntless I pursue.

VI

THE RISE OF CONSCIOUS ART

I HAVE said that criticism affects taste : and affects it alike in the author and in the reader. When a writer begins to know what he is doing—when he criticises his own work—he can no longer write as he used to write. And when the reader, or rather the hearer, knows what the author is trying to do, he can no longer be influenced by him in the old fashion. Many have held that the result is unfortunate. Macaulay, it is well known, believed that poetry declines as criticism advances : and there is much to be said for his view. It is indubitable, at any rate, that the habit of constant criticism does occasionally spoil enjoyment to some extent : and it is probable that in certain cases extreme fastidiousness, due to this habit, has even prevented some men, who might have been good writers, from writing at all. Some, again, have been deterred from writing through fear of the criticism of others. But the almost universal result, when writing *has* been practised, has been the rise of what is called rhetoric. I shall try in the following chapter to say a little on this subject.

It is of course not till long after works of art have been composed that men begin to analyse them. Poetry, in particular, which would seem to be almost as natural to man as error itself, arises and advances, perhaps through many centuries, more or less unconsciously. Thousands of 'scops' and 'skalds' make verses, introduce novelties, and even devise improvements, being guided in part by their own untutored inclinations or talents, and in part by observation of the effect of their verses on the hearers. A 'school' thus arises, but there is hardly any direct teaching, no particular curriculum, and pupils who are little more than mere imitators : its doctrine is inchoate and informal, and heresy is detected simply by failure to please. The hearers like or dislike they know not why, and the reciters, though more keen-sighted, certainly cannot formulate the laws according to which they succeed or fail. At times, we may imagine, some great genius arises, who, receiving from his predecessors a tolerably fixed vocabulary, and a tolerably well-defined form, produces a poem which is recognised to be far beyond what has been hitherto achieved : but even he, like the Syrian archer, though he has hit the mark, has drawn his bow at a venture, 'in his simplicity.' He is an artist, but his art has been that which Shelley ascribes to the skylark—unpremeditated. Rarely, even in far more introspective ages, do we find in one man, mingled in equal proportions, the powers of a critic and of a poet : and high as the powers of this bard must have been, we may be sure that the Plato of his day, if such there were, would put down his sublimest flights to a divine madness. Nay, some of the most deliberate and sophisticated writers, in civilised times, have often gained their effects without purposed or conscious effort, and, like other sinners, have been surprised at what they have done. No great poet was ever more of a critic than Goethe : but it is certain that many of Goethe's lyrics were written with the uncritical side of his mind ; he tells us with truth that he piped like the birds. It is well known also that so careful an artist as Tennyson piped or sang in linnet-fashion ; and we are told that often, reading criticisms on his works which pointed out subtle alliterations or delicate avoidances of the banal, he recognised that he had done this or escaped the other, but declared that, till the critic informed him, he had been quite unaware of what he was doing. Much more must this have been the case with poets like Homer, the authors of the *Edda*, or the creators of *Beowulf* and the *Seafarer*. They saw *how* their hearers were moved, but the *why* was hidden from them. They lived in the ages of ' tactile ' taste, before criticism had arisen. I do not suppose, for instance, that Homer had the slightest conception of his own preference for the *oratio recta* to the *obliqua*. So far as we know, this was not seen till the days of Plato. The poets, like the Spartans, did what was right ; the hearers, like the Athenians, saw that it was right when it was done.

Now as soon as criticism really set in, its influence, both conscious and unconscious, upon writers of prose and poetry, as well as upon hearers and readers, began to make itself felt ; and it soon became strong and overmastering. It can, I think, be traced in 'Homer' himself. It is hard, for instance, to believe that the highly rhetorical speeches of Achilles in the Ninth Book of the *Iliad*—speeches that might have come out of Livy or Tacitus—are the product of pure undiluted inspiration. They seem rather to be born of discussions in some Ionian ' Mermaid Tavern,' between a Chian Jonson and a Milesian Shakespeare : they are reminiscent of arguments, rejoinders, sur-rejoinders : and to me they appear to provide a far stronger proof of the comparative lateness of that book than any of the more objective reasons usually advanced. Almost as easily could one imagine the debate between Ajax and Ulysses in Ovid's *Metamorphoses* to have been written by a ballad-monger of the regal period, as ascribe those speeches to the author of the original *Menis*. In any case there can be no doubt that the marked difference in style between Thucydides and Herodotus is due to the irruption of professional rhetoricians into Athens during the twenty years that separated the two historians : and it is a common-place that something of the same sort explains, to a great extent, the difference between Æschylus and Euripides. From the time of the visit of Gorgias to Athens in 427, with the ferment the orator's speeches provoked, it was impossible for writing or speaking, as for reading or hearing, to retain its old simple char-acter. Pericles had thundered over Greece and shaken the arsenal like the Olympian Zeus : but Zeus himself was now being doubted, and his credentials asked for ; and his earthly incarnation was being analysed also. ' He ever left his sting behind in his hearers,' said Eupolis ; but people now began to discriminate one bee-sting from another—and incidentally to note that this very phrase of Eupolis was the thing which had been recently caught, pinned to a board, and named a ' metaphor.' Similarly the sayings of Pericles, that ' Ægina was the eyesore of the Piraeus,' that a city which has lost its youth in war is a year without a spring, that Athens was the schoolmistress of Greece, were now recognised as figures with names and char-acters ; and the change was portentous. At the very moment when Pericles, the last of the great artless orators, was speaking in Athens, Corax in Sicily was

I

drawing up his treatise on the *technë* of oratory, and a new world had been discovered. Thenceforward art, with all its good and all its evil, became a catchword like ' complex ' or ' inhibition ' to-day ; and the seed was sown of that vast growth of mingled sincerity and humbug, sense and nonsense, poison and nutriment, which has since, like the tree of Mandane, overshadowed the whole earth, magpies, daws, and ravens lodging in the branches thereof. The style of Herodotus differs little from that of talk. That of Thucydides is a language which can never have been spoken in ordinary life ; and his recurring antithesis between ' theory ' and ' practice,' which sometimes wearies the reader, is by itself enough to show that the rhetorical teacher was abroad in the land. Æschylus is full of metaphor ; but his metaphors are the natural overflow of a powerful and imaginative mind. When Euripides uses metaphors, we may be sure he knows what he is doing. In the market-place the change was probably equally great. Audiences began to listen critically. Plays were dissected into their component parts and functions assigned to each ; plots were analysed, and choruses pulled to pieces. If we may trust the evidence of Aristophanes, the satirist could rely on his hearers to follow him when he compared his favourite playwright with the one he detested, and to weigh his judgments with knowledge and intelligence. Orators were subject to the same close inspection. Their speeches were not only heard but watched, to see whether they conformed to rules ; whether the ' pistis,' the ' prooemium,' the ' epilogus ' turned up in their right places and acted up to their characters ; climax was expected and its absence noted ; audiences, metamorphosed into literary detectives, waited to catch the interrogation or oxymoron, and expressed their satisfaction as their desire was met : some even marked an hiatus, or, noticing the intrusive rhythm of an iambic or epic line, cried out like Jaques, 'Nay, then, God be wi' you an you talk in blank verse.'[1] Even when Demosthenes told them that sincerity, and not rhetoric, was the sign of the true orator, they wanted him to say so rhetorically, and received what they wanted. From this time, if I may employ for a moment the figure called hyperbole—and I wish the reader to bear in mind the innumerable exceptions which prove the statement to be hyperbolical—oratory, and with it poetry, tends to be less spontaneous, and becomes studied, inspiration gives way to craftsmanship, and we are gradually prepared for the advent of a Callimachus, who 'ingenio non valet, arte valet.' At the same time, by an inevitable law of nature, there are those who weary of the artificiality and cry for simplicity. I am not disputing the unequalled genius of Demosthenes ; but it was not for nothing that Æschines told his hearers to be on the look out for his rival's practised devices. Among those hearers there must have been some who distrusted ' art ' ; and we know that the plain and rugged Phocion, who despised every trick of rhetoric, was the one speaker of whom Demosthenes was afraid. ' See here the man who pulls my periods to pieces.' There were Antonys, even then,

---

[1] The famous anecdote about Demosthenes, though not exactly to the point, illustrates the attention with which the crowd listened to the speeches. ' Is Æschines a mercenary or a friend ? ' said he. (πότερον ὑμῖν, ὦ ἄνδρες Ἀθηναῖοι, δοκεῖ μισθωτὸς Αἰσχίνης ἢ ξένος Ἀλεξάνδρου ;) But he was careful to pronounce μισθωτός with the wrong accent, as if he had said ' mercénary,' whereupon the crowd cried ' mércenary.' ' You hear what they say, Æschines,' said Demosthenes (ἀκούεις ὃ λέγουσιν).

who began their speeches, however really artful, with the assertion that they were not, like Brutus, orators : and there were poets whose one law in poetry was to forget all about law. For a time, however, and a long time, the artists had things pretty much their own way.

The rules, inevitably, were like the ' theoric ' of Henry V, founded on the ' practic ' of the acknowledged masters : and, in my opinion, at times laid too great stress on merely accidental features of that practic. Aristotle, for example—I am obliged to choose his work because other critical documents have been lost—when treating of the epic, has recourse to Homer, and dwells strongly on the ' unity ' of the *Iliad* and the *Odyssey*, pointing out that these poems, though really dealing with long spaces of time, contrive, by means of episode, to compress this length into apparent brevity. But this brevity, I believe, if not the invention of arrangers who put the poems into order, is not improbably due merely to the necessities of recitation. No chief would listen to the whole *Iliad* or *Odyssey*, still less to the whole saga of Troy, at one stretch. He called, therefore, for a well-marked portion—the poet was to begin from the point where Achilles strove with Agamemnon, or, as the *Odyssey* puts it, ' from some point or other.' This compelled the bard to divide his work into well-marked sections, and the most convenient means of so doing was to adopt the episodic system. But there was no reason why a *writer* should adopt such a method for *readers*. It is but a trick after all, and a trick which called forth from William Morris one of his most celebrated and pithy objurgations against the ' classics.' You have to get the incidents in, and you may as well get them in chronologically. But it was this accident of circumstance that led Aristotle to lay down his rule, and accounts for the artificial construction of epics, from the *Æneid* and *Paradise Lost* to Cowley's *Davideis* and Blackmore's *King Arthur*. It is also, in a measure, responsible for those stories within stories which adorn, or disfigure, *Don Quixote* and *Tom Jones*.

Again, if we may judge from Aristotle, plays also were regulated by reference to the recognised exemplars. These, being contrived after a pattern dictated by accidental circumstances, decided the form when the circumstances had ceased to exist. You will notice that Aristotle measures all plays by a foot-rule : he criticises like a man of science, and determines merit by very superficial characteristics. Is the plot well balanced ? then the play is good. Has it the right sort of Recognition ? good again. What to us are the higher qualities he passes over. And if this is the case with Aristotle, we may be sure that it was more so with inferior men I doubt not that the judges gave the prize to Xenocles rather than to Euripides because Xenocles kept to the rules, and Euripides did not. Criticism was tending to be the destruction of originality and passion.

But to turn from this highly controversial digression, with which I do not expect all my readers to agree, I will pass to a very different literature. Different as it is, however, I believe we shall be able to detect that it passed through similar phases, and for similar reasons. Hebrew literature never distributed itself into clearly-marked forms as did the Greek. The lyric, the epic, and the dramatic—nay prose and poetry themselves—are constantly intermingled. Nor, so far as we know, had the Hebrews any Gorgias to point out that every time they opened their mouths a trope

flew out—though, as a matter of fact, they were far
more given to the habit than the Athenians themselves.
I will find three metaphors in a Hebrew poem for every
one in a Greek poem of the same length. But they
passed through an experience which must have been
even more decisive for their mental future than the
visit of a fluent sophist. The Babylonish exile, pro-
phesied as a penalty, proved like many penalties to be
an education. Meeting in captivity a culture far
higher than their own, they assimilated much of it—
a theory of numbers, a system of astrology, a doctrine
of angels, a modicum of science—and turned it to their
own uses. But, as so often, a culture thus acquired
was more favourable to the production of superficial
cleverness than to the growth of genius. They became
skilled in enigmas, allegories, and maxims : but they
did not grow in imagination. The effect is visible,
even to-day, in their poetry, which, as compared with
that of their fathers, is sometimes—for again I would
not exaggerate—mechanical, icily regular, and null
without being splendid. The glorious freedom and
sublimity of Isaiah, the rushing descriptiveness of
Nahum, have all but vanished, and in their place we
find sententiousness, occasional epigram, obscurity not
redeemed by profundity. Worse still, we find conceits, ' kennings,' riddles, and lyrics hardly to be distinguished from riddles, the whole culminating in the
endless repetitions and trivialities of that huge acrostic
the hundred and nineteenth Psalm. As if the alphabet
had but newly been invented, and shone before the
eye in all the glory of a freshly purchased instrument,
these poets played with it and rang their changes on it
like the Elizabethans rejoicing over a verbal quibble.
The lamentations over the solitary and ruined city

of Jerusalem fell into this artificial form and ' came out' like the calf in Horeb ; the praises of a virtuous woman ran neatly from A to the Hebrew Z ; the very prayers took on the desired mould.[1] Rarely does the poet move lightly in these self-imposed fetters. Indeed, if we may believe the scholars, very early must readers and editors have wearied of their perfunctory ingenuity. The ninth and tenth Psalms for example, and the first chapter of ' Nahum,' appear to have been originally in acrostic form ; but as we now possess them they exhibit additions and alterations which have, perhaps, improved their meaning at the expense of their arrangement. It is pretty clear that it was not long before men felt that ' technique' has its perils, and too easily runs into excess. We know nothing of the criticism of those times ; but it is not impossible that there arose an Addison with a Hebrew essay in ' False Wit' which put an end to the vogue of these Jewish *bouts-rimés*.

When we leave Jerusalem for Rome, we meet, *mutatis mutandis*, the same phenomenon, if possible, intensified. When the Romans had leisure to pause from conquest, and to sit down for a while behind the closed gates of Janus, they began, like their tutelary god, to turn their faces in two directions. They looked at themselves, and observed a great lack ; they looked outward, and saw a great abundance. Studying the civilisation they had subjected, they found that it was far higher than their own, and spoke a language richer and more expressive. Here was a

[1] I doubt not that from these Psalms sprang the ' Abecedarian' hymns of Sedulius (' A solis ortus cardine ') and other Church poets, as well as the A.B.C. of Deguilleville in his *Pèlerinage*, so familiar from Chaucer's translation.

poetry more profound and sublime, an art altogether
beyond their attainment, and a criticism far advanced
whereas theirs had not even begun. They took over
this great inheritance as they took over the Macedonian rule, or rather, to use the words in which
Horace put it once for all, the vanquished nation led
captive the victor ; and straightway they set to work
to imitate it, to constrain their own language into
some approach to the Greek lissomeness and grace,
and to build a literature upon an almost entirely
foreign foundation. It was as if every cultured Roman
had been a Naaman, carrying with him two mules'
burden of earth from an alien land, in order to build
thereon a shrine in his own country. Only a few were
left to maintain that Abana and Pharpar were better
than Jordan : and those few were soon silenced or
came over to the enemy.

Thus we have here the astonishing and I believe
unique case of a nation starting to form its literature
when it has reached its highest point socially and
politically. In all other cases, however much a nation
may have borrowed from others, it has founded its
literature on its own soil. Our own, to take one
instance, may have been for a time driven underground
by foreign conquest, but it emerged, if loaded with
accretions, essentially *itself*. Even Chaucer, with all
his pillages from abroad, used them not for building
his house but for adorning it : and the classical,
French, and Italian influences which have *moulded*
our poetry have never been more—to change the
figure—than graftings upon a native stock. But
Rome deliberately *made* its literature, and on a foreign
model. It can hardly be said even to have poured the
imported wine into old bottles : the bottles themselves

were so patched and repaired as to be almost new. Though it is a Latin maxim that *poeta nascitur non fit*, the Latins might seem to have set themselves to refute it.

We learn from Cicero—himself one of the chief agents in this mighty change—what immense pains the men concerned took in bringing it about : how they toiled both at Greek and at Latin, how laboriously they strove to supply the defects of the one by studying the other, how they rejoiced when they discovered those strong points which, they hoped, might be yet further strengthened, how they enriched it with invented words and phrases that might save the necessity of actual borrowing. Whenever Cicero has occasion to discuss a philosophical entity for which there is no Latin expression, with what care does he fashion one, and how justifiably does he boast when he thinks he has succeeded ! Nor was he without coadjutors. To take but one example, his treatise called the *Orator*, addressed to Marcus Brutus, is one long proof both of his own devotion to these problems and of the equal zeal, if lesser ability, with which Brutus himself and many others attempted their solution. In great points and in small, in pressing the essentials of eloquence and its minutiæ, in asserting the necessity of conviction on the part of the orator and in giving hints as to the arrangement of his smallest words, this essay shows how Cicero trained his own mind and how he found others to listen to his exhortations.

Nor less visible is this effort in a work which Cicero is said, if not actually to have edited, yet to ' have seen through the press,' the *De Rerum Natura*. In one of the best-known passages in Latin, Lucretius complains of the difficulty he finds in treating his subject ' propter egestatem linguae ' : and though, as Munro has shown, he certainly exaggerates the poverty of the Latin *poetical* vocabulary, yet, as the same great authority declares, in the technical portions of his work he invents hundreds of new words, some of which are but Greek words in Latin dress. It must not be forgotten, further, that the *form* of his poem was borrowed from Ennius, and that Ennius had, by a marvellous *tour de force*, compelled the Latin language, as it were against its will, to accept Greek rhythms, and the Roman theatres to accept Greek themes for their plays. Lucretius, following in his master's footsteps, compelled the Latin language not only to bear a Greek form of versification, but to convey a Greek philosophy.

Now if this was so—if orators, prose writers, and epic and philosophical poets were thus of set purpose *creating* a style—it was inevitable that the later poets, in carrying on the work, should conceive of poetry as hardly anything else than a branch of rhetoric, for which the Greek poets provided the models and the themes. For it is next door to impossible to transfuse the *imagination* of a poem, or its native glamour, from one language to another : but it *is* possible to give it a rhetorical colouring—to render it into a style *superficially* ' poetical.' We can almost hear Virgil, Horace, Pollio, Varius, saying to themselves, ' Greece has poetry : Rome must have poetry too.' It is said that some years ago a great Head-Master, whose boys had won unparalleled distinction in scholarship, found that other Head-Masters, far from envying him, were boasting of the triumphs of their boys in cricket and football. ' You get Fellowships,' said they : ' we train Blues.' ' If that is so,' replied he, ' my school shall be as good as any of yours in games also.' He

went back, made games compulsory, organised them
as he had organised his classes, arranged matches,
hired coaches, and threatened to flog any boy who
showed the white feather in football. In a short time
he turned out very respectable elevens and fifteens.
Something of the same kind—except that it was trans-
forming athletes into students—happened in Rome
under Augustus and Maccenas.

But the poetry that resulted—I am not denying the
genius of many of its writers—was hot-house poetry.
It did not spring unforced from the soil of the country,
but was brought to birth by intensive cultivation. And
such poetry is rhetoric : nay, in many cases, it is direct
mimicry of Greek poetry which was already rhetoric
and little else. The poets chosen for imitation were
mainly the critic-poets of Alexandria and Cos: invoking
'Callimachi manes et Coi sacra Philetae'; that very
Callimachus who was strong not by nature but by
art, and that Philetas who was, as far as we can see,
not less artificial and not more natural. Even Virgil
began, continued, and ended as a copyist; and if he
copied better models, and showed more inborn genius
in his copying, it was yet his highest ambition to be to
Rome what Homer was to Greece. His Eclogues are,
it is true, imitations of a charming original, and themselves usually charming : but—though one dislikes
saying a word that may seem to depreciate Theocritus
—he, too, to quote Munro again, 'repeated parrot-
like forms which he did not understand, because their
meaning had been lost for centuries.' Horace, again,
as a lyric poet, claimed to have naturalised Greek metres
in Italy ; and his *Art of Poetry* is apparently little else
than a versified transcript of some Greek lectures on
the drama. As for the *servum pecus*, the apes of Virgil

and Horace, what but mere prize-exercises could be expected of *them?*

If these seem hard sayings—as, in a sense, they seem so to their writer—I would appeal to the Romans themselves, and to competent critics of modern times : though such an appeal will certainly be needless for any who have tried to read Valerius Flaccus or Silius Italicus. Quintilian, we know, ' giving it as his own opinion,' ranks Lucan rather among rhetoricians than among poets : and assuredly Lucan, though the most superb of rhetoricians, whenever he tries imaginative writing becomes merely bombastic. His contemporary Persius is not even rhetorical : he is as contorted as a Sibyl without her inspiration. In the *Thebaid* of Statius Macaulay found *one* passage worthy of a great poet : though it is true that Chaucer found several which a great poet might transmute into poetry. But there were some, even as early as Quintilian's time, who held similar views about Virgil himself. We still have a fragment of a dialogue of Hadrian's reign, by Annius Florus, entitled ' Vergilius, orator an poeta ' : and if, as is said, Florus wrote a ' poem ' in praise of Domitian, he must have known at least what an ' orator ' is. In the fifth century Macrobius treats Virgil almost exclusively as an exemplar for rhetoricians to follow, and that not merely in the speeches. To pass to a much later age, in the eighteenth-century Virgil supplied a model and a storehouse to Burke, the prince of rhetoricians, who not only, in a memorable conversation, upheld his claims against those of Homer, but never went a journey without a dog-eared Delphin copy in his portmanteau, in which he rarely failed to find a clinching verse to point a paragraph. It is hardly possible to read ten pages of Burke's speeches without lighting on a Virgilian quotation, which is always in harmony with the balanced and ' rhetorical ' structure of the context in which it is embedded. Burke would have agreed with Voltaire that if the *Æneid* is Homer, it is Homer's greatest work.

And Mr. Garrod in his excellent Introduction to the *Oxford Book of Latin Verse*, points out that even in the passionate and romantic Fourth Book of the Æneid, where if anywhere, we might expect the purest emotional poetry, we get instead a formal, regulated verse. ' Analyse any speech of Dido. Dido knows all the rules. You can christen out of Quintilian almost all the figures of rhetoric which she employs.' And, like Virgil's profound admirer Sellar, Mr. Garrod notes how significant it is that our Parliamentary eloquence was so long dominated by the fashion of Virgilian quotation. Not only Burke, but Pitt, the most stately—almost perhaps the heaviest— of great House of Commons orators, rarely failed to point a climax with half a dozen lines of Virgil ; and Fox, the most spontaneous, capped his rival's verses with others. All will remember the famous duel between Gladstone and Lowe on the Reform question, when the Trojan horse leapt backwards and forwards over the benches, and threatened to overwhelm London as it had overwhelmed the city of Priam. You do not thus bandy Burns or Catullus to and fro in Houses of Commons and Chambers of Deputies.

Now, as Mr. Garrod goes on to say, this rhetorical poetry has for one of its parents or nurses the art of recitation. Augustus, having as his aim the gradual attraction of Rome into the orbit of his new Principate, gathered round him a small bodyguard of poets, listened kindly and patiently to their performances, and at times condescended himself to recite. Like Wordsworth, he knew that a sonnet might become a trumpet, and urged men of talent to blow from it the due imperial strains, alas! not too few. All poets, therefore, who looked for favour had to give their works that power of instantaneous appeal which is the special prerogative of forceful rhetoric. They had to be immediately effective, or fail utterly. The executants soon learned to provide the music, and for a hundred years we find the desired quality in ever-increasing measure. The effect was achieved by Virgil through a rhetoric so beautifully disguised as scarcely to be recognisable, haunting and waylaying the hearer without startling him ; by gentle repetitions in varied phrase, by melody returning upon itself. In Ovid and Lucan the epigram and antithesis often kill the poetry ; in Statius all the arts of the trained declaimer are combined. When, in fact, Augustus, to use the famous phrase of Tacitus, gave peace to eloquence along with everything else, the orators, silenced in one direction, found in ' poetry ' their channel of expression, until all the indignation of Juvenal, reinforced by a huge note of Professor Mayor's, scarcely suffices to portray the magnitude of the Deucalionic deluge which drowned the marbles and plane-trees of Fronto.

Such is the almost invariable result of a system of royal patronage, imitated, of course, by all the great men of less than royal rank. Every poet, seeking his ' sportula ' by flattery, tends to become a poet-laureate : in other words he ceases to be a poet. A congratulatory ode is not the place for inspiration : but it *is* the natural receptacle for all the external trappings and paraphernalia which, at a first hearing, may be mistaken for inspiration. A thousand examples could be given, from Martial's eulogies of Domitian, through Boileau's *Ode on the Capture of Namur*, to Southey's *Vision of Judgment* and Wordsworth's *Inaugural Ode*.

The builders of the Tower of Babel have much to answer for : but not the lightest of the evils they have brought upon the world is this, that while the suggestions conveyed by words, and the atmosphere they breathe, cannot possibly be transfused from language to language, these rhetorical flourishes and ornamentations slip over the border almost without exception, easily enough, and lose but little in the transit. Whereas rhythmical beauty and verbal charm must shiver eternally on Ellis Island, the whole apparatus of rhetoric presents its passport and is welcomed. You cannot possibly convey the essence of Virgil's charm into English or German ; but you can hand over bodily his personifications, metonymies, hypallages, or synecdoches. The same is true when the translation is less obvious—when the language is apparently the same, but has suffered the changes insensibly wrought by place or time. The deception is here more subtle than when we have to deal with a tongue recognised as foreign : for the general sense of the words presents no difficulty, and we fancy we understand our author because we perceive his meaning without effort. We are not, in fact, on our guard. This is the case with the average reader of Shakespeare to-day : the phraseology is apparently English ; but not for a long time, if ever, are the associations caught and felt. Nor, to be precise, is even the mere phraseology always apprehended : how many people are there who know the real meaning of ' One touch of nature makes the whole world kin ' ? But all can see that the poet is using a

' transferred epithet ' when he says, ' Every man hence
to his idle bed.'

By a process which it is the business of history to
explain, it happened that Roman literature became
the glass of fashion and the mould of form to the whole
of Western Europe for more than a thousand years.
The Latin language was the Esperanto of all educated
persons, who could understand one another from
Bangor to Bari : who wrote and spoke Latin as their
second mother-tongue, and who attended lectures
one year in Oxford and the next in Bologna without
finding any linguistic difficulty. It is not likely that
Bernard and Abelard could have understood each
other's vernacular dialects : but the vagaries of the
heretic were easily detected, in their Latin dress, by
the orthodox saint. And this state of things lasted
down to the time when Bacon had his books translated
into Latin to secure at once their permanence and
their universal vogue, and when Spinoza learnt the
language in order to understand Descartes and to
refute him.

This knowledge of Latin, easy, colloquial, and free,
was just of the kind to perpetuate that conception of
poetry as something rhetorical and artificial of which
I have spoken. The language, understood in a measure,
carried with it all that can be carried through a millennium ; the salient points. The half-tones, the
suggestions, the magic, are lost : the associations of the
words, being different, are all wrong. These things
belong to a language learnt at one's mother's knee, and
to no other. If anyone doubts this, let him compare
the few lines of Latin which Dante wrote when he
thought of writing the *Comedy* in a ' fixed and changeless ' dialect with the opening of the poem as it now

stands.[1] That Dante, like Spenser when he was composing the *Faerie Queene* in English measures instead
of hexameters, had his Gabriel Harveys to contend
with, may be seen by any who will look at Toynbee and
Gardner's *Dante and Del Virgilio*. ' Thou sacred voice
of the Pierides,' writes Del Virgilio, ' who unfoldest
Orcus to the guilty, Lethe to them that seek the stars,
the " epiphoebia regna " to the blest, why castest thou
these weighty themes to the vulgar, while we pale
students shall read naught of thee ? Sooner shalt thou
stir the curving dolphin with the harp, and Davus
solve the riddles of the ambiguous sphinx, than
unlettered men shall picture the precipice of Tartarus
and the secrets of the pole scarce unsphered by Plato.
Why write in laic verse, which clerks despise ? ' I refer
to this because nothing could better illustrate what I
have just been saying than the very poem of Del
Virgilio in which he thus complains. Every figure of
speech that the classics used is there, and the poem
swarms with allusions to Virgil, Horace, and Terence.
Gibraltar is the Gades of Alcides ; a storm is Nereus
stirring the Tyrrhenian Sea ; war is the champing of
Mars ; the poet himself is the clerk of the Aonian
muses, the vocal slave of Apollo. Every ornament,
in fact, that rhetoric can supply is there : and yet the
poem is one of the dullest ever written. There is no
true word in the whole poem but one of those modest
ones so often spoken in vanity. We shall all agree

---

[1] Ultima regna canam, fluido contermina mundo,
   Spiritibus quae lata patent, quae praemia solvunt
   Pro meritis cuicumque suis.
But Dante soon saw a better way. ' I laid down the lyre upon which
I had relied and prepared another suited to the perceptions of the
moderns : for in vain is food that needs chewing offered to the mouths
of sucklings.'

K

with the bard when he says, ' I am the rash goose cackling to the clear-toned swan.' Yet Del Virgilio promises that if Dante will but write in Latin and come to Bologna, he shall receive a laurel-crown from the University and the applause of multitudes.

Dante refused both invitations. Like Milton, he hailed his native language that by sinews weak had taught his first endeavouring tongue to speak ; threw aside the flatteries of so-called scholars, and gained immortality instead of momentary applause. Other poets, however, were less wise, and among them one who actually did receive the crown of laurel. Take one glance—you will certainly not take two—at Petrarch's *Africa*, and compare it with his Sonnets. *Africa*, on which Petrarch rested his chief hopes of wide and lasting fame, obeys all the rules, has every figure and turn in its right place, and, in the words of an Old English alliterative poem, is ' as dead as a door-nail, to deme the sothe.' It is like the Earl of Galway, the hero of Almanza, who, according to Macaulay, thought it more honourable to fail by rule than to succeed by innovation : ' who drew up his troops according to the methods prescribed by the best writers, and in a few hours lost eighteen thousand men, a hundred and twenty standards, all his baggage and all his artillery.' Historians, I believe, have corrected both Macaulay's numbers and his judgment of Galway ; but no critic has yet arisen to reverse the general opinion as to *Africa*. Dante, fortunately for himself and us, checked his ' gouty hexameters ' ere they had tottered far, and fell back on his native Tuscan. But we can still see what he admired in the classical Latin poetry. Among the honoured five in the limbo of the noble but unbaptised heathen, to whom he is proud to make a sixth, Homer, whom he had not read, is the sovereign, Virgil the ' altissimo,' Ovid the third, and Lucan the fourth : while for Statius is reserved the still higher renown of being his guide in Purgatorio.   Horace he knows but as satirist.   Three, then, of the six, are confessedly rhetoricians : and with the five he enters, not the Palace of Imagination, but the seven-walled Castle of Knowledge, including Logic, Grammar, and *Rhetoric*.

The classical Latin poets being thus the acknowledged models, and the visible quality of their work being the rhetorical, one expects, and one finds, among their imitators and admirers, this quality in superabundance. Not merely is this true of those who wrote in Latin— though of them it is only too painfully true—but of many of the vernacular poets the same may be said. Those who have read but a few specimens of Renascence Latin poetry will inevitably have noticed how all the figures of speech, the personifications, and even the heathen divinities, of classical times reappear, galvanised into a semblance of life : and these now almost unreadable performances were the object of unbounded admiration at the time of their appearance, often bringing their authors sinecure bishoprics from enthusiastic patrons.   But we can trace the same influence even more widely.   The two favourite Latin poets, in our own Elizabethan age, were Ovid and Seneca : and the extent to which these two affected our rhymers and playwrights need hardly here be emphasized.   The chief merit of Ovid, apart from his delightful gift as a story-teller, is an astonishing antithetical skill, exhibited equally by his warriors and by his distressed and lovelorn heroines.   As for Seneca, he is the epigrammatist *par excellence*, and almost every other line of his plays might be taken from some book of quotations. Had his plays been lost, and only his ' sententiae,' like those of Publilius Syrus, survived, we should have missed little that could not easily be spared. But these plays were the recognised models for a whole school of dramatists, and, as has been shown so comprehensively by Professor Cunliffe and others, have left many marks on Shakespeare himself. Not merely in the ghost-scenes and horrors, not merely in the Cornelias of Kyd and the Cæsars of Lord Stirling, but in the antitheses and forced figures of Shakespeare's early plays, nay in *Macbeth* and *Lear*, the Senecan influence is plainly discernible.

When we leave the Elizabethans, and come to their successors the Augustans, the case is even more striking. There were, of course, many more forces than one that tended to the creation of what we call Augustanism ; but the very name suggests the chief of them. To the whole school, from Dryden to Johnson, Latin literature, both directly and as interpreted by French poets and critics, was almost the only standard of judgment : and to some extent the models selected were even more rhetorical than before. There is much in Dryden of Juvenal, and more in Johnson. Addison's criticism of Milton is not much in itself, but its constant references to Virgil and Homer as models prove that his readers would hardly accept Milton as a poet until he had proved *Paradise Lost* to be a good copy of the *Iliad* and the *Æneid*, and especially of the latter. His own *Cato* is still less of a success than his criticism, but it obeys the rules of Horace, and has some speeches which are not bad as rhetoric. Whether Pope, the chief versifier of the age, was a poet or not, has been, and still is, vigorously disputed : but no one has ever denied that he was a rhetorician. Still more, he read rhetoric into books where there was little or none, and plainly fancied that Homer was as rhetorical as his own translation of him. That translation was, as Bentley said, a very pretty ' poem '—that is, a poem as the age understood the word—but it was not to be called Homer, precisely because it was deliberately and consciously art.

But when art degenerates, as it is always apt to do, into artificiality, when rules are kept because they are rules, and not because they answer to some real demand of nature, then men begin, fortunately, to weary of it. As with the imitators of Virgil, so with the imitators of Pope. They could catch his mannerisms, but not the talent that redeemed them. The externals, the devices, were easily mimicked, but not the force and life. Hence, as again happens too often, the master was blamed for the faults of his disciples ; and the whole rhetorical school was swept away because its lowest class was perceived to be bad.

And then once more the swing of the pendulum is seen. Men weary of lawlessness : they look before and after, and pine for whatever is not at the moment. Rhetoric, once discovered, cannot long be ignored : she has one thing in common with Nature, that you may expel her with a pitchfork but she will return. Forward to the future means back to Methuselah ; advance from the nineteenth century means return to the eighteenth. There is at the present time every indication that Pope is returning to his dominion, and the young poets of 1940 may well supply future teachers with as artful examples of figures of speech as those that crowd the pages of the *Essay on Criticism*.

Before I leave this branch of my theme, I should

like to touch briefly upon a subject which, if not the same, is allied to it, and will illustrate the phenomena, of which I have been speaking, in both its good and its evil sides. The later Renascence, which may be dated about three-quarters of a century after Petrarch and Boccaccio, and which is chiefly associated with the rediscovery of Greek literature, had its repercussions upon Latin. It was inevitable, when Latin was in such common use all over Western Europe, that it should be of the free and easy kind—that it should suffer those vulgarisations which are the invariable concomitants of colloquialism. As the *Lingua Franca* of the Church, it had to admit words and constructions as different from the classical as a Gothic cathedral from the Coliseum. It was the language of law, of medicine, and of what then passed for natural science : it was employed by University lecturers, by students, by playwrights, and by the authors of any works which aimed at an international circulation or at an immortality of fame : in fact every man with any pretensions to culture both wrote it and spoke it. So late as the end of the sixteenth century Montaigne named it as a living tongue, almost from his cradle, along with the French he caught from his mother : and long afterwards University plays and prelections were declaimed in Latin and were easily understood. We know that King James split his sides at the jokes in Ruggles's *Ignoramus,* performed in 1615 in Cambridge. King James was a scholar of a high order : but everybody else laughed too, and not merely because the King had laughed first. But this Latin was not the Latin of Cicero and Cæsar, nor even that of Petronius or Tertullian. What it could become when employed by ignorant tongues and pens is hardly exaggerated by

Ulrich von Hütten and his friends in the *Epistolæ Obscurorum Virorum*—a book well worth reading by all who have a modicum of Latin and can enjoy some good fun. 'Si deberem vobis scribere omnes guerras que sunt de hoc libro, Olympie me tempus sit defuturum. Simpliciter plures dicunt quod non est possibile quod Pfefferkorn composuit istum librum, quia nunquam didicit unum verbum Latinum. Respondeo quod hac obiectio nihil valet, quia Johannes Pfefferkorn ea potest annotare que audit, vel quando studentes veniunt in domum suam, vel quando ipse vadit in balneum!' This might seem to be the language of Chaucer's drunken summoner; but it is easily to be paralleled from many a serious sermon or epistle of th times. De la Marck's 'Si non payatis, brulabo monasterium vestrum' is scarcely below the level of some of these performances. Not a few of the Church hymns are all but macaronics; and even the Latin of the Missal is hardly more classical. As Macaulay says, it is doubtful whether even Claudian would have understood the language of the Communion service.

With the advent of the Renascence, a natural reaction took place, and, as is almost inevitable with reactions, went too far in the opposite direction. The strange sect of the Ciceronians arose, with the determination to use no word not in the vocabulary of the Roman orator. Like Charles Fox trying to write his history without a word he could not find in Dryden, 'only more so,' they were reduced to strange shifts. For 'faith,' *fides*, they used *persuasio*, and for 'excommunication' interdiction from fire and water: nay for Christ himself they had to say 'Optimi Maximique Jovi's interpres ac filius.' It is significant that the chief opponents of this craze—for I think *taste* too

noble a word for it—were the finest scholars of the
time. Muretus, carefully searching through Cicero
for words the dictionary-makers had overlooked, introduced them into a lecture, received the expected hisses,
and then revealed the source whence he had taken
them, thus turning the laugh upon the critics. But
the *coup de grâce* was dealt by a still nobler hand.
Erasmus, in his famous dialogue *Ciceronianus*, with that
mingling of wit and learning which characterises all
his writings, attacked the absurd pedantry : and,
though he did not live to see his complete victory,
achieved that triumph which so many controversialists
have missed. The folly which he assailed is still remembered because of the brilliancy of the attack that
killed it.

On this famous quarrel some thoughts arise which
are fully relevant to my subject. First, were we to
run through the names on each side, it would be seen
that the view of every man could have been confidently
predicted from a knowledge of his character and circumstances. Knowing the man, we should have known
his taste. Trifling as was the issue involved, it provided, as do so many trifling issues, the opportunity
for the expression of the man's whole personality ;
and a question of taste is once more perceived to be in
essence not a question of taste merely, but of one's
whole attitude towards life. The *mere* scholar—who is
therefore less truly scholarly than his rival—is found,
as is inevitable, to take the petty and pedantic view :
the wide-minded man, trained not only in the study but
by contact with all sorts and conditions of men, gifted
with a sense of humour that has been developed by
travel, by experience of human vagaries, and by insight,
equally inevitably takes a broader, more common-sense

survey. But the whole story shows how a strange fashion in taste may arise through a special concatenation of events, and die out as things change. This trivial example, which Addison might have considered among the rest in his essays on False Wit, shows once more how futile it is to deal with æsthetics in the light of æsthetics only. To understand changes of taste, or even taste in stillness, we need to refer to the general tendencies and special circumstances of mankind.

VII

HYPERBOLE

VERY closely allied with the taste for rhetoric, indeed strictly but a part of it, is the taste for exaggeration and over-emphasis. Exact equivalence between fact and statement, such as one might suppose would be desired by both writers and readers, gradually palls as ' criticism ' develops, and as comparisons are made between one author and another. Men begin to ask first of all for force, and do not discriminate closely between force and its substitutes. Calm and quiet speech, human nature being what it is, proves to excite the hearer little, and the demand is ever for violent and more violent expression. He who exaggerates, either in diction or in delivery, is found to have, with the *blasé* and the ignorant, a vast and palpable advantage over the precise and cautious. Exaggeration is the special weapon of orators, and is therefore the special weapon of writers who adopt the devices of oratory. It must be confessed, indeed, that it is the special mark of most poetry : and this, I think, is the main cause of that antagonism which is so often seen to arise between the poet and the man of science. ' I dislike poetry,' said a physicist to me once, ' because it does not *measure* its words.' He had himself been accustomed, for thirty years, to precise measurements of phenomena, and to precise admissions that his measurements were never *quite* precise. The result was that the loose statements

and *unmeasured* language of poets had come to appear
to him like the rash and reckless guesses of sciolists
who jump to conclusions without careful testing of
results. 'Take one example,' said he. 'Byron says
love is woman's *whole* existence : a wild hyperbole. It
probably did not occupy more than a tenth of the
existence of Venus herself. Poets should study
statistics.'

I could not deny that there was much truth in my
friend's strictures. And certainly there is constantly
seen an upward tendency in the strength of the
language of poets—until the tendency overreaches
itself, and the violence is discovered to defeat its own
ends. There may then be a return to simplicity and
exactness, but only for the process to begin all over
again.

The earliest poets whose works we know are, as a rule,
marked by a certain restraint. For all we can tell,
this may be a mere accident. Their quietness, perhaps,
was due to a reaction against the noise and over-vigour
of still earlier poets whose works have perished. Be
this as it may, it will I think be generally admitted
that Homer and Hesiod are distinguished by a tolerable
equivalence between deed and word. Pass on, however,
some centuries, to a time when conscious art had been
developed, and we shall find a great change. I have
spoken of Virgil as a rhetorician ; and, if there were
no other proofs of his rhetorical turn, examples of his
hyperbole would be sufficient. He wished to be the
Latin Homer, and to be a Homer to the Latins of his
time he soon found that it was not enough to reproduce
Homer *exactly*. He had to *strengthen* Homer whenever
he reproduced him ; and in almost every case where he
quotes him he adds a touch of additional force. Thus

Homer tells us that Diomede hurled at Æneas a stone of considerable mass :

> Not two strong men the enormous weight could raise,
> Such men as live in our degenerate days.

But Virgil, in order to show us the might which the dying paroxysms gives to Turnus, makes him lift a rock which

> vix lecti *bis sex* cervice subirent,
> Qualia nunc hominum producit corpora tellus :

and though the hero fails to hurl it, yet the poet is careful to remark it is not through native weakness but through the fatal influence of the Dea Dira. Again, Homer, in asking the help of the Muses before enumerating the thousand ships which Helen launched against Troy, says that by himself he could not accomplish the task if he had ten mouths and ten tongues. But this is poor and single business for Virgil. Arriving with Æneas at the creaking gates of Tartarus, he finds that a hundred tongues, a hundred mouths, would fail him to sum up all the forms of crime and all the penalties.[1]

But whatever one may think of Virgil, none will deny the rhetorical capacities of Pope : and here again we find, among the scores of other rhetorical devices, this of hyperbole. ' Translating,' or at any rate manipulating, that same passage of Homer about the catalogue, Pope, as usual, took a glance at Ogilby's version ; for,

---

[1] Incidentally, it may be noticed that it is a kind of hyperbole, and a peculiarly rash one, when he makes Otus and Ephialtes pile Ossa on Pelion and Olympus on Ossa. As Pelion is much smaller than Ossa, and Ossa only half the size of Olympus, the two youths showed a remarkable ignorance of the laws of equilibrium, and deserved to fail in their attempt. Homer shows more sense, and more orographical knowledge.

though he ridiculed Ogilby in public, he was careful
to consult him in private. He found that Ogilby had
been beforehand with him, and had multiplied Homer's
ten into a hundred. But Pope is not going to be out-
done by a mere printer. Accordingly he multiplies yet
again, and we now read the couplet which I have
already once quoted in this volume :

> To count them all demands a thousand tongues,
> A throat of brass, and adamantine lungs.

The tendency to seek to gain attention by assuming
the voice of Stentor, and to trust that by enlarging
your statement you may secure belief in at least a
fraction of it, is, of course, practically universal. We
find it in the tongue-doughty Harapha, and in the epic
poem of the Egyptian Pentaur, who thinks to flatter his
master Rameses by informing him how, when his whole
army had been scattered by the vile Hittites, the mere
sight of his solitary majesty had driven the enemy back
in ignominious rout. We find it in Ariosto's description
of the deeds of Orlando :

> And ere the evening settled on the plain,
> Full fourscore thousand by his arm were slain :

a feat which, if we allow twelve hours to the labourer's
day, means two slaughtered Saracens per second. We
find it as almost the only figure of speech employed
habitually by English schoolboys. It is also habitual
among Asiatics ; and here, if nowhere else, East and
West meet. Oriental hyperbole, in fact, may almost
give points to the Transatlantic variety. It is familiar
to us through the Bible, as well as from the reports of
astonished travellers. ' Cities walled up to heaven,'
Chaldean soldiers ' swifter than leopards, fiercer than
evening wolves,' ' we were in our own sight as grass-

hoppers,' 'all I have is thine,' 'after whom is my lord
come out, after a dead dog, after a flea?' 'I am the
least in my tribe, and my tribe is the least in Israel,'
'as the sands of the sea for multitude': these are but
a few random examples. Christ himself, an Oriental,
and speaking to Orientals, avails himself of this style;
and it is possible that, by taking him literally, we have
sometimes mistaken his meaning. 'If any man come
to me, and hate not his father and his mother':
here we can perceive and allow for the hyperbole.
But the exact interpretation of 'If a man smite thee
on the one cheek, turn to him the other also,' as of
many other maxims of like kind, may perhaps best be
left to our Bishops and Curates by the congregations
committed to their charge.

This will be enough to show one danger of hyperbolic speech : the form of hyperbole adopted in certain
times and places may be strange or difficult to men of
other habits of mind, although exaggerations equally
wild rarely impose on those to whom their special
character is familiar. De Quincey tells us that, passing
through a village of about four hundred inhabitants,
he saw a crowd, and was, a little later, informed by an
old lady that the crowd numbered about four million.
He was not imposed upon : and, though exaggerations
are not usually so extreme as this, they scarcely ever
convince the hearer to the extent of their literal meaning. But when we do not know our author, 'his object,
scope in every page,' we may easily run the risk of
misunderstanding. Still oftener are we deceived when,
his wing being damped, he descends to literality.
Having become accustomed to discounting his too
vigorous assertions, we discount his plain statements.
He has cried Wolf so often that we pay no attention

when the beast is really on him. This is one of our difficulties in the study of medieval history. Knowing, for example, that the hundred thousand said to have followed Edward to Bannockburn are more than could have been crowded into the field, unless like the devils in Pandemonium they had 'reduced their shapes immense to smallest forms,' we are embarrassed whenever we come to deal with medieval calculations, even though they may not be intrinsically improbable. The same embarrassment overtakes us when we deal with many modern authors, who, with less excuse, magnify not all, but half, they describe. It would be easier for us if they magnified everything.

Such extravagance may of course arise from a mere childish love of display; and in Orientals may be associated with the fondness of jewellery, fine colours, and over-adornment generally which we Westerners are accustomed to notice in the East. We find it in our own literature, certainly, at times when the love of such extravagance is manifest in other than literary spheres. The Elizabethan age, with all its merits, was not above boastfulness, ostentation, and a certain vulgar magnificence : and the writings of the age do not, as a rule, err by over-modesty of expression. Shakespeare himself, when he thinks himself specially fine, is specially flamboyant : indeed, as Macaulay says, whenever he tries to write well, he rants : it is only when he forgets to write his worst that he writes his best. Even so sympathetic a critic as Bradley maintains, and I think rightly, that Shakespeare saw no bombast in the Player's Speech in *Hamlet*, and that in many of his most seriously intended speeches there are passages fully as high-falutin' as that of the Player. With Marlowe, as everyone knows, youthful vigour con-

stantly runs into the wildest frenzy. In the *Jew of Malta*
we have a stage-direction, ' Enter three Jews,' followed
almost immediately by the exclamation of Barabas,

> Why, how now, countrymen?
> Why flock you thus to me *in multitudes?*

This is typical of what happens throughout almost
all Marlowe's plays : the simple three is constantly
treated, as if, after the manner of the ' little one ' in
the prophet, it had become a thousand. Like Cosroe
in *Tamburlaine the Great*, every word of his seems to

> rid its royal shoulders
> Of such a burthen as outweighs the sands
> And all the craggy rocks of Caspia.

This is youthful exuberance, the ' Cambyses' vein ' of
a boy : but it exactly suited the minds of an audience
young in hope, and with the prospect of a new world
opening before it. It must be remembered, also,
that the sounding speeches of *Tamburlaine* were, in all
essentials, orations : they were mouthed by the actor
at the far end of the ' apron,' with every oratorical
accompaniment of voice and gesture, to an audience
thirsty for rolling periods and ' mighty lines ' :
an audience that felt it could not cough or look away
without the danger of missing a thunderbolt of diction.
One can imagine how the groundlings ceased to crack
their nuts, and the young aristocrats on the stage
forgot to whisper their euphuistic repartees, as the
actor, no longer an actor but a reciter, flung out these
magnificent hyperboles.

> Now clear the triple region of the air,
> And let the majesty of Heaven behold
> Their scourge and terror tread on emperors.
> Smile, stars that reigned at my nativity,
> And dim the brightness of your neighbour lamps !
> Disdain to borrow light of Cynthia !

All this is the sublime rant of a poet in harmony with an age which fancies it is beginning the world over again, and that the morning-stars must sing together to celebrate the new birth of things.

For hyperbole at such a time there is every excuse. It reminds one—though indeed it stands immeasurably higher—of the wild hysterical eloquence of the orators of the French Revolution, overjoyed at being alive in such a dawn, and unable to keep their rapture within bounds : many of them rejoicing for the first time in the full liberty of unlicensed speaking, and sub-consciously resolved to make the most of their oppor-tunity. One cannot demand the calm of age from the boys of Lynn when just released from school. In almost every case, when such a release has come to a nation, the literature has been of this excited kind. I was about to make an exception in the case of Athens after Salamis : but I remember that if ever the Attic tragic stage lost its dignity and repose, it was when the grave Æschylus brought out the *Persae*, the end of which might be a Carmagnole.

But natural and often excusable as this extravagance may be, there can, I think, be little doubt that when it arises from mere competition and emulation, when it is a case of shouting in order to be heard above a din, then it marks some defect alike in those who indulge in it and in those who accept it. In the present day, when an English book has every year thirteen or fourteen thousand rivals, it is hard for the still small voice to prevail above the earthquake : and too many, both of our prose-writers and of our rhymesters, confuse noise with speech. The author's constant endeavour on the one hand, to compel attention, and, on the other

L

side, the hearer's inattention to whatever does not by
sheer violence compel him to listen to it, shows an
indifference to truth which indicates that something is
wrong with ourselves, and therefore with the style
which expresses ourselves. I could, I imagine, easily
give a hundred examples from living authors : but it
may be as well for the present to confine myself to
those whose voices, once so loud, are now silent. I do
not for a moment agree with those who hold that
Macaulay's History is inspired by the desire to let the
Tory dogs always have the worst of it : but I do think
that colour is lent to the charge by his habit of over-
statement, to which he was led not by political parti-
ality but by ' the cherished lure of pomp, and proud
precipitance of soul.' To say that Boswell was a great
author because he was a great fool, that the dull and
placid English nation heard, with ' transports of
delight,' how an Englishman had been elected Pope,
or that to the seared conscience of Marlborough the
death of a man caused no more uneasiness than the
death of a partridge, may seem strong, but is really
feeble. Macaulay's rival Carlyle said that Rhadaman-
thus would order him four dozen lashes for his treatment of Marlborough ; but Carlyle himself is guilty of
Macaulay's sin in double measure. As Lowell said, he
is for calling down fire from heaven whenever he cannot
lay his hand on the match-box ; and his eternal shriek-
ings show rather a futile exasperation with fate than
the true strength of the silent Prometheus he fancied
himself to be. So too the vapourings of Byron
struck one of his shrewdest friends as rather silliness
than the Lear-like madness which the poet was vainly
trying to mimic. But the worst of all out-Heroders
is Swinburne, who, if he had lived in Dryden's day,

would probably have received at least one of the
characterisations of Zimri :

> So over violent or over civil
> That every man with him was God or Devil.

Let any one read Swinburne's eulogies of Marlowe or
Charlotte Brontë, and his denunciations of the ' addle-
pated' or ' long-eared ' people who have the ill-luck
to disagree with him, and he will see hyperbole at its
most hyperbolic. A passage or two from his little book
on Shakespeare, however, will do equally well. ' The
majestic and impassioned poetry of the graver scenes
(in *Henry IV* and *Henry V*) should not, if it is possible
that it should not, be overshadowed in the sight of
students young or old by the presence and the rivalry
of the greatest comic figure that ever dawned upon
the conception of the greatest comic poet ever born.
. . . The multitudinous magnificence of variety in
creation which makes it difficult if not impossible for
any not immodest and irrational criticism to attempt
an estimate of this trilogy can be compared with
nothing else in poetry or prose. . . . The flawless
equity, the impeccable intelligence, the illimitable
sympathy and the infallible apprehension of noble
nature and of living truth, none need seek elsewhere,
but all may find in Shakespeare. The radiance of right-
eousness distinguishes the judgment and the treatment
of character which cast all other men's into the shade.
Shakespeare is himself alone : he could have taken up
Homer in his right hand and Dante in his left.' It is
strange that Swinburne did not see that this is not
criticism at all : it is no more like a balanced judgment
than the courtiers' salutation, 'O king, live for ever'
is an exact chronological summary of the reign of

Nebuchadnezzar. Or take another dithyramb, the excuse for which is less easy to find than in the case of Falstaff. 'Though Perdita may be the sweetest of all imaginable maidens, Imogen is the most adorable woman ever created by God or man. Her single figure might well suffice to distinguish its designer as the supreme creator of imaginative life in human and immortal character . . . (Cymbeline) is to be ranked among the great works of Shakespeare.' Again, ' *The Merchant of Venice* is perhaps the greatest and most perfect example of tragi-comedy on record.' Æschylus was one of the greatest of poets, but that ' in all patriotic literature there is nothing of its kind comparable with the *Persae* but *Henry V* ' is a more disputable proposition. The only effect of all this declamation is to make the reader, however enthusiastic an admirer of Shakespeare he may be, pause and ask himself whether the sun has no spots. One admires, of course, the amazing profusion with which adjective is piled upon adjective like a dozen Pelions on Ossa ; but in the long run they carry less weight than a measured sentence of Johnson. The bow has been strained too often and too rashly.

It is not easy to surpass Swinburne in this respect : not much easier, in truth, than to surpass him as a melodist or rhythmist : but the present generation has made the effort, and not fallen far short of success. With a few noble exceptions, the novelists of to-day would appear to desire each to overgo his predecessor, if not in the force, yet in the strength, of his language as well as in the startling or shocking character of his plot. Novel-writing might seem to be a war after Lord Fisher's heart, in which violence from first to last is the essential. A novelist is a strong man armed, who

keeps his castle till a stronger than he cometh : nor is
the would-be teacher behind him. It would seem to
be the general belief that the truth of a prophet's
message is to be decided by the wildness of his con-
tortions, and that if you but foam at the mouth you
will be accepted as a minister of Apollo. I cannot but
think that all this is in actual fact a sign of weakness :
that the constant forcing of the note proves the in-
sufficient training of the voice : and that those who
shout so loudly have often little to say that is worth
hearing. To many of them might be applied the
description an old Elizabethan novelist gives of a
braggart : ' of presumption a giant, of power a gnat.'
They are like the losel who made off with the spear
and steed of Sir Guyon, but could not borrow his
strength or skill. At any rate, one remembers that the
writers whose voices have carried furthest down the
centuries have usually been those who have spoken
most quickly. Here, if anywhere, we may learn from
the Greeks, of whom one could use the phrase in which
Dowden describes the mature style of Shakespeare ;
they contrived almost invariably to attain ' a perfect
harmony between thought and expression.' In an
excellent paragraph of an excellent book to which I
have already referred, *The Classical Tradition in Poetry*,
Professor Gilbert Murray points to the conspicuous
absence of strain and over-emphasis as a characteristic
of classical Greek literature from first to last. ' The
language,' he says, ' is so free from bombast and exaggeration that it generally disappoints a modern reader,
accustomed to the habitual over-emphasis of modern
fiction, not to speak of newspapers and advertisements.'
Professor Murray may here, misled by his love of the
subject which he has made his own, be indulging very

slightly in the hyperbole to which he objects : but in
the main he is right. He is right also when he draws
attention to the habitual exaggeration which is the
sign-manual of Romanticism. 'Romanticism,' says a
French critic, '*c'est le faux*. As contrasted with the
classic style, Romanticism is never happy unless it
exaggerates. Dumas' Antony, when annoyed, drives
his dagger through an oaken table. Victor Hugo's
Hernani offers people his head, but refuses to take his
hat off.' We shall, of course, have to define our word
Romanticism pretty carefully before we admit the
truth of this indictment : but within the requisite
limits it is true enough. Whether the present age, the
age of the Nine-fifteen, is Romantic or not, I am not
prepared to decide ; but that much of its most popular
literature has this romantic quality needs no proof.
From the hoardings on which it endeavours to induce
people to waste their money, from the garish headlines
of the newspapers, to the most elaborate of novels or
the most recondite of poems, its one object is to startle :
if it can startle in no other way, it attempts to shock.
To use the slang of the day, it tries endlessly to ' beat
the record.' All its adjectives are superlatives, and all
its verbs are in the tense which in the grammars of
some languages is called the ' Energetic.'

Fortunately there are always, even in the full tide
of such a frenzy, some who remain calm and unmoved,
and refuse to be taken in by these thrasonical out-
pourings. There are authors, even to-day, who endeavour to say what they mean with precision, and
there are readers who, learning gradually that these
authors do say what they mean, come to trust them and
so to enjoy them. Men learn, slowly but surely, the
lesson of the Mosaic orator, that when truth is an ally,

a quiet five can be more than a match for an hundred, and a mild hundred can put to flight a noisy ten thousand. It would, happily, be easy to name a dozen novelists of to-day who are as gentle and unobtrusive in their style as Jane Austen herself. Two or three would seem to have adopted as their model the plain and unadorned simplicity of De Foe and Swift ; and many others are beginning to perceive the superiority of the rapier to the bludgeon. Nor is the capacity to see this superiority less visible in certain of the critics whose opinions are valued by the public at large. But the lesson is learnt, not merely by a few, when the everlasting bawling has wearied the ear, and eternal hyperbole has cloyed the palate, of a whole generation. We then get the reaction which always follows too much action ; the swing of the pendulum which is as visible in literature as in politics. Nothing, in spite of Oscar Wilde, succeeds less permanently than excess : it inevitably provokes its opposite. Few rhetorical writers are more justly admired than the great preachers of the seventeenth century. Donne, Browne, Jeremy Taylor, Milton, and the whole host of Puritan and Anglican divines—where can one find loftier prose than theirs ? But it had the defect of over-statement ; and it inevitably wearied, with the natural result that it gave way to the simple prose of Dryden, Tillotson, and Addison. Instead of the stately Claren-don we have the homely Burnet ; instead of Harring-ton the ' genuine Saxon English of Asgill.' And the effect lasted throughout at least the first half of the eighteenth century. Nowhere is there a more quiet and direct philosophical style than that of Hume or Berkeley, one more plain and colloquial, yet vigorous, than that of Bentley, one more exactly adapted to its end than that of Middleton, one more delicate, clear, and precise than that of Goldsmith. This, too, gave way, it is true, to the ponderous oratorical periods of Pitt, to the gorgeously elaborated rhetoric of Burke, and to the balanced and overwrought style of Johnson : but once again there came a reaction. There is hope, then, that to the loose and frenzied style so common to-day may succeed, if only for a time, a style more restrained and more exact.

Rarely, however, does the pendulum of taste stay long in the happy mean. It is swung to and fro by a force which it appears unable to resist. We often find a studious and ironical meiosis taking the place of an hyperbole ; and this is but hyperbole in another form. Habitual understatement, although, since hyperbole and violence have worn themselves out, vastly more effective as a weapon of style, has some of their disadvantages, and wearies the reader even more quickly. It becomes a mannerism, and tends to be regarded as an affectation. It has the same purpose as hyperbole : that of drawing attention to something which, described simply, would pass unnoticed, and often deserves to pass unnoticed. A consistently ironical style would be perhaps more tiresome than any other that can be conceived. Such a style is very rare : but when the ironical vein begins to be exhausted, the reader is in the same bewilderment as when the exaggerator tells the truth.

There are other devices for startling the reader with which, if space allows, I may briefly deal later. Such are paradox, antithesis, and epigram. Scarcely ever were they more rampant than now : and the only wonder is that the authors who deal in them have not long since tired of the eternal monotony. It would

appear, however, that nothing is more difficult than
to be simple.   At any rate simplicity is but seldom
found : and the explanation may lie in the great
sentence with which Spinoza closes his *Ethics* : ' All
things excellent are as difficult as they are rare.'   It
is not my purpose to assert that other styles have not,
in due season, their merits : but it might almost
seem as if, amid the welter of conflicting opinions,
we have here lighted on one certain and irrefragable
critical doctrine, that simplicity is good *per se*, always,
in all places, and for all.

VIII

THE TASTE FOR THE PRECIOUS

As writing becomes more and more self-conscious, and as the author applies more and more criticism to his own work, all sorts of consequences appear. I have spoken, in the last chapters, of the rise of rhetorical writing as one of these consequences : a phenomenon combined of evil and of good, producing admirably artistic work but ever tending to the artificial and over-elaborate. It is of course impossible to draw up a history of such a process : it goes on differently in different individuals, and what is a comparatively early stage in one literature may be late in another, while each stage shades off so gradually into the next that definition is out of the question. There is, in fact, nothing in which reaction follows action more confusedly and irregularly than in this. A man reacts against his own rhetoric, as Ruskin, for example, reacted against the adornment of *Modern Painters ;* and often, in his very next work, reacts against his simplicity, and turns to rhetoric again.

But let us, leaving historical points on one side, consider the question as if it were possible to view it *in vacuo.* Let us isolate the phenomenon as a man of science tries to isolate, in his experiments, the causes of the effect he wishes to study. Suppose that writing has been reduced to rules, and suppose that words have been more or less fixed in meaning. Imagine that the old days when there was no king in Israel and every man did what was right in his own eyes are over; that the Republic of Letters has admitted rulers, and that the medieval anarchy has been subjected to law. It is precisely then that a new anarchy sets in, that men begin to aim at a new kind of independence. 'I don't like the French Sabbath,' a friend of my youth used to say; 'it's impossible to break it.' But he had an irresistible impulse to break the Scottish Sabbath under which he had been brought up. As work was forbidden on that day, he wanted to work on it— though never on other days—and as play was forbidden he wanted to play. That is human nature. Set up a fence and you want to cut it down; make a law and you want to jump it. Even the Psalmist, seeing a troop ran through it, and seeing a wall leapt over it. And this tendency, working in the literary sphere, leads to two results which, in the nature of things, cannot arise in unsophisticated ages. On the one hand men begin to play with their thoughts, to invert them, to combine them, to distort them; even, in some cases, to make fun of them without ceasing to believe in them. This is what we call the making of conceits, and is a fashion which arises every now and then in all peoples at a certain stage. Some may call it a disease of civilisation: at any rate it does not appear until the literature has become civilised.

Men may also begin to play with their words. Here again there must be a more or less fixed foundation on which to build their play. Seeing that the words have a certain fairly precise significance, and that their associations have been tolerably defined, so that readers, when they see the words, expect a certain train of thought to be aroused, these men see a chance of startling. They invert the words, displace them, combine them in curious patterns, wrest them into new meanings and associations. Hence arises what we call a 'precious' style. It is clear that not till men have been accustomed for a long time to thinking can they thus play nicely with their thoughts, and not till words have attained a certain fixity can men venture to disturb them.

As a parallel I may compare metre. It is not, for example, possible for a writer of blank verse to venture on complicated variations on its pattern until he is sure that his readers are accustomed to that pattern, and have it so fixed in their minds that they know what it is that is being varied. And similarly, while all good musicians break the rules of harmony, the teacher of harmony makes his pupils learn these rules, if only that they may see when they are being broken. Beethoven, it is said, rebuked one of his pupils for perpetrating a ' false relation.' Next day the pupil showed the master exactly the same thing in one of his own works. Beethoven was unperturbed. ' *I* can do that,' said he ' but *you* can't.' In a less legitimate fashion the old Eleatic philosophers invented their paradoxes. Reasoning having been reduced to rule, with the object of discovering truth, they said ' We will show you how your boasted rules lead to anarchy and demonstrate obvious falsehood. We will give the tortoise a small start and prove that Achilles will never overtake it. We will prove that motion is impossible, and that space both ends and does not end : that the universe must have had a beginning and can never have begun.' These are examples of the distortion of the thinking capacity. Preciousness and conceits, in like manner, are the distortion of a style and of a thought

which are *there* already, waiting, so to speak, for sophistication to be applied to them.

One does not consider the Eleatics as men who have
contributed greatly to the advancement of philosophy.
They are ingenious, and nothing more.   In the same
way neither the precious writers nor the *concettisti*
have done much for the improvement of taste.   It
does not follow, because a man can play with his
thoughts, that he has many of them, or that they
are particularly profound.   The contrary may be the
case, and in fact usually is so.   The two early ' heirs of
Shakespeare's invention,' *Adonis* and *Lucrece*, are full
of conceits : a few commonplace ideas are dressed
up like a child's doll, re-dressed, and dressed again.
But who goes to these poems for profundity ?   You
will find more real deep thinking in ten lines of *Hamlet*
than in all the three thousand lines of these poems.
As Shakespeare thought more he said less.   Similarly
with Milton.   His earliest poem, short as it is, is
tricked out in full Elizabethan fashion, and decked
with so many clothes that it can hardly walk in them.
In *Samson Agonistes* there is the utmost abundance of
ideas with the severest economy of words.   The fact
is that poets are like the king's servants in the Parable
of the Pounds.   The man with ten thoughts makes them
produce many others, while the man who has but one
thought very often tries, in order to disguise his poverty,
to wrap it up in a napkin of many colours, and to exhibit
it in such a way that though single it may appear multitudinous.   This is the method of Petrarch—the first
and perhaps the greatest of modern *concettisti*.   His
ideas, especially in his love-poems, are amazingly few,
but every one of them is presented in innumerable
aspects : and it is not till you begin to count that you

observe how skilfully the kaleidoscope has been used. Here he is the exact opposite of his great compatriot Dante, who, when he has said a thing—in the fewest possible words—has done with it, and leaves the reader to do the multiplication.

All know the period in which this style flourished in England, and how popular it was. It pleased both authors and readers : the authors because it tickled their vanity to see how ingenious they were, and the readers because, while tickling *their* vanity also, it saved them the trouble of *advancing* in thought. They were like schoolboys who, having once mastered an algebraical rule, love to stick to exercises on that, and dislike going on to another and a harder rule. To do a score of sums on Proportion or Division *seems* like advance, but is in reality nothing but going round the circle for ever and ever. Similarly, to read Cowley's *Mistress* or Petrarch's *Sonnets*, with the endless variations on one theme, *seems* like reading new poems, but is really only doing the same sum over and over again, with a for x and b for y. Nor is it easy to imagine that such circular tours mean real interest in an end to be reached. Cowley's *Mistress* we know was a mere phantom, a false Florimel that dissolves at the touch of the real. Cowley was never in love but once, and was then too shy to utter his passion. Petrarch's Laura, indeed, was a real woman ; but you often doubt it when you notice how the poet is more intent on his own skill than on her. His is not the way in which Catullus speaks of Lesbia, nor the way in which Burns speaks of Jean or Highland Mary.

It may perhaps be desirable to take a few examples of these conceits, though the reader may well be familiar with most of them. Many will have read, in Johnson's *Life of Cowley*, his little essay on what he calls, after Dryden, Metaphysical Poetry, where he collects a number of conceits from the Jacobean and Caroline poets : and for some these will be sufficient. To others there is a very keen pleasure in watching the aberrations of such writers as Cartwright and Cleiveland, while Quarles's Emblems, especially when supported by the delightful old illustrations, are a mine of endless interest. Two other poets, Crashaw and Donne, show how possible it is to combine absolute sincerity and real depth, with a quality that in others would be a sure sign of the absence of truth. There is more dispute as to the real power of George Herbert ; but this at any rate must be said of him, that whether himself a true poet or not, he inspired one of the truest in English literature. Without George Herbert we should have had no Henry Vaughan.

But I will take Cowley, who is the best for my purpose because, if he was not, as Johnson thought him, the greatest of the school, he was by far the most prominent, and is in fact one of the stock instances of that variability of taste about which I am speaking. No poet ever enjoyed more popularity, and none ever fell into oblivion more suddenly. When he died, Milton was just publishing *Paradise Lost ;* but there was no doubt who was the greatest poet of the age. Yet a few years later, Pope uttered his famous rhetorical question, ' Who now reads Cowley ? ' and if, for the next few years, some people did read him, it was simply because Pope had said that nobody did.

Take then first the *Davideis,* an epic poem in which all the rules are observed, even to calling David Jessides. Here we have the correct episodes—the plunge *in medias res,* the previous history told by pictures as

in the *Aeneid* or by the tales as in the *Odyssey*, the
future foreboded by useful prophets. You could illustrate every epic device from that poem ; nay, because
Virgil left some lines unfinished, Cowley deliberately
does the same ; and he would have given us the
requisite twelve books if he had not wearied of it after
four. But the poem was of its age, and that is why
it is not for all time : it is crammed with conceits
from beginning to end. If Cowley has to describe
the murder of Abel by Cain, he says

> So huge a stone he threw, as if he meant
> At once his murther and his monument :

if he has to describe the music of the spheres, he must
assign the parts :

> Water and air he for the tenor chose ;
> Earth was the bass, the treble flame arose.

After a description of the sacrifice of the ram instead
of Isaac, he cannot stop. Abraham is like an Argentine
ranch-man ; he utilises every part of the animal :

> On his horns the ransomed couple played,
> While the glad boy danced to the tunes they made

Even the sublime loneliness of God before the Creation
must be described with a quip :

> Full of himself the Almighty stood, his own
> Palace, and, without solitude, alone.

Asahel would run so fast ' that Time itself perceived
not what was done ' : when the Egyptian giant fell
by Benaiah's staff, ' the earth, as if worst strook, did
loudest groan ' ; when Aeneas carried Anchises on his
back, he took ' a richer prey than all the Grecian
forces bore away ' ; when the lightning is harmless

it ' bears a shining winter in its flame ' ; when Samson
slew the Philistines, ' he grew half-dead with toil of
giving death.'

If this, and much more than this, is what Cowley
can do with a story of which the smallest details were
already supplied to him in Scripture, no wonder that
in the *Mistress* there is a congestion of conceits as close
as that of the Jews on Holy Cross day.   Never was a
girl, even one who never existed, turned into so many
different things : the transformations which Ovid in
his Metamorphoses distributes to a hundred are here
endured by one : and whatever be true of woman in
reality, it is certain that Cowley's woman is ' varium
et mutabile semper.'   She is now an island, surrounded
by the waves of pride and hauteur ; the next moment
he is waging with her a Peninsular war : shortly
afterwards she is China, closed to the foreigner, or at
best admitting him but to a treaty-port.   Her very
body alters ; it is now straight, like Cupid's dart, now
crooked, like his bow.   She is a tulip, good neither for
physic, for smell nor for taste ; she is a thief who robs
him of sleep, she is the letters of the alphabet written
in gold, and he is Midas who perished by possessing
them ; she is human, but she is so divine that to buy
her is to be a Simon Magus ; she is the North Pole
to which he ever turns like a compass, and she is manna
that tastes of everything at once ; she is lightning that
has not disdained to burn the furze, and she is a city
that cannot be taken ; she is a grenado shot into a
magazine, and a queen reigning despite a Salic law.

On everything else he is equally ingenious.   Describing the mortality due to the Civil Wars, he says,

> Charon sweated at his trade,
> And had a larger ferry made.

M

On a bad picture of Prometheus, which he thinks good for nothing but to be burned :

> Pity him, Jove, and his bold theft allow ;
> The flames he once stole from thee, grant him now.

The love of gold is a jaundice of the soul, which makes it see all things yellow. Great men never see the sword of Damocles because they cannot imagine that anything is above them. The chair made out of Sir Francis Drake's ship is an illustration of Pythagoras's doctrine of the transmigration of souls. When he sees the fish with their silver scales in a stream, he thinks of the scales as coins enriching the river. To an absent friend he writes,

> By every wind that comes this way,
>   Send me at least a sigh or two :
> Such and so many I'll repay,
>   As shall themselves make winds to get to you.

The feature of all these fancies, and of a thousand others that might be given, is that the poet first seeks a far-fetched image, and then pursues it into its ramifications. He is like those commentators who, in explaining a parable, seek for a hidden meaning not merely in the main story but in its accidental details. As there have been men who have seen a profound significance in the five, two, and one of the Parable of the Talents, or a special symbolism in the ring that the father gave to the repentant prodigal, so those poets *invent* details to which symbolism may be forcibly attached. That these are not of the essence of poetry may be shown by the fact that one of the least poetical of great men, Francis Bacon, is richer in such comparisons than any three of these poets put together, and that one of the least poetical of great poets, Samuel

Butler, pours them out in *Hudibras* with a careless profusion which shows at once his mastery of them and his contempt for them. Ingenuity only too easily passes into pedantry and thence into absurdity.

Not that I would speak contemptuously of each and all of these writers. True critics always avoid scorn. I am far from denying that many of the *concettisti* have been true poets : a few of them have been not only true but great. The rank of Cowley is settled by judgments beyond appeal—the admiration, and the sincere flattery which consists in imitation, of scores of later poets. Even Milton has not disdained to borrow from him, and as for other poets, from Pope and Gray down to Coventry Patmore, they have robbed him without scruple. He has been to them what Spenser was to him : the poets' poet. ' Hither as to a fountain other stars repairing, in their golden urns draw light ' ; and stars do not draw light except from suns.

If it be true that bards can find in the strict bonds of rhyme and rule not bonds but wings, so, many poets have found in the narrowness of conceit no prison but an enlargement. Some villanelles and virelays have been great poems in spite of their cramping rigidity of form ; and it has proved not impossible for men to achieve imaginative beauty while aiming merely at point. As George Herbert might have expressed it, they have meant a tree and hit the sky : nay, sometimes, aiming at the most pedantic branch of the Tree of Knowledge, they have hit the Tree of Life instead. I know few poems, anywhere or by anybody, more sublime than Cowley's ' Hymn to Light ' : and, by the side of Cartwright's dreary witticisms on a gnat that got into a lady's eye—lucky creature, it received tears from her, while we miserable men earn only scorn—there are some real poems, penetrating and imaginative, and some almost as charming as Herrick's. Here, for example, is one—perhaps the only one ever written by a poet to a lady many years older than himself—'To Chloe, who wished she were young enough for me':

Chloe, why wish you that your years
   Would backward run, till they meet mine,
That perfect Likeness, which endears
   Things unto things, might us combine?
Our ages so in date agree,
That Twins do differ more than we.

There are two Births, the one when Light
   First strikes the new-awakened sense;
The other, when two souls unite;
   And we must count our Life from thence:
When you lov'd me, and I lov'd you,
Then both of us were born anew.

Love, like that Angel that shall call
   Our bodies from the silent grave,
Unto one Age doth raise us all,
   None too much, none too little have:
Nay, that the difference may be none,
He makes two not alike, but One.

But to go far higher than Cartwright or even than Cowley, he would indeed be a bold man who should deny the name of great poet to Petrarch, whose reputation, all over Europe, stood higher for five hundred years than that of any other poet since Virgil; who earned the devotion of Chaucer, and who fell back into a secondary place only in the last century and a half. So, too, amid all the differences of opinion about Donne—however much his crabbedness of diction may irritate some judges—it is, I think, fairly certain that the criticism of recent years is right, and that he possessed in rich measure many of the highest and most essential elements of poetical greatness.   I should like also to say a word for Crashaw, who is at times as conceited as Cowley himself, but who contrives somehow to reconcile even conceit with something not far removed from sublimity.   Take, for instance, the little epigram upon the ass that carried Christ into Jerusalem :

> Why else had Balaam's ass a tongue to chide
>   His master's pride,
> And thou, heaven-burthened beast, hast ne'er a word
>   To praise thy Lord ?
> That he should find a tongue and vocal thunder
>   Was a great wonder ;
> But O, methinks 'tis a far greater one
>   That thou find'st none.

Of Christ's silence before his accusers he says :

> God spake once when he all things made,
> He saved all when he nothing said :
> The world was made by nothing then,
> 'Tis saved by nothing now again.

It is true that sometimes the conceits are quite intolerable ; as when he says the martyred Innocents of Bethlehem would find milk on the path to heaven— along the Milky Way : but on the whole, with all his fancifulness, Crashaw is one of the very few religious poets who are not *nearly always* intolerable : and he is this, not in spite of his conceits, but I verily think often *because* of them.   At any rate it was certainly because of them that he gained his popularity.   Catholic as he was, Protestants welcomed him as they welcomed Francis Thompson three hundred years later ; and for the same reason.   He was in the style of the time, and he hit the prevailing taste of the time. For fifty years, if one wished to please, one had to write in this fashion. If Cartwright desired to gain the favour of King Charles and his court, he had to mould his poems in this fashion, and if Cleiveland meant to win hearers, he had to follow in the same path. A score of lesser writers, with none of the genius of these men, could at least mimic their external characteristics, and, for a time and in a small circle, pose as poets. Why the style did please, it would be hard to say : no one, I believe, has yet fully analysed the causes of this strange vogue ; but that these writers were immensely popular goes without saying. The works of Donne circulated by hundreds in manuscript, and were so skilfully imitated that even now we are not sure whether many of them are his or another's ; those of Cartwright were set to music by Lawes, and were belauded by Vaughan, by Shadwell, and by everybody in fact who could set up any claim to be a judge.

I say that I do not know anyone who has yet analysed the causes of this strange popularity, and that I am by no means sure that I know them myself. But it has often struck me that there may well be some connection between the literary tendency to conceits and the theological debates, so often turning on minute points, which flourished at that time. It will, I think, be agreed that theology, more than almost any other science, has to be expressed by means of metaphors, and that great ingenuity has often been shown in the choice of these metaphors. Never, since the days of the early councils, was that ingenuity greater than in the controversies of the Reformation time and its sequel the Puritan time in England. If we read the sermons and polemical tracts of those days, we shall

light on conceits, comparisons, and fancies, even in
prose, no less remarkable than those of Donne or
Cowley in verse.

Let anyone, for instance, take up the *Contemplations*
of Bishop Hall of Norwich, and he will not have gone
far before he will fancy he is reading Quarles in prose.
Hall had the misfortune to be the enemy at once of the
High Anglicans and of the Puritans ; he was attacked
by Milton and suspended by Laud ; but take either side
of the controversy and you will find the combatants
equally quaint and curious in their volumes of forgotten lore. And as for Fuller, more delightful even
than Hall, where can you find more ingenious quaint-
nesses, more undefiled wit, than in the pages of his
Church History? Remember also that *everybody* was
then interested in such controversies—that Chilling-
worth was popular, and that Fuller never wrote a
work that was not eagerly purchased and devoured
by multitudes of readers ; that the mental energy
now expended on discussing the style of a cricketer
or the chances of a tennis-match was then devoted
to analysing the differences between Arminius and
Calvin ; that the washerwoman or the milkman chat-
tered on Supralapsarianism or Sublapsarianism, and
that prevenient grace or imputed guilt was talked
about over the dinner-table—remember this and none
will, I think, be surprised that Crashaw could give a
conceited twist to a text, that Cartwright could turn
an astronomical allusion into a compliment, or that
Cowley could discourse on chemistry to his mistress.
I do not know that I am right : but I am sure that
conceits flourished when theological quarrelling became virulent, and died out when people ceased to
bother about it : and I throw out the suggestion, to

be proved or disproved, as a possible subject for a thesis.

I may have more to say of this peculiar taste when I come to speak more specially of the cult of Ingenuity : but I will add here what I take to be the truth, that a taste for conceits is usually short-lived. It arises from temporary causes, and passes away as the causes vanish. Nothing wearies so quickly as surprise, and the man who has admired a dozen conceits will reject the thirteenth at sight. Even in the very height of the Caroline craze there were many who despised it. Carew remarked how pitiful it was to see so many poets taking so much trouble to be dull : and, not unnaturally, many writers who practised the trick themselves, despised it in others. One of the greatest masters of the art, speaking of Fletcher's wit and cleverness, which he says made all his hearers ' wonder how the thing would be until it was, and delight in the endless cheats,' in the very next poem tells us that Beaumont, Fletcher's very *alter ego*, considered so much wit was unfit to come upon the stage, and deliberately blunted it to please the taste of the audience. Where it refused to be blunted, he took a sober sponge, and erased it altogether. As with detective novels to-day, the people disliked over-amplification. One thing is pretty certain, also, that if men want real ingenuity, they will, if they are wise, go elsewhere than to literature. I said at the beginning of these chapters, that downright hard crushing thought is not the mark of the literary man as such : and neither is consummate skill in the combination of thoughts. It belongs to the mathematician, the inventor, or the chess-player ; and when the writer strays beyond his proper field into mere cleverness, his insufficiency is speedily detected by those who know what real cleverness is. They soon weary of him and turn aside.

The taste for the precious differs from that for conceits only in this, that as the *concettisto* tries to wring out of a thought or a fancy more than it holds, so the precious writer tries to make words do a little more than their proper duty. They are to be more than the unprofitable servants in the Parable : in addition to the work for which they are paid they must throw in a supererogatory service. He is like the epicure who will never eat fruit in its season, and fancies it shows delicacy of taste to reject strawberries in July and welcome them in March. If a word, and especially an adjective, is the natural one, he will have nothing to do with it. Like Flaubert, he is always searching for the *mot juste*, with this difference, that when he has found it he throws it aside and seeks for another. He wants his readers to be constantly surprised by his choice of the word, and yet somehow to regard it as felicitous. He is simple when we expect adornment, and ornate when we expect simplicity. He is always applying force, and yet hopes that the constrained phrase will seem as if it came there of its own accord. He is Procrustes pretending that the limbs of his victims have not been stretched.

This, like so much that is not good, is after all but an exaggeration of what *is* good. It borders so closely on precision and exactness, that it is often hard to say where the border has been passed. It will be remembered that Virgil himself, one of the great ' lords of language,' was accused by many of his contemporaries of just this fault, though the word preciousness had not yet been invented. If Virgil did not quite escape it, it must indeed be near to virtue. Dante said that, while he had never used words for the sake of a rhyme, he had sometimes compelled them to express more than they usually *did* express : and Milton rarely uses a word without making it yield up its whole store of associations, classical, historical, derivational : with the result that every reading seems to reveal more depth of meaning than the one before. The precious writer is only trying to do the same thing, and over-doing it. But there are seasons and places at which the overdoing is not perceived, or if perceived is admired. Nor is it by any means always easy to be sure that the due limits have been overpassed or regarded. Churton Collins, for example, accused Tennyson of preciousness in the lines

> Where the kneeling hamlet drains
> The chalice of the grapes of God.

He ought, said Collins, to have been content to say ' Where the villagers take the Sacrament.' I am by no means certain that Collins was right. Again, in that love-song in the Princess,

> Now sleeps the crimson petal, now the white,
> Now winks the gold fin in the porphyry font,

I have known some people object to the second line, at least, as fantastically elaborate. Here, again, I am not sure that they were right : but I am sure of this, that Tennyson's first readers—the true judges—would not have agreed with them. The fact is that a great phrase-maker—and if Tennyson was not a great phrase-maker there never was one—always runs the risk of startling too much. The appropriateness may be too complete to seem natural, and men suspect,

very often quite unjustly, that a little more labour
has been spent than is right. On the other hand, the
time may be ripe for such labour, and for the full
appreciation of it. It may have been that an era of
carelessness has preceded, and that men will welcome
an excess of care—that is, what at other times would
be thought such—as a change. I have known two
preachers share the charge of a church—as Erskine and
Robertson shared the charge of Greyfriars ; one of
whom was extemporary, free, and careless in language,
trusting to the furor of the occasion to carry him
through ; the other memoriter, cautious, and rigid in
the choice of words. No division of labour could have
been more satisfactory : the congregation took one as
a foil to the other, and enjoyed both. Similarly with
literature of a more permanent kind. After the laxity
of Dickens and the heaviness of George Eliot the world
was ready for Stevenson : the harshness of Carlyle
and the hammer-beats of Macaulay prepared the way
for Pater : and not long afterwards a small but devout
congregation listened reverentially to Mrs. Meynell
herself, every one of whose adjectives was daintily
unexpected. I have heard people quote Stevenson's
phrases about Mr. Utterson : ' Men liked to sit awhile
in his unobtrusive company, practising for solitude,
sobering their minds in the man's rich silence ' ; and I
have heard them praise that epithet ' rich ' as Ned
softly, in Addison's story, praised the ' Ah ' which he
would rather have written than have been the author
of the *Aeneid*. I am not depreciating Stevenson's
genius, any more than I am depreciating *Marius the
Epicurean*, when I say that ere long it was precisely
such tricks as the one shown in this word ' rich ' that
set some people against the authors of them. People

weary of so artificial an appropriateness, as you come to suspect the over-urbanity of a man who talks to you as if he had lived his life with no other object than to have the honour of meeting you. And then comes the inevitable change. We pine for a more free and easy style, though it be as lax and unadorned as Scott's at his hastiest. ' Is so much care worth while ? ' as Shelley asked when he saw the fifty-six variations of the first line of Ariosto's *Orlando Furioso*. Is not something of the freshness of youth lost with all this particularity and servile diligence ? We reject it, as we reject the close air of town, and seek the country. Times have altered ; and Time, as Ulysses says, is a host who slightly shakes his parting guest by the hand, and with his arms outstretched as he would fly, grasps in the comer. We are like Time—we receive a style for one night into our caravanserai, and in the morning bid it farewell.

IX

THE TASTE FOR THE INGENIOUS

BOTH the Conceited and the Precious are but varieties of the Ingenious : and it may be as well, before proceeding further, to consider the taste for Ingenuity in general. Not that Ingenuity, any more than anything else, is ever universally admired. There is never a time at which all men, even all men with pretensions to taste, think alike : and there is no time, in which one kind of taste largely predominates, that is not quickly succeeded by another, in which another taste holds sway. Nothing illustrates this truth more clearly than the oscillations of feeling with regard to ingenuity. At one time ' all the world '—that is, the apparent majority of a certain coterie—is for cleverness at any price, and writers respond to the demand. I have no doubt, for example, that Ovid was prouder of his ability to get anything whatever into an elegiac couplet than of what to us appears his true poetic gift. This was because such dexterity was what the plane-trees and marbles desired. We know that St. Bernard thought he could not have completed the exacting pattern of *Hic breve vivitur* without a special measure of divine grace. This, considered closely, is a disguised form of self-satisfaction. Ingenuity is in the air, like an influenza. And then, like influenza, it passes, giving place to ' new,' that is, older, forms. Apollo fulfils himself in many ways.

The fact is that, in the decay of inspiration—and inspiration, like other things, tends to wear itself out —men are driven to other means of mental excitement. It may be that even the highest forms of inspiration, if long continued, would ' corrupt the world,' and it may be better that lower forms should have their innings. It is, certainly, hard to conceive anything much worse than a world overpopulated with geniuses. It is the average man that keeps things going, as it was the superabundance of giants that brought about the catastrophe of the Flood. But, fortunately or unfortunately, inspiration *does* fail. Sometimes, as in England during the fifteenth century, it flags in whole peoples and for generations : sometimes it ceases to work in the individual man of genius, it may be for a few months, it may be for years. A few of these men may have the strength of mind, at such times, to lie deliberately fallow, and produce nothing ; but many, the habit having obtained the mastery over them, or the need of money being insistent, go on writing, though probably conscious that what they produce is unworthy of them. It is tolerably certain that even Shakespeare was occasionally guilty of this sacrilege. *Measure for Measure* appears to have been begun in a rush of the divine frenzy : it was finished, or rather was huddled up, when the frenzy had ceased but the stage-manager was still pressing. If the author of the *Odyssey* wrote the last book, it would seem that he had really finished, in the last but one, but could not stop. Every reader can supply scores of examples of cases where the author would have done well to give his pen a rest.

Not seldom, again, when there is a widespread flood of genius, men without genius are caught in it, and hurried along like the cattle, described by Virgil, in an inundation of a Lombard river. Everybody is writing, and none can resist the impulse to write. Pindar has sung, and they will sing too, though the result may be merely to christen some glassy sea. In all these cases the *cacoethes scribendi* exerts its power ; and it shows itself in a multitude of ways : now in tasteless imitation, now in equally tasteless revolt against the accepted models, now in gaseous nothings to which the writer is unable to give a local habitation. Perhaps most often, when some great man has shown the way, it appears as mere technical skill in the use of a popular form, the substance and the life being absent. When Chaucer feels that for the time being a *Legend* or a *Canterbury Tale* is beyond him, he produces intricate and difficult examples of metrical cleverness like those in *Anelida and Arcite ;* mechanical and lifeless toys. When Martial is bringing out his endless stream of almost perfect ' epigrams ' his envious rivals, unable to compete with him in his own line, devote themselves to palindromes and Sotadeans, which Martial justly regarded as but a waste of time.

When a whole age uneasily feels itself incapable of works of lofty thought, it puts Virgil into ' cristate ' or ' leonine ' hexameters, rewrites the *Odyssey* in twenty-four ' lipogrammatic ' books, or compiles centos from the *Iliad* into lives of Christ. It is well known that so true a poet as Ausonius was once guilty, under pressure from the Emperor, of an epithalamium made up of scraps of Virgil.

It is not always, of course, that the taste for ingenuity takes so fantastic a form as this. What we see oftener is a phenomenon like that of the so-called ' Silver Age ' of Latinity, in which simplicity appears dull and flat, and the demand is for something startling. I have already spoken of that age when treating of the vogue of a rhetorical style : and indeed ' rhetoric,' when carried a certain length, is but a form of ingenuity. Any device by which the force of a statement or of a reflection is heightened, may be called a rhetorical device : and a certain amount of skill is necessary in order to employ this rhetoric with effect. We find then, inevitably and invariably, that when for any reason the simple style fails to produce its due impression, all sorts of means are used in order to stimulate the jaded palate of the reader : antithesis, the harsher the better, epigram, the smarter the surer to be welcomed, paradox, the wilder the more satisfying. Sometimes a studied brevity is affected, though it be at the cost of exactness or intelligibility : anything, indeed, as long as it is clever, and stirs a momentary admiration. Such a style may vary from something not far off the highest to the lowest degradation. We find every possible variety in the so-called poetry of Lucan—the epigram that sums up in a few words a whole philosophy, and the strained metaphor that disgusts by the feebleness of its would-be force. In the plays and essays of Lucan's uncle Seneca we have examples, in even greater abundance, of similarly contrasted character. Even in Tacitus, who was a man of greater sincerity and power than either, there are occasions when we feel that truth is sacrificed to print ; though, from his very love of effect, he was usually careful to set his ingenuities against a background of sheer simplicity. If we had more works of inferior writers, we should probably see the style carried to still greater excess.

There can be no doubt that all this suited the average

taste of the time.   It was, like the rhetorical style in
general, a natural result of the habit of public recitation, in which momentary success was imperative ;
and it was the inevitable development of the style of
Virgil and Livy, itself a reaction from the severity of
Cæsar and the plainness of Catullus.   But the time was
to come when the perpetual straining, in its turn,
wearied the hearers, and the plain style came back,
in exaggerated plainness.   Nay, there seem to have
been some, in the very height of the fashion, who disliked it.   If we may judge from the incidental criticisms, and actual practice, of Petronius, the very
' arbiter elegantiarum,' there were in the days of
Seneca himself a few who sighed, like so many who
were cloyed with Apician luxury, for a Saturnian age
in which men were satisfied with simple fare and
unadorned dress.   We must never imagine that a
fashion, however prevalent, carries everyone away, or
that the coming reaction is not foreboded even when
the action is strongest.   All things carry in them the
seeds of their own decay, and there are men who foresee the autumn in the spring.

A very curious phenomenon, to which I have referred
elsewhere, is that exhibited in the literary history of
Iceland.   Here we see, more clearly I think than anywhere else, the two tendencies, to simplicity and to
excess of ingenuity, working simultaneously in the
same man.   It is as if Diabolus and Emmanuel had at
one and the same time gained possession of the human
city, and the little state were suffering ' the nature of
an insurrection.'   No plainer and more direct style
can be conceived than the prose style of Snorri in his
Edda and other sagas.   The words are exact representa-
tives of the thoughts, and none are wasted.   He tells

N

his tale as the author of Genesis tells the story of Joseph—and no higher praise can be given. And Snorri seems to have been but the best among a crowd of story-tellers hardly less simple than himself. But turn to the contemporary poetry. It is ' Gongorism ' run mad. No mere description will be of any use in showing its character : it must be studied, like a wild animal, in its native home if its character is to be fully understood. Suffice it to say that the basis of this poetry is the ' kenning,' or riddling description of the thing—a conundrum the answer to which the hearer is to guess. The king, for example, is ' the despiser of the flame of the street of the hawk.' Here the street of the hawk is the hand, on which the falcon rests ; the flame of the hand is the gold ring or bracelet ; and the despiser of the gold is the king, who must despise it so thoroughly for himself that he bestows it on the poet. Similarly, the sword is the ' sun of the helmet,' flashing round it ; or it is the ' icicle of the baldric,' which glistens in the ' play of the iron '— the battle—while the arrow—the ' bone-gnat '—bites into the flesh, and the ' wave of the sword '—the blood—comes hissing from the wound. In this fashion ten or a dozen lines express merely the fact that the king defeated his enemies in battle, and another dozen tell us that the royal ship sailed over the sea.

A more obscure style is hardly to be imagined, and the last chapter of Ecclesiastes is easy in comparison. Yet who was the man to collect an anthology of these verses, and prepare a dictionary of the phrases to be used by the poets who desired to shine in the courts of the chiefs ? None other than the same Snorri whose prose I have just described. No stranger example could well be found of the eternal conflict between the simplicity of genius and the obscurity of mere cleverness. That the courts, the critical tribunals of the age, preferred this terrible style is proved by the rewards they gave to the bards, and by the words of unstinted praise, which are occasionally recorded. When, in the inevitable reaction, the poet Eysteinn produced his exquisite lyric ' The Lily,' he had to apologise for its lack of obscurity, and to plead for a hearing ' though the rules of Snorri had not been observed.' But the whole thing shows once more the fascination exerted by riddling ingenuity upon mankind. It would seem that there is an irresistible impulse to it in human nature, and that from time to time it will predominate in literature.

All nations, apparently, catch this disease at one stage or another, and we in England have had our attacks of it. With all the abundance and genius of the Elizabethans went a love of conceits and an ill-regulated ingenuity, which is of course most clearly visible in the Euphuism of the beginning of the period, but is to be seen, in various forms, right to the end. Lyly can make his Euphues declare his constancy in terms like these : ' Though the stone cylindrus at every thunderclap roll from the hill, yet the pure sleek-stone remaineth at the top : though the rust fret the hardest steel, yet doth it not eat into the emerald ; though Polypus changeth his hue, yet the salamander keepeth his colour : though Proteus transform himself into every shape, yet Pygmalion retaineth his old form ; though Aeneas were too fickle to Dido, yet Troilus was too faithful to Cressida ; though others seem counterfeit in their deeds, yet, Lucilla, persuade yourself that Euphues will be always current in his dealings.' But the same, or a similar, fashion

prevailed long after Lyly's death.   It is no longer
generally held that even Shakespeare escaped it : and
if, as was once believed, he laughed at it in Armado,
he might have been laughed at for it himself.   At any
rate there were other and perhaps worse forms of
would-be cleverness in which he and his contemporaries indulged without stint.   In Shakespeare's later
plays there is, as has often been noticed, a tendency
to choose the most out of the way expressions of his
ideas : a great contrast alike to the floridity of his
earlier work and to that ' exact correspondence of
thought and phrase ' which marks his middle period.
I might give a hundred examples.   One, from *Winter's
Tale*, will be sufficient.

> Affection, thy intention stabs the centre :
> Thou dost make possible things not so held :
> Communicat'st with dreams—how can this be ?
> With what's unreal then co-active art,
> And fellow'st nothing ; then, 'tis very credent
> Thou must conjoin with something, and thou dost.

Not only is this unnecessarily obscure, it is affectedly
and ingeniously so : it is certain that it is the very
last style likely to be adopted by a real Leontes,
consumed with a real jealousy.   The only thing to
be said in its favour is that, though the meaning is
hard to discover, a meaning there is.   With some of
Shakespeare's contemporaries, however, there is often
a similar perversity without a similar excuse.

Other forms of ingenuity, equally to be deprecated,
are not difficult to find in these same writers.   One
of these I need scarcely mention again.   The pun or
quibble was the Elizabethan will of the wisp, which
led even the greatest astray : and it was this weakness
which specially disgusted the succeeding school of

criticism. Shakespeare, said Dryden, though ' many times he has written better than any poet in any language, is the very Janus of poets,' and often sinks lower than the lowest. Ben Jonson, having the whole range of classical authors before him, and being therefore without the excuse of lack of models, yet ' often falls into meanness of expression. Nay, he was not free from the most grovelling kind of wit, which we call " clenches," of which *Every Man in his Humour* is infinitely full ; and, which is worse, the wittiest persons in the drama speak them.' Now ' clenches ' or puns, if they are, as Dryden thought them, the most degraded form of ingenuity, are nevertheless ingenious ; the search for them, in Elizabethan times as in others, was an attempt to be clever, and we find them profusely scattered in the writers of that age, from Philip Sidney to Milton. There can be no doubt that they were popular : every indication we can find of the feelings of groundlings and gentry alike is that nothing raised a cheer, and stopped the cracking of nuts in the theatre, more certainly than some wretched pun, which the most contemptible pantomime clown to-day would despise even while he uttered it.

Why a jest based on a similarity of word or sound should be worse than any other, is however hard to say. It is certain that the taste for it constantly dies out, but it as constantly recurs. There are scores in Aristophanes, few or none in Menander : plenty, as we have seen, in the Elizabethans, few in the next hundred years. In the first half of the nineteenth century they came again, and were probably regarded as the chief form of wit. They died out again, and revived with Burnand, who carried them to an amazing excess, and with Gilbert, who indulged in them less freely, but in the opinion of the twentieth century too often. How can we tell that we shall not, in 1950, see new Tom Hoods and Theodore Hooks, bringing out whole poems, and whole volumes, made up almost exclusively of puns, and winning unstinted applause on that very account?

But Dryden might, had he chosen, have found many other kinds of ' false wit ' to reprove in writers more nearly allied to his own class. In the early works of Dryden himself are plenty of conceits worthy of Cowley and Quarles at their worst : the famous lines in *Annus Mirabilis :*

> Amidst whole heaps of spices lights a ball,
>   And now their odours armed against them fly ;
> Some preciously by shattered porcelain fall,
>   And some by aromatic splinters die,

might have called forth a severer censure than any ' clench ' in Jonson : and much later poems, especially those done to order, are crowded with petty ingenuities hardly better. The description of Charles II's death, for instance, is a typical example of what happens when a clever man is called upon to do a Laureate's duty and justify his pension and his butt of sack.

> The sons of art all medicines tried,
> And every noble remedy applied,
> With emulation each essayed
> His utmost skill, nay more, they prayed :
> Never was losing game with better conduct played :
> Death never won a stake with greater toil,
> Nor e'er was fate so near a foil.

Had Dryden lived a few years longer, also, he might have found much cleverness both to admire and to blame, in the verse of Pope and his imitators, much of which, indeed, is often rather clever than poetical. But my present point is that it was popular. Epigram, smartness, neat combinations of ideas, were what the reading public looked for and what it received. The demand created the supply, and, as so often, the supply in turn stimulated the demand. What to most of us to-day is wearisome was then satisfying, and images which are now trivial then appeared sublime.

We ourselves, however, have little right to pass censure on all this, or to boast that we are not as our ancestors were. Already we are seeing in criticism the inevitable reaction in favour of the early eighteenth century, and there are judges who give to Pope's terse and pointed ingenuities the name of inspiration. A reaction is visible against romanticism in all its forms, and against the whole school or schools of poetry which used not to ' fear to speak of '98.' How far this reaction may run no one can say, but it is there. Nor less visible is it in our writers than in our critics : nay, it is perhaps even more visible and possibly far more blameworthy. It can hardly be denied that there is in many authors of to-day too little clearness, directness, and simplicity of style. The bubble reputation is sought by startling the reader : and the writer is given to strange ideas and marvellous collocations of words. As in our music the aim of the composer seems often to be the concealment of the melody, and as in our painting the puzzle is to detect the subject, so in our literature. Many of our authors, whether really clever themselves or not, demand cleverness in their readers ; for they appear to write with the set purpose of hiding what they are writing about. The meaning, if meaning there be, lies *perdu* in the recesses of a jungle of philosophical terms, and the reader, if he thinks it

worth while to make a path through the forest, has to
hew it out like an explorer in the Brazils. Our writers
imagine that obscurity of language is the same thing
as profundity of thought, and that everything that has
to be dived for is a pearl. They wish to be admired
less for what they say than for the astonishing manner
in which they say it. True wit, it would seem, is
nature dressed to disadvantage ; what oft was thought,
but ne'er expressed so darkly. It is indeed amazing
with what skill they contrive to clothe their ideas in
language that sounds as wonderful as a Delphic oracle :
but too frequently it turns out that the whole thing is
as empty as the proverbially vacuous King's Speech at
the opening of Parliament, or a party programme in
a general election.

Almost worse than this is the endless epigram and
paradox, unparalleled perhaps since Seneca, in which
certain popular writers indulge ; and their popularity
is a sign that ' my people love to have it so.' If the
universal consensus of those who have studied the great
books of the past is worth anything, the prevalence of
this style, and the admiration of it, prove a degradation
of taste. It is true that some of these writers show great
compensating merits ; and the very cleverness of the
paradoxes proves, as in the case of Donne and Cowley,
liveliness and vigour of mind. But too probably it is
not the merits that have gained the audience. For
one person you hear praising their real talents, you
hear ten praising the ' stultus labor ineptiarum.'
' I know nothing,' says one of these authors with a
certain captivating audacity, ' so contemptible as a
mere paradox, a mere defence of the indefensible ' :
and he follows up the statement with a series of paradoxes and defences of the indefensible which might

win cheers from the Oxford Union, but which earn
nothing but languid amusement from those who have
learnt to admire Herodotus and Plato. 'Men of the
world do not understand the world'; 'imagination
does not fill lunatic asylums, but reason does';
'poets do not go mad, but chess-players do'—an
assertion either ignorant or deliberately provocative—
'if thy head offend thee, cut it off': these are a small
selection from the gems scattered over the following
three or four pages; and fully twelve score could be
chosen from the remaining two hundred.

Authors of this kind are among the most popular of
the present day; and their vogue, like that of detective
novelists, seems to show that this species of cleverness
strikes an answering chord in the minds of the public.
And yet, as usual, it is impossible to draw an indictment against a whole nation. Some of these very
writers, with the advance of years, have become notably
less epigrammatic. Like Ruskin, they have begun with
brilliance and end with plainness. Many readers, also,
unquestionably prefer this later style in their favourites
to the earlier. And that very return to the eighteenth
century of which I spoke above, and which is clearly
seen in so many of the critics of to-day, perhaps indicates in certain cases a recurrence to simplicity.
While in part, undoubtedly, due to an ignorant and
foolish prejudice against the nineteenth century, it is
probably due also to a real desire to recover the straightforward clearness which is so conspicuous in Hume,
Berkeley, Middleton, Goldsmith, and in fact in almost
all the eighteenth-century prose writers. We may well
see, in the coming years, a rebirth of that vanished
plainness. Older authors will prepare the way for it,
and the younger, though the courses of their youth

promise it not, will perhaps follow. If they do, we shall be blessed in the change.

But here again I find it desirable to qualify. Though my personal preference is all for simplicity, and though I feel a mild resentment whenever I have to take more trouble in reading a book than I finally discover it to deserve, I realise that there is something to be said on the other side. I dislike cleverness for its own sake, and I do not care for adornments that are rather disguises than aids to beauty. But reason will reassert itself, and I perceive that there are different ways in which men may express their ideas. I would therefore not wish to be understood as casting an absolute and dogmatic censure even on the over-ingenious style so prevalent now. Though I look forward somewhat eagerly to the coming swing of the pendulum, I know that no style is perfect and that no vogue is lasting. Nor do I believe that there is any infallible and unvarying standard of taste The one safe rule is that which Yahweh laid down for Laban, ' Take thou heed that thou speak not to Jacob either good or bad.' As I claim for myself the right to have a preference, so I give the same right to others. And yet—to express freely my own preference, as others may express theirs—to me the baldest and crudest representation of thought, the barest and clumsiest arrangement of words, provided it enables me to grasp the meaning at once, seems vastly better than the most brilliant of epigrams or the most striking of paradoxes which even momentarily confuse the mind or which show a straining after effect. Bareness, at the worst, allows the facts to speak for themselves ; but a style that constantly puts the facts in an inverted fashion is like a glass through which we can only see

darkly. I prefer to see the meaning ' face to face.'
Nor is bareness by any means always at its worst. In
youth, perhaps, we think Cæsar's *Commentaries* too
austere, uninteresting because of their haughty lack
of ornament, and without force because their strength
is so rigorously concealed. Turning to them in later
years, we find that very lack of ornament a beauty,
and realise the strength in the deliberate restraint.
I do not know that we do not come in time to prefer
Cæsar's utter plainness to the most elaborate and
finished perorations of Cicero. It has a lasting, un-
wearying power, and holds us with the cords of a man.
There is, on the other hand, something that, in the
long run, cloys and tires in perpetual stimulants. Even
those who at first welcome them tend to become, like
Mithridates, fatally inured to them. They ought
rather, like Hannibal, to have kept them for the decisive need ; for too often it is found that they have lost
their efficacy at the very moment when that efficacy
is most desired. A writer of the kind I have described
is like a soldier who forgets to reserve his fire for the
culminating moment : the final defeat is in these
cases certain and deserved.

The fact is that the literary man should be content
with his advantages and should realise his limitations.
So far as he is literary he can, as I said above, never
hope to vie in ingenuity with men of a different cast
of mind. Be he as ingenious as he likes, he will never
attain to the ingenuity of the mathematician. The
most cunning plots ever woven for a detective novel,
the craftiest involutions of style, are child's play compared with the problems solved in the Theory of
Numbers, and inferior to the intricacies unravelled
in a quite ordinary game of chess. This may be a hard

saying, but it is a true one ; and it would be well if the literary man would recognise its truth. He has many compensations : his reputation, for instance, is far wider than that of these others : but in sheer mental power he is quite ' out of the running ' with an Euler or a Gauss, and cannot keep pace long with the mere maker of arithmetical puzzles. Little as Swift knew it, the Laputan professors were cleverer even than the inventor of Laputa. In ' tricks to show the stretch of human brain ' the literary man will always come off a bad second ; and he will do well to leave dealings in ' curious pleasure and ingenious pain ' to the men who are created by nature for them. His object is not to strain the intellects of his hearers, but to give them enjoyment by revealing beauty—whatever beauty may be. Those who desire problems, enigmas, or conundrums will go elsewhere, and will scorn the trivial puzzles presented to them by a poet or novelist who strays beyond his proper field.

But if I have myself this preference for the plain food, and if, in accordance with the universal tendency of mankind, I prefer also to think my own taste the purer, I can give no binding *reason* for my preference —I can say nothing to *prove* my case. Impartial reflection compels me to admit that my taste is not the only one, and that others, by the same human law, will think theirs the best. To the beldam who ' knaps ginger,' ginger, though ' hot in the mouth,' will necessarily be more palatable than cakes and ale ; while the schoolboy will always reject the meal provided by the authorities in favour of the dainties provided by the ' tuck-shop.' To try to impose your own preference is waste of labour, and a stupid waste. There are seven ages in the life of the race as in the life of the individual :

what attracts the lover will repel the justice, and what the justice wants will be scouted by the soldier. We may fondly call in Time to justify us ; but the call is empty. Time brings in his revenges, but he moves in cycles. ' Jam redit et Virgo, redeunt Saturnia regna ' : and Time, like Saturn, has a habit of devouring his own children. But, like Saturn, he devours them to restore them to life, and having restored them, destroys them once again. He putteth down the mighty from their seats, and exalteth the humble and meek ; but ere we can say behold, the mighty are in their seats again, to fall once more into momentary humiliation.

X

THE TASTE FOR ALLEGORY

I IMAGINE that when men discovered the possibility of saying one thing and meaning another they felt a certain exhilaration, not unlike that which schoolboys feel when they get hold of a form of words which may preserve the literal truth yet deceive the master. At what time this discovery was first made—it must of course have been made at different times in different countries—we cannot tell : but we are not without analogies which enable us to conjecture the sort of Eureka which the discoverer would utter when the first equivoque swam into his ken. We have already seen how keenly the Elizabethans and the Hebrews enjoyed a pun—which is one sort of equivoque ; and we all enjoy skilfully disguised flattery, which is often another. The prophets who told Ahab that Ramoth-Gilead would be delivered into the hands of the king—they did not say *which* king—must have plumed themselves on their dexterity ; and it is not hard to picture to ourselves the grim smile on the faces of the priests of Delphi when they hit on a sentence which would satisfy Crœsus and yet be compatible with either result of the campaign. If we may believe Herodotus, Crœsus himself learnt the lesson : for, years after his defeat, he paid his Persian conqueror an ingenious compliment which at first sight appeared a censure, but, examined more closely, turned out to be subtle flattery. We are told that Cambyses and his courtiers admired the ambiguity greatly : this was plainly because they recognised a new capacity in language.

Such equivoques may in certain cases have been the skilful invention of some member of an oppressed nation who hit on this method of venting his feelings or conveying messages without betraying himself to his masters. As Disraeli at once soothed his own vanity and flattered the literary bore who plagued him with the gift of his novel, by saying ' I will lose no time in reading it,' so a helot who understood the tricks of language might relieve his mind at the expense of his tyrant without running the risk of the whip. The equivoque would in such a case be allied to the crypto-gram or the code-signal. Understood by those in the secret, it might bear a perfectly innocent meaning, or no meaning at all, to those whom it was intended to deceive. Such cryptograms certainly existed among the Jews. When Jeremiah used the word ' Sheshach ' for ' Babel ' or Babylon, simple as his system was,[1] he must have meant his compatriots to understand and the Babylonians to be bewildered : though one can hardly believe the Chaldæan soothsayers to have been so stupid as not to be able to solve so easy a riddle. When, centuries later, the author of the Apocalypse devised his famous piece of ' wisdom,' the arithmo-gram six hundred and sixty-six, he must have had a similar design : the Christians were to know and their Roman masters not to know. A score of similar in-stances will at once occur to the reader.

It may have been, in certain cases, from some such origin that the more literary allegory sprang. We

---

[1] It is the ' Athbash ' system ; the last letter of the alphabet for the first, the last but one for the second, and so on.

know, for example, that it was a very necessary caution
which compelled Rabelais to clothe his terrific attack
upon the Church in a garb of sheer nonsense : only
by some disguise of the kind could he, with any safety,
give vent to the dangerous wisdom with which his mind
was teeming. Similarly, also, De Foe, in his *Short
Way with the Dissenters*, posed as the most violent of
High Churchmen—unfortunately, however, with less
success than Rabelais. We have no reason to believe
that similar devices were not adopted in much earlier
ages. A coterie of more or less philosophical people
framing an esoteric language for the inner circle,
would welcome such a method of at once revealing
and concealing the doctrines of their sect. All know
that the Pythagoreans spoke in such a dialect : and a
still more famous example is familiar to every reader of
the Gospels. It is certain that Pythagoras was not
the first to clothe his message in symbols, as the Illu-
minati and other societies of our own time will assuredly not be the last. We find the Hebrew prophets
and psalmists describing the Jewish state by all sorts
of images, as a vine that once flourished but has now
decayed, as a human being passing unscathed through
a fiery furnace, as a house, as a city : while the oppres-
sing kingdoms are goats, rams, graven images. Living
rulers were veiled under the names of the dead :
Antiochus appears as Nebuchadnezzar, Domitian as
Nero ; the reason being obviously the same as that
which made Juvenal seek his victims among those
whose urns lined the Flaminian Way. Nor would
such a style of speech disappear when the occasion
that gave it birth had died. Poets, having felt the
enormous enlargement of power which this symbolism
lent them, would seize upon it, hold to it, and carry

it to lengths of which its inventors never dreamed. Such an allegory, for instance, as that of Phœnix in the *Iliad*, about the lame and wrinkled Prayers which follow Ate, or that other, of the two jars in which Zeus keeps the fortunes of men, look very much like products of early and crude philosophising : allegories invented by thinkers and borrowed or adapted by poets, who have been plagiarists ever since there was a predecessor to steal from. And it is noteworthy that both of these allegories are found in parts of the *Iliad* which, on independent grounds, are commonly believed to be later accretions : they certainly read strangely if compared with other portions of the poem. And if later, they will mark a change in *taste*, as if both authors and readers were demanding something different from what had satisfied previous generations. To use an exaggerated term, men were becoming a little sophisticated : their critical palate was asking for something ' acrid.' It is just this which, from the point of view of our inquiry, claims our interest : it is plain that passages like this were inserted for the benefit of those who had realised the attractiveness of the *under-meaning*, who had come to appreciate a certain measure of *ingenuity* in the poet, and to delight in their own exercise of ingenuity in inter-pretation. They desired at least an occasional relief from the plain and straightforward narrative style, even though the relief had to be purchased with a certain amount of mental strain. The strain, of course, was not intense : but we can not improbably detect here the beginnings of a form of poetry which, as we shall see later, was to culminate in the obscurities of Lycophron, and which was to perish of its own excess. At what stage such divergencies from absolute

o

simplicity add to the legitimate pleasure which it is the task of the poet to give, and at what stage it begins to swamp poetry under a load of extraneous philosophy, it is the hard lot of the critic to decide : nor will the critic succeed without a study of the psychology both of the poet and of the readers.

We must, it need not be added, distinguish carefully between such allegories, which are at best ornamental additions to poetry, and the simile or metaphor, both of which are of the very essence of poetry, and in fact the warp and woof of language itself.   So soon as speech advanced beyond mere mimicry of natural sounds, it became inevitably metaphoric.   The human race, at the stage in which it could not discriminate between the animate and the inanimate—in which winds, trees, animals, stars, and stones were alike human—could not even begin to speak without using, in a literal sense, a vocabulary which later would be interpreted metaphorically.   Men's world was a world of myth, and they spoke mythology without knowing what they were speaking.   When they said ' Fire devoured,' they conceived of fire as a monstrous animal actually eating, as Logi in his match with Thor ate up both meat and platter : and their early customs, like the laws of our Anglo-Saxon ancestors, punished fire as men punish a thief.   Storm was an imprisoned warrior escaping his bonds and thirsty for vengeance : hunger a wild beast gnawing the vitals of its prey. Language, thus formed, fell to be employed by poets who, half knowing what they did, and half in ignorance, retained its personifications, and turned myth, once the most fearful of realisms, into the romance of poetry. A famous and characteristic passage of Carlyle shows how this necessary feature still marks all our speech.

' Metaphors,' says he, and in so saying himself uses a
metaphor, ' are the muscles and tissues and living
integuments of the Flesh-Garment, Language. An
unmetaphorical style you shall in vain seek for : is
not your very *Attention* a *Stretching-to?* ' And, to
make but one out of a score of possible choices, Mr.
Prescott's recent excellent work on ' Poetry and Myth '
draws out in detail this inevitable dependence of the
poet on the animism which we may fancy we have discarded, but which is rooted in our nature, and from
which no amount of scientific investigation will ever
entirely sunder us. Even the most ' conceited ' of
poets, seeking to deliver us from the tyranny of ancient
metaphors, falls back, in the very moment of concocting
new ones, into the old. Cleiveland, when reducing
the sun to a mere coal-pit, cannot help calling him a
charioteer.

As the poet, and his hearer—who, to be an attentive
hearer, must himself be something of a poet—develop
knowledge and self-consciousness, the metaphor tends
to yield place to the simile. Fire is now *like* a devourer,
the lion *like* a warrior, the wind *like* a runner, the ship
walks the waters *like* a thing of life. The reciter is
no longer deceived into imagining that similarity is
identity. And this is true even when he does not
actually use the words denoting likeness : while he
retains the form of metaphor he thinks in simile.
There are, indeed, languages, such as Hebrew and
Arabic, in which the *phraseology* is habitually that of
identity, though there is no reason to think that the
hearers or speakers are deceived. I find, for example,
in Driver's *Hebrew Tenses* a long list of appositions
which to us sound strange, and which are in fact usually
disguised in our versions. ' The whole earth was one

speech,' 'we are yesterday,' 'all thy garments are myrrh,' 'I am prayer,' 'cities are separations,' 'all the people shall be peace,' 'O tongue, deceitfulness,' 'the vale of Siddim was slime-pits': these are but a few random specimens illustrating this peculiarity—the retention, *in phrase*, of an identity which is really a mere general likeness or loose relation. But such a retention is sufficient to show that to our earliest ancestors a likeness *was* an identity : precisely as, to children, the sight of a man is enough to call forth a somewhat embarrassing recognition of a father. Simile, then, is later than metaphor, and is due to a power of discrimination which did not at first exist. As this power developed, the poets made liberal, or even rapacious, calls upon it : for mental wealth, like material, is the ready prey of the tax-gatherer.

Allegory, however, demands a much keener and better-educated sense, not only of likeness but of difference, than either metaphor or simile. There must be a clear perception of the region common to the compared thing with its parallel, and a distinct idea of the points at which the two part company. They are to resemble each other not in one particular only but in a series of particulars ; while at the same time we are called upon to realise that they are not one but two. To maintain the parallelism requires not so much genius as ingenuity, and to see the boundaries not so much insight as a certain logicality. The combination of powers is a matter of practice and training such as is not always found in the greatest of uneducated minds. The similes of Homer, unsurpassed as he was in poetical genius, are keen enough in the likeness, but forget the differences : they constantly run far beyond the limits of appropriateness. This is because he saw *clearly* but not *distinctly:* his poetry outstripped his logic. Precision, when found in early poets or fabulists, does not last long. The simile may, and often does, in early stage, stretch out into a fable like that of Jotham, but it does not often take the elaborate form of allegory proper : and when it does, it speedily loses itself in irrelevancies. Popular thought, which invents proverbs, can also invent brief apologues such as those ascribed to Æsop and Pilpay ; but it cannot go much further. As the maxims of La Rochefoucauld could not have arisen in a simple society, so the allegories of Prodicus or Plato are the deliberate work of a highly cultivated mind.

I shall not here dwell at any length on a much later and more difficult development of allegoric literature—that known as the Symbolic. To define a symbol is notoriously next to impossible. It certainly rests on a supposed resemblance between one thing and another, but the resemblance is often slight and remote : and, when a symbolism has once been established, the resemblance may become slighter still. A poet who uses symbolism may be led by association of ideas very far from his original conception, and indeed so arbitrary is often his choice of emblems that interpretation becomes all but impracticable. The Cross, for instance, is a symbol of Christianity ; but to a man who does not know the history of the Church it is as meaningless as the symbol π to a non-mathematician. Salt is, in many countries, the symbol of friendship : it is easy to conceive circumstances in which it might stand for hatred. There is not a single vocable in the language of flowers which might not very easily be transferred from one flower to another. Hence in early poetry, which was recited and therefore had to be intelligible, symbolic language is not to be found. It was left for the trained and somewhat distorted mind of Porphyry to discover hidden meanings in the *Odyssey*, to interpret the Cave of the Nymphs into fantastic cloud-visions, and the sleep of Odysseus into a philosophic rapture.

But this very arbitrariness in symbolism, this very fact that a symbol might mean anything whatever, made it peculiarly useful for the purposes of concealment or for esoteric teaching. An ordinary allegory, having many clues, is an enigma that admits of easy solution : a set of detached symbols is a different matter, and is therefore specially adapted for a secret association, which desires to keep its members in touch with one another, and yet to avoid the too close attentions of a suspicious Government. Sometimes this kind of writing has survived the dangers of its earlier years, and has emerged as literature : nay, for one reason or another, it has often established itself as a literary form, and has gained the flattery of imitation. Of such forms of symbolic writing far from the least important is the Apocalyptic, to which so much attention has been directed in recent times. Its history is remarkable. It sprang from prophecy, of which in actual fact it was a modification due to special circumstances : but few children have been less like their parents. Prophecy sometimes employed symbolic *action :* a Zedekiah might make himself horns of iron to betoken the strength with which Ahab would push the Syrians till he had consumed them ; an Isaiah would go naked and barefoot in sign of the coming captivity of Egypt or Ethiopia ; a prophet would strike another, or urge another to strike him, to symbolise battle or disaster ; but the actions were reinforced by words

as plain as the most daring prophet thought it prudent
to use. With apocalyptic, on the other hand, the
vision and the symbol were everything, and the lesson
had to be unravelled from a tangle of processions,
triumphs, spectacular images, sieges, defeats. Very
different are the visions of Ezekiel from the predictions
of his contemporary Jeremiah : and Daniel confesses
that he needed an angel to explain to him what he had
seen. But, as I have said, that the visions might admit
of several explanations was often all to the good :
it was just as well that while the initiates should comprehend the profane should be at a loss. Amid the
persecutions of Antiochus Epiphanes the righteous
needed consolations unintelligible to the persecutors.
The end aimed at was not unlike that sought in the
' Mysteries ' to which almost all religious have been
prone ; gibberish to the world, full of meaning to
the church : but to the Jews at a certain period they
were even more necessary, for the spy was everywhere
and the need of union among the scattered faithful
was crying. Nor less necessary, for the same reason,
were they to the early Christians, whose very secrecy
and love of retirement aroused the darkest suspicions.
Such Apocalypses, therefore, it is well known, were the
main form of Jewish literature for the two hundred
years before Christ and the hundred after : and the
Christians borrowed, imitated, and adapted them for
their own use. They arose out of very special conditions, and perhaps no other form could have met the
necessities of the case. Their influence was tremendous,
and has not even yet been exhausted.

What is still more notable, however, than this
influence of both allegory and symbolic upon subsequent literature is their *retrospective* influence. Once

established as *a* form of literature, they bade fair for a time to annex almost all other forms. Since they, by their nature, bore at least two meanings, it was assumed that all others, even the simplest and plainest, must admit of two or more interpretations. The clearest parts of the Old Testament, the baldest genealogies, the directest narratives, the most personal lyrics, were read as if their authors had written under the allegoric spell. The greatest minds—Philo, Clement, Origen— wasted their energies in unearthing the inner significance of the simple story of Hagar, the flight of Jacob into Egypt, the three hundred and eighteen servants whom Abraham armed against Chedorlaomer, the spoils given to Melchizedek. St. Paul himself, who was learned in the lore of Gamaliel, drew from the history of Genesis a great deal of profundity that would have astonished the author of the book. As for the weaker men, like the so-called ' Barnabas ' and the author of the ' Shepherd ' of Hermas, their vagaries are almost beyond belief. One example out of a thousand will be sufficient. The ceremony of the Scapegoat, says Barnabas, is a type of Christ : and the scarlet wool wound about the goat's head signifies that Christ was to die for us. ' For as he who would take away the scarlet wool must undergo many difficulties, because the thorn was very sharp, and but hardly attain his end, so they, says Christ, that will see me and come to my kingdom must through many afflictions and troubles reach unto me.' After this, that the broken pottery which Jeremiah saw renewed by the potter should stand for Christ's death and resurrection, will surprise nobody.[1]

[1] This allegorising tendency had another use : it enabled the Church, without losing hold of its past, to advance intellectually, and in a measure to keep pace with science. When Celsus told the Christians

I dwell on this because in my opinion it was the steeping of the Church in allegory that was the real source of the allegorising literature of which the Middle Ages are full. Anyone who has read, for instance, but half a dozen sermons of St. Gregory knows that the medieval theological mind must have thought allegory, dreamt allegory, and pictured allegory : and it is well known that one chief task of the Renaissance scholars was to break the tyranny of this ruinous system of Biblical interpretation, and to substitute for it plain literality.

The great Jew Maimonides, by using allegorical exegesis to explain away certain rigidities in the Torah, had in a fashion turned allegory against itself, with the purpose of liberalising Judaism : and something of the same kind was attempted by Moses Mendelssohn many centuries later. But the scholars of the Renaissance rejected allegory altogether—not without shocking the orthodox. When Erasmus said that his aim was to discover the *literal* meaning of the Old and New Testaments, it appeared to the pious as if he was overthrowing Christianity itself. That the fishers of Galilee actually drew a hundred and fifty-three fishes out of the lake—this the conservatives might accept : but that the statement had nothing to do with the Trinity—when the Modernists said this, it sounded like a blasphemy. They might—as indeed some did—go further, and deny that St. Peter's ' two swords ' had anything to do with the Empire and the Papacy : and where would the Church be then ?

Now from about A.D. 400 to 1500, the Church was the great literary educator. The laity, when it learnt

that the story of Adam and Eve was absurd, Origen answered that it was no history but an allegory : and the same method was very recently adopted in order to reconcile the Pentateuch with geology.

anything, learnt it, like King Alfred, from ' Asser my bishop, and from Grimbold and John my mass-priests.' Even its arithmetic was priest-taught and priest-controlled. But the Church spoke allegory, taught parable, founded its dogmas on symbolically interpreted texts, which—to parody the words of St. Peter—it ' wrested ' to its own defence. In our own country, Aelfric, following Gregory the Great, explained the Bible stories of the Flood and of Abraham's migration into apologues of moral or religious truth. Natural history, if such it can be called, was taught in Bestiaries, in which every animal was allowed a more or less accurate portrait, a description, and an allegorisation of the description. The Phœnix was Christ, Leviathan or Fastitocalon the Devil, who tempts sailors to land on him, and then, submerging, plunges them into hell. And similarly, *mutatis mutandis*, with the elephant, the unicorn, and the partridge. Even secular history was manipulated in no dissimilar manner. Orosius, whose work Alfred translated into English, is constantly calling in the Biblical story to make a balance to the profane : and such parallelism is itself a kind of allegory. What more natural, then, than that the poet, the most worldly as well as the most religious, should appeal to his audience as the preacher appealed to his congregation ? Without allegory, he would hardly be able to pose as a poet at all ; and to call things by their plain names was to write oneself down as a bungler in one's art. Hence the enormous number of allegorical poems —the *Pèlerinage de la Vie Humaine*, the *Romance of the Rose*, the *Pearl*, and—greatest of all—the *Divine Comedy*, which is but the supreme medieval imitation of the Apocalypse of John, declaring to its readers those things which must shortly come to pass. Every device of mystical symbolism is employed in the *Comedy* —and deliberately. Not only, as the poet himself confesses, have 'both heaven and earth set their hand' to it, but the worlds of philosophy and fancy have lent their aid, and the light that never was on sea or land. The well-known passage in the *Convivio* will here bear re-quotation. 'The written words, it must be understood, may have a fourfold meaning, and must be so explained. The first sense is the literal, which goes no further than the letter. The next is the allegorical, which points to a truth concealed under a pleasant fiction. The third is the moral sense, which the readers must pursue with eagerness. The fourth is the anagogical or super-sensuous, which appears when a passage which even literally refers to heavenly things is lifted yet higher into spiritual meanings.' These four methods of interpreting Scripture, already for centuries applied to Holy Writ, Dante means to be applied to his own writing, which in this sense, as in others, is a ' poema *sacro* : and hence we often find in his work several layers of possible exegesis, some of them simple and natural, others crabbed and even perverse. It is significant that occasionally, when the narrative is itself somewhat grotesque or laboured, he pauses, to beg the reader to look below the surface :

> O voi, ch' avete gl' intelletti sani,
> Mirate la dottrina che s' asconde
> Sotto il velame degli versi strani.

It is as if he had said, ' The *literal* meaning is clumsy enough, and I cannot deny it ; but use your brains in accordance with the accepted principles of theological

commentary, and you will find that there is *something*
in it after all.' Unfortunately, too often so many
meanings were open to the commentator that it became
all but impossible to be sure which was the right one.
Of the very passage from which I have just quoted the
preface, some dozens of different interpretations have
been given by the ' sound intellects,' to whom Dante
appealed, and the doctrine still remains hidden under
the strange words. Even he was not always free from
the tendency to confuse obscurity with profundity,
and to fancy that you turn a commonplace into a reproductive truth by wrapping it in mystical folds. He
certainly felt some pride in the ingenuity of his conceits. In a famous passage he says, with a mixture of
irony and vanity,

> My song, I fear that thou wilt find but few
> Who fitly shall conceive thy reasoning,
> Of such hard matter dost thou entertain :

and we know that some people found the lyrics of the
Vita Nuova beyond their comprehension. It is a curious
fact that the prose explanations which the poet afterwards appended to these *canzoni* have been held, in
certain cases, to be mistaken : the author himself had
forgotten what they originally meant. Nothing could
show more clearly the dangers of symbolism. But it
shows also, what is more to my immediate purpose,
the compelling influence of the visions of Ezekiel
and of St. John the Divine on the author of the
Comedy. Equally clear is the influence of the medieval
allegorisation of Virgil's epic on the whole texture of
the poem : and the ' living creatures,' pageants,
double and treble emblems, and in fact the very essence
of the work, are but the prophecies, apocalypses, and

old classical writings, read in the 'darkness visible' of an allegorising method which pervades the whole millennium from Constantine to the Emperor Henry VII.

The child of a too-ingenious theology—I do not censure the whole in passing this judgment on this one aspect of the medieval order—the work of Dante became in turn the parent of a long line of descendants. But even the Florentine had less influence, for the time being, than the Frenchman Jean de Meung, whose enormous poem was in part translated by Chaucer, and whose disciples are to be found all over Western Europe. There may, indeed, appear to be very little religious meaning in this worldly, cynical, and even poisonous work, which seems to have been designed to attack everything the Church held sacred.

> Se bien veulx et chastement vivre,
> De la Rose ne lis le livre,

cried Christine de Pisan : and many a Father confessor must have echoed her cry. But if, like Caliban, Jean had learned to curse, he had been taught his language by the Church : and his quest of the Rose, unholy as it is, is carried out as *theologically* as Dante's quest of the Love that moves sun and stars. It is not hard to trace in the *Romance* all the four methods of interpretation which Dante derived from Gregory or Aquinas, and expected us to apply to his sublime but enigmatic poem.

Now both the *Comedy* and the *Romance* were at once the effect of a *taste* already established, and the cause of the spread and continuance of that taste. Poets desirous of an audience had to satisfy the appetites of their hearers, and their hearers, for some time, would accept nothing else. What the public wanted, the poets offered, sometimes probably with a sub-conscious reluctance. Chaucer himself, the most concrete and matter-of-fact of all great poets, long followed the fashion, and gave the world allegory after allegory, dream after dream—the *Death of Blanche*, the *House of Fame*, the *Complaint of Mars*, the *Prologue to the Legend ;* until at length he found himself, and renounced the style for ever. None the less, immense as was the fame of Chaucer, those who most admired him still pursued the allegorical track. King James's *Quhair* is an allegory, Dunbar's *Thrissill and Rose* is another : the crowds of anonymous imitations are yet others : Sackville's *Induction* is a magnificent specimen ; and so on till we reach the crowning achievement of the *Faerie Queene*, with, in turn, Spenser's multitudinous progeny of *Purple Islands* and *Britain's Idas*.

Let me take as one example the *Pearl*, which is my favourite among all English medieval poems. We can draw from it no argument as to the popularity of allegory among readers—for we have no evidence that more than a single copy was ever made of it. But it is, I think, a typical instance of the compelling force exerted by the allegorising tendency of the time upon the poets themselves. It has been held that the whole poem is an allegory—that the Pearl itself is a mere emblem, and the child a personified quality. I do not for a moment hold this view : though if it is correct, it strengthens my argument. What I believe is that the poem is an expression of real sorrow for a real loss, that Margaret was his own daughter, and that he felt her death as a father does feel such a fearful sorrow ; that he sought consolation, being a poet, as Milton and

Tennyson sought theirs, in the way natural to poets. But the way natural to poets then was to allegorise : and the *Pearl*, though not an allegory as a whole, allegorises in detail everywhere. All remember how he begins. He does not say ' My child died ' ; but— ' Pearl pleasant in princes' pay, closed in clear gold : no Orient gem was ever her peer : wheresoever I judged gay jewels, I set her alone and unrivalled : Alas, I lost her in an arbour ; she fled from me through grass to ground ; I pine, wasting in longing for that precious pearl without a spot.' And, though we find her as a maiden in heaven, a child whose body, sown an earthly one, has been raised as spiritual, filled like Beatrice with heavenly and theological learning, yet the symbol of the Pearl is kept constantly in mind, and recurs at intervals throughout the hundred stanzas. Recollections of Dante, of the *Romance*, and above all of the Apocalypse of John, show clearly whence the poet's inspiration was drawn : and this is the more to be noted because his *real* sorrow, and his *real* consolation, cannot be concealed ; and because, as I believe, and as is held by most scholars, he was not *primarily* a symbolic poet, and even avoids symbols that come directly in his way. Had he lived at another time there would have been no more allegory than there is in *In Memoriam*. But he was a medieval writer, and allegory was the medieval vehicle for poetry.

Whoever he was, he does not seem to have been well known. But there are others who were ; and they teach the same lesson No better example, either of the *genre* itself, or of its popularity among the common people, can well be found than the *Vision of William concerning Piers the Plowman :* and if, as Professor Manly thinks, the poem is the work of several authors,

my point is but made the stronger. That poem, with
all its formlessness and want of distinct plan, is a moral
lesson conveyed by a dream, within which is an allegory
not too hard to unravel; and within the allegory
itself are enlarged personifications like those of the
Seven Deadly Sins, fables like that of Belling the Cat,
and political views conveyed by symbol. It is in fact
a nest of Chinese boxes, one within the other, with
just enough difficulty to titillate the hearers, and
just enough explanation to save too great a demand
on the ' intelletti sani ' to which it appealed. There
can be no doubt that the poem was vastly more effective for its purpose than if it had been a direct statement of its case. It was a long sermon in popular
' rum, ram, ruf ' verse, and the hearers, accustomed
to hear from their pastors the stories of the Scriptures
explained in allegorical manner, had their palates
ready to relish it. The gently enigmatic presentation
provided the hearers with the satisfaction schoolboys
feel when set a sum they can do : and the poet himself,
doubtless, took a modest pride in the skill with which
he drew his parallels and expressed his ' heavenly
meaning ' in an ' earthly tale.'

Allied to this, and indeed exhibited in *Piers the
Plowman* itself, was the beast-story, of which the
Bestiary and the Æsopian fable were the forerunners,
but which gained a strong impetus from the general
vogue of allegory. The imitators of Langland knew
the power of it : and such poems as Chaucer's *Parliament of Fowls*, Clanvowe's *Cuckoo and the Nightingale*,
Nicholas Guildford's or another's *Owl and the Nightingale*, and all the rest, down even to Dryden's *Hind and
Panther*, or even Anatole France's *Ile des Pingouins*,
thin as is the veil which divides the inner meaning

from the literal, are all alike due to one impulse—the belief that an idea is at once more profound in itself, and more likely to seize attention, if it is expressed in a roundabout manner. It is, in fact, the same impulse as led Joash to rebuke Amaziah in a contemptuous parable rather than to tell him plainly what he thought of him—though it is true he did the latter as well : and a feeling so old, and so unconscionably long in dying, must be rooted in some essential quality of human nature. I have already, perhaps, given illustrations in over-abundance, but I cannot resist the temptation to add yet another. Few compositions are livelier, even to read, than the Mystery Plays—the Towneley, the Chester, and others. They are full of humour, vigour, and invention, and they must have been still more attractive when acted than they are in the study. How then can we account for the success of the Moralities—which, with few exceptions, are dull and wooden allegorisations—with audiences accustomed to the Mysteries, unless there is in truth something in human nature that demands such things and welcomes them when presented ? Herod, Noah, Noah's wife, are real men and women, such as could be seen every day. Repentance, the Flesh, Riches, never existed and never will exist : yet plays with these ' characters ' were popular for centuries, and even survived the Reformation. That some of them are ' good,' and bear revival to-day, only reinforces my argument : it shows that there is in such themes, empty as they may appear, enough ' matter ' to kindle an author to inspiration, and to rouse the enthusiasm of an audience. It can be no mere fashion which led not only men of no capacity, but writers like the poet of *Everyman*,[1] to

[1] I have seen a German version, with ' 75th edition ' on the title-page.

P

adopt this method of appealing to the world. Nor less powerful must have been the motive which stirred men like Dante and Bunyan, who in addition to their genius had wide experience of men, to employ allegory as their medium, not once nor twice, but often. If it be a fashion, it is not one of those that speedily pass away.

But—and here I return to my point—there can, as I have hinted, be little doubt that all these allegorists, and the scores of others I have not named, regarded the allegorising as *in itself* a poetical beauty, nay, as of the very stuff of poetry. As in our own day there are many who, resembling Dante in nothing else, resemble him in thinking darkness to be depth, so, in the times of which I am speaking, allegory not merely added a charm to poetry, but was the philosopher's stone which turned brass to gold. To find some analogue, the remoter the better, for a quite ordinary event—a royal marriage, the death of a princess, a victory—was with these bards to turn it from prose to poetry. It mattered not that in other respects their epithalamium was no better than a newspaper report—it was allegory, and that was enough. Verses that had no merit other than a mild kind of cleverness in working out a parallel between a queen and a flower, an obstacle and a castle, idleness and a porter, were written, copied, read ; and have endured to this day, ' ut pueris placeant et dissertatio fiant.' As one for many, let Hawes's *Pastime of Pleasure* stand : it has neither metre, nor unity, nor beauty : its very meaning is trifling, but as it is two-fold, the author fancied he had produced a poem. So, both before and after, men have hitched prose into rhyme, and imagined they are Homers.

Thus, as is usual with literary modes, allegory

survived as a fashion after the life had gone out of it :
and it has exerted a strange attraction on poets, even
on some of the greatest, at all times. Shakespeare himself yielded to the influence when he wrote that curious
epitaph on 'married chastity' entitled, in true
medieval style, *The Phœnix and the Turtle :* and all
know how Tennyson half ruined the *Idylls of the King*
by wavering hopelessly between the Malorian treatment of the story and a symbolic 'shadowing of sense
at war with soul.' It was a feeling of the same kind,
though cruder and more stupid, which was at the
bottom of Mrs. Barbauld's criticism of the *Ancient
Mariner*, that it lacked a moral—a criticism which
drew from Coleridge an elaborate defensive mono-
logue, and from Lamb a brief and emphatic
monosyllable.

This is not to say that, in due subordination, a touch
of what may be called allegory is not almost *an* essential
element in poetry. If nothing more is meant than
meets the ear, if the mere literal significance is all,
the poem may attain prettiness but rarely the higher
beauty. Even the *Ancient Mariner* itself, if it had not
a *suggestion* of unhappy far-off things and of conflicts
long ago, would lose its charm. The concrete and direct
Paradise Lost, superficially a history in verse, is really
from beginning to end almost as much an allegory as
its episode of Sin and Death : Satan is rebellion, Adam
is mankind, the story is a doctrine. If *Endymion* were
but an ancient myth retold, it would deserve all the
censures that have been, by unsympathetic readers,
passed upon it. The lightest of Herrick's songs, if it
carries us away, if we desire to read it again and again,
will be found to have about it a breath of mystery, a
message from the other world. As, when we meet a

saint, though he may look like other men, we yet
have an inexplicable sense that there is something
more in him, as if this man had been in heaven, so
with poetry. The poet's words may be common, his
story plain, but if he is speaking as a poet there will
abide with us the feeling that he has read a prophecy
in a diviner language, and is translating it to us. His
tongue is the tongue of the dying, and enforces attention like deep harmony.

A word or two may be ventured on that ally, or
rather perhaps dependent tributary, of Allegory
which is known as Personification, which so often serves
in the train of Allegory, but which oftener still appears
as a solitary knight-errant. This, too, from being an
ornament of poetry, has tended to be regarded as of
its essence : and with more excuse, for originally it
was of the essence of poetry. Like metaphor, it is a
development of Myth, and arose in that stage of human
mentality in which everything was a person. In that
stage it was real and vital, and ought not to receive the
stigma of being called a ' figure of speech ' at all. It
was the literal representation of actual belief, and in its
true character neither exclusively prose nor exclusively
poetical. Reciters and auditors were alike unconscious
that there was anything out of the common in it, and
accepted its appearance as phlegmatically as a child
accepts a fairy-tale. As men advanced to a dim conception of abstraction, when not merely the concrete
thing but some of its qualities gradually isolated themselves in thought, it was inevitable that Dream, Sleep,
Anger, War, Fear, Flight should don the personality
that had always been given to winds, trees, and rivers :
nor is it possible to tell at what point the personification was recognised as such, or at what later point it

degenerated into a mere trick of ornament. We see quite clearly that to Ovid the cave of Morpheus or the Temple of Fame was a conscious sophistication ; but he would be a bold man who would say how far the Sleep and Death that carried the body of Sarpedon to Lycia, and the Dream sent by Zeus to delude Agamemnon, were viewed by Homer as persons or as personified abstractions ; or how far, on the other hand, the Athene who checked the wrath of Achilles, audible to him alone, stood to the poet as a restraining impulse of the hero's own mind. When Deimos and Phobos, Fear and Flight, accompanied Ares to the war, did Homer visualise the phantoms more clearly than Milton visualised the Expectation that stood in horror as Satan and Michael addressed themselves for combat, or than Gray visualised the Amazement, Flight, and Solitude that attended the scourge of France ? There can be no doubt that in *some* cases the abstract was to Homer as real as his gods and goddesses : but at other times I believe that he drew the distinction as clearly as we do to-day. It is when the imagination of the poet flags that we feel the weakness of this kind of figure : and it shows every grade of force from the full vitality of Shelley's images to the emptiness of ' that school of poets who conceive it sufficient for a personification to begin a word with a capital letter.' There is no need to fling one's net wide in order to find examples of every sort. The works of Gray, few as they are, will be sufficient. He has many personifications that are illuminating, natural, and strong : and many also that are as useless, perfunctory, and feeble as those of Mason. But that is just my point. Had there not been an appetite for such things, neither Gray nor Mason would have endeavoured thus to satisfy it. For in poetry, as in other concerns of life, the demand creates the supply, and the supply in its turn strengthens the demand.

But Appetite, as Gilbert remarked—nor do I imagine that he was the first to remark it—has the capacity of being satisfied, and finally satiated. Your hunger, like the ghost in *Hamlet*, is here, and is here : you eat your dinner, and 'tis gone. So with the appetite for certain poetical dishes—for allegory and symbolism, for extremes of metaphor and personification : it arises, it may even grow with what it feeds on, but it departs. There is, however, a difference between the mental and the physical varieties. When William Pitt, under the influence of an indefinite number of bottles of port, made a sad exhibition of himself in the House of Commons, one of his admirers suffered terribly under the shock. ' A mysterious dispensation of Providence,' said Pitt : ' I have the wine and he has the headache.' This is rare in the physical world : but it is the rule in the æsthetic. A style retains its charm with those who are obviously having a surfeit of it : it is their successors who get the indigestion. The fathers eat the sour grapes, and like them : the children's teeth are set on edge. A fashion arises, and captivates a whole generation : the next generation wearies of it before even giving it a ten minutes' trial. People are bored with Tennyson without reading a hundred lines of him, and with Swinburne after the first three verses of *Dolores*. And so it has been with the taste for allegory. Other men indulged the taste : by all the rules of justice *they* ought to have sickened of it, but there is no sign that they ever did. *We* never had it ; but we have rejected it with nausea none the less.

XI

THE GROTESQUE

THAT taste which finds pleasure in incongruity—in
violation of the recognised conventions of art—is
one of the few tastes of which, so far as I know, little
or no trace is to be found among the ancients. There
is indeed something not far removed from the grotesque
in Hebrew literature : but, as there does not appear to
have been much sense of *rule* among the Jewish
writers, so we can hardly expect to find among them
a defiance of rule. Where they are grotesque, they are
grotesque by instinct and not of set purpose. In
Greek and Roman literature I remember hardly any
poems or prose writings which seek to excite pleasure in
this peculiar fashion. There were the satyric dramas,
to us incongruous enough ; but I doubt whether the
incongruity struck the hearers, any more than some
very remarkable religious services to-day strike the
devotees as ridiculous. The much later works of
Lucian *do* aim at a kind of incongruity, but the incongruity is in the substance and not in the style, which is
as Attic and regular as Lucian could make it. There
were at all times burlesques, parodies, and any number
of farces and comedies ; but very little which we, at
least if we exercise our historic imagination, and put
ourselves in the place of contemporaries, would call
grotesque.

It may be, of course, that this deficiency—if such

it be, is only apparent : that there were once specimens of Greek or Latin grotesque of which the caprice of Fate has deprived us. Aristotle, for instance, tells us that the painter Pauson, the parodist Hegemon, and Nicochares the author of the *Deliad*, represented men as ' worse than they are '—a phrase which may denote that they dealt in what we should call the grotesque. Chæremon, again, whose *Centaur* was a medley of all sorts of metres, may have been a sort of Butler composing an earlier *Hudibras*. But all this is a matter of guesswork : what one can be sure of is that such Greek art as is left to us is for the most part of the ' legitimate ' kind : and the traces of an art that laughs at itself are few indeed. On the other hand, ever since the early Middle Ages, we have rarely been long without grotesquenesses in sculpture, in architecture, in painting, in music, and perhaps not least in literature. It will, I imagine, be generally agreed that the grotesque is far from extinct to-day.

One cause both of its absence at one time and of its presence at another may perhaps be suggested by the derivation of the word. The Italian for cave is *grotta*. The medieval Italians, having their own conceptions of art, finding in caves or catacombs drawings or sketches belonging to an older civilisation, gave to such art the name of *grottesca*, cave-work. Now such art, being strange, almost inevitably appeared lawless, terrible, or more usually, comic. The foreigner, whether foreign in time or in space, is, at first sight, either ridiculous or terrible. But, as familiarity banishes contempt and fear, such art grows upon the spectator : he perceives it has a power of its own, and also that, if used as a foil or contrast to *his* own, it is capable of giving pleasure by variety. It tends, therefore, to provoke imitation, and starts a new taste either for itself alone or as a revolt against the established code. In particular, sculpture and architecture very early endeavoured to imitate the ancient forms. The gargoyle is the transference to later times of a very old and perhaps crude or tentative art.

Let us imagine that a man of artistic capacity lights, in some *Caverne des Trois Frères* or *La Tène*, upon an ancient picture of the Horned God or of Cernunnos. To him, with his Christian ideas, such a picture, once the expression of a serious piety, would appear both ridiculous and terrible. It would carry with it those mingled feelings of contempt and fear which the thought of the devil always aroused in the medieval mind. The Horned God *was* the devil, with cloven hoofs, bestial disguise, and every requisite Satanic appurtenance. He was also fraught with black magic : a danger to all who incautiously approached him. But his magic could be nullified. He could, like so many other heathen deities, be made a slave of the Church he hated. To copy him, to transfer him to the safe precincts of a cathedral, would be a pious act : you would at once draw out Leviathan with a hook and bind him to the service of your maidens : you could turn ugliness into an ornament, and wickedness to good. So to speak, you passed your conquered enemy under the yoke—you had captured him, and in the fashion of old warriors you made him an object of ridicule. The story of the workman who was engaged at Magdalen College, Oxford, is a later setting of what may have happened scores of times in the thirteenth century. Exasperated by one of the dons, he put his portrait above the cloisters, thinly disguised as a devil. He took his revenge, and at the same time destroyed the force of any spells the don might use against him.

Now these gargoyles, though in one way hideous, unquestionably exercise a certain fascination over the beholder. I am not sure that the most attractive features of Notre Dame are not the numerous devils who grin at us from the parapets. Men of all sorts, though not sculptors, or architects, would feel this attraction, and, if they had talents of their own, would wonder whether a similar attraction might not be found in the application of similar principles to other arts. 'That grotesqueness,' they would say, ' has a peculiar power : can I not gain a like power of being grotesque in my own style ? '

Now imagine this man to be a poet : we can see here the origin of many of the deliberately grotesque poems that were written, particularly in Italy, in the Renaissance period : a grotesqueness which took sometimes the form of burlesque, sometimes that of parody, sometimes that of purposed contortion. A poet of this kind, in English, is I think Skelton, who found this kind of ugly attraction to be specially adapted for his satirical aims.

We must, of course, distinguish this purposed grotesqueness, such as we find in Skelton, Tassoni, or Pulci, from the accidental grotesqueness which is due simply to antiquity or foreignness. It is I think certain that when we approach Chaucer for the first time we think him grotesque : that is because his language is old-fashioned. After a time, we become so familiar with him that he is no more grotesque than Tennyson, and far less so than Masefield or Miss Sitwell. Much of Dante, such as his pictures of Minos or Geryon, and some of his descriptions of Paradise (drawn, by the way, from medieval architecture) is still, I think, grotesque to most of us : and the account in *Patience* of Jonah in the whale, though amazingly vigorous, is grotesquely so. There is something grotesque, also, in the story, as in the metre, of the same author's *Gawayne and the Green Knight.* It is tolerably certain, however, that there was none of this grotesqueness in the intention of any of these authors.

Nevertheless, a later writer, approaching these poets from a modern angle, may well receive from them an impulse towards *deliberate* grotesqueness. Just as those medieval sculptors, modelling themselves on ancient art which had been once serious but had become strange, produced their gargoyles and demons, so a modern poet, studying an old author whom time has made quaint, may model himself upon him and produce a purposed quaintness. I do not imagine, for example, that Philip Quarles thought himself quaint : but a modern writer who should imitate the *Emblems,* would be quaint and know it. I have seen one or two modern imitations of George Herbert's more fantastic poems. In these imitations the fantastic, being conscious, is staring and exaggerated.

I am not so bold as to think that these few conjectures adequately explain the rise of the grotesque. But however it arose, it was speedily found to satisfy certain demands of human nature. It appeals, as psychologists tell us, to the love of Power. There is a pleasure in degrading the lofty ; for it negates that sense which in modern jargon is called the inferiority complex. There is a grim satisfaction in seeing those who have surpassed us, or kept us in subjection, brought to our own level. Even the righteous, says the Psalmist, shall see the deposed tyrant and shall laugh at him :

much more those who are not righteous : and we all know Hobbes's definition of laughter as a sudden glory which arises from a feeling of superiority to others. Hobbes might have added that it is also a sudden relief arising from the removal of a sense of inferiority. In any case, the removal of constraint, the discovery that a law is a bogey that may be defied with impunity, is a source of real gratification to us. And I think that it is this which lies at the root of our enjoyment of the grotesque, as distinct from our enjoyment of the merely comic. If humour lies in the detection of incongruities, and wit in the discovery of unsuspected likenesses, then the grotesque lies in the domain of humour rather than in that of wit : it accepts a position, and shows what happens when a foreign element is introduced. When Lucian puts the gods in degrading situations, or when Carlyle deprives our senators of their sartorial dignity, we feel that this is not comicality, but a humorous grotesqueness. And the grotesqueness is felt more distinctly when we still, with the other half of our mind, retain some respect for that which is thus degraded : we have thus the opportunity of contrasting two opposites. We do *not* feel that Swift's picture of the Yahoos is grotesque—the contempt is too obviously sincere. But there *is* grotesqueness, I think, in the account of the Laputians, so far as it is a successful account. That of the Lilliputians, I take it, is neither grotesque nor ferocious : it is comic, and the draughtsman feels some sympathy with his victims. Similarly, the little jests at which Addison indulges at the expense of women—the Fan Exercise *par excellence*—are, if grotesque at all, relieved by their humanity. Much of Peacock, especially *Sir Oran Haut-ton*, is grotesque in intention, if not always in effect : and the practical jokes of Peregrine Pickle would be grotesque if they had a little more genuine humour about them. The classical example, however, of a grotesque art which contrives to combine the height of humour with the depth of human feeling, is unquestionably Don Quixote. But it is not given to everybody, as it was to Cervantes, to elevate our idea of the human race while systematically appearing to lower it.

Similar considerations will apply to deliberate violations of the dignity of style and phrase. When an author, of set purpose, uses in dealing with one subject the style which custom has appropriated to another, we experience the same sense of relief from constraint, we make the same discovery that law is not so inviolable after all, and our hearts leap, at least for a moment, in the same sudden enjoyment of liberty. Above all, perhaps, there is a sense of enlargement—a realisation of an increase of power. When we thus perceive that a style, a metre, a rhyme, a set of phrases, hitherto associated with serious things only, can be applied equally, by a dexterous twist, to the purposes of ridicule, we have the same sense of enlargement as when we pass out of prison into the open air. The prison may have been comfortable, and the jailers human—but the open air is better. If a man whom another has girded, and carried where he would not, is suddenly given permission to gird himself and walk where he wills, he feels as if youth is restored to him, and youth-like he may even go too far.

But notice that to break the laws you must know them. Parnell said that he learnt the rules of Parliamentary procedure by breaking them. This is not the case in literature, nor was it quite the case with the Irish obstructionists. In a certain sense the taste for the grotesque is a sophisticated taste. It postulates a knowledge of the conventional rules of the art in question, and a determination to gain an effect by violating them. Even in the case of the gargoyle-maker, whom we need not suppose to have been always a highly-educated man, we must assume that he had enough knowledge to be able to satirise his art, and to realise what he was doing when he flung an ironical dab of contrast upon the stony canvas which others had provided for him. The spectator, again, to appreciate the irony, must have formed a fair conception of the rules that are being laughed at. He will otherwise be simply bewildered, and find none of the acrid pleasure which the artist means to give him.

In literature we must assume the same thing. Both author and reader must bear clearly in mind the more or less established rules, if they are to appreciate the way in which they are here observed and there defied. For example, if we are to enjoy Disraeli's *Ixion in Heaven*, or an imitation of it like Erskine's *Private Life of Helen of Troy*, we must know the conventions of the old myths and the Homeric epic, in order to savour the incongruity between them and the modern ideas with which they are satirically crossed. In a very clumsy way, as I think, a similar effect is aimed at by Mark Twain in *A Yankee at the Court of King Arthur*: the contrast there is between the chivalry of the medieval romance and the modern American notions. That book fails, in my opinion, because the contrast is *too* crude : but there is no doubt that Mark Twain *meant* to achieve the same sort of grotesque end which the gargoyle-artist actually achieves.

If we turn to a much higher example we see more clearly the working of the same principles. The success of Butler's *Hudibras* was, of course, mainly due to its satire of a cause which, though fallen, was still sufficiently alive to be worth satirising. Butler and his readers had suffered under the tyranny of the Saints, and their souls still felt the iron. Most of them also could appreciate the varied learning which was brought in at every turn to diversify the poem and relieve its monotony. But a large part of their pleasure was derived from the constant recognition of incongruity between the apparent form of the poem and the reality. It was externally a romance of chivalry— ' knights, squires, and steeds had entered on the stage ' —and everywhere the chivalry was ridiculed. It had the metre of the old romances, and that metre was everywhere suggesting the old simple dignity and everywhere ' letting it down.' All the readers had formed a conception of the laws of rhyme appropriate to such a romance, and had the continual enjoyment of seeing those laws skilfully turned to a sarcastic purpose. The rhymes were ridiculous because the intention of the author was to turn his subject into ridicule : but the ridiculousness consisted in this, that in the old romances the rhymes were serious.

What adds to the force of Butler's work is the fact, which is repeatedly visible, that he could write in the conventional artistic form when he liked. I do not say that he could have written a highly romantic or imaginative poem. But he could—and did—write in the accepted style of the time : and he makes it plain that, if he had chosen, he could have written a Satire on the Presbyterians in the manner of Oldham's *Satires on the Jesuits* or of those pieces which Marvell wrote but thought it desirable to keep anonymous. There is certainly a feeling in all of us that grotesque art is best done by those who are capable of doing what is ordinarily called ' better work.' If, for instance, you write bad rhymes, the reader must not imagine that you do so from incompetence : and if you sculpture a demon, there ought to be enough technical skill in it to prove that you could, if you pleased, produce a Madonna. There is, in Butler, proof that he possessed this power ; and I think the same will be admitted in the case of others whom I shall adduce. There is, for instance, no need to demonstrate that Byron had the true poetic gift. And this is manifested not only in so serious a poem as the *Giaour* or *Parisina*, but also, amid all the grotesqueness, in *Don Juan* itself. The hint for this, as is well known, came from Frere's *Monks and Giants*, in which, with ability but a certain crudity, the Butlerian method was adopted. But much besides had been learnt from the burlesque Arthurian romances of Italy. Byron had studied these with interest, and had even translated the first canto of Pulci's *Morgante Maggiore*, in which the old chivalrous poems had been turned to ridicule. That poem adopts the natural metre and style of romance ; the metre and style afterwards adopted by Boiardo and Ariosto. In *Don Juan* Byron borrows the Pulcian manner, and puts it to the purpose we all know. The poem is the Arthurian or Charlemagnian epic, turned to the uses of modern satire ; and it ridicules not only the manners and morals of Byron's times, but itself. As I have already pointed out in an earlier chapter, whenever by any chance, or by the secret influences of Byron's poetic temperament, it *falls* into real poetry, the succeeding verses make fun of it ; and

the style, answering to the intention, deliberately
vulgarises the context. As one might expect, there is
an abundance of Hudibrastic rhymes—if in the middle
of good ones all the better—the purpose of which is to
cast scorn on the whole conventional rhyming system,
and to degrade a recognised ornament into a deformity :
precisely as the choice of a hero and of a subject is to
cast scorn on the conventional themes of poetry. The
effect, at least in certain cantos, is amazing : those who,
by nature or by nurture, have the taste for these
strong condiments, feel an admiration for this poem
hardly less keen than that which others, or themselves
in other moods, feel for the ' legitimate ' poetry of
Paradise Lost. But it is worthy of notice that you
must have the requisite training if you are to feel thus.
The Countess Guiccioli, we may remember, urged
Byron to give up the ' horrid wearisome Don,' and
present her with a fifth canto of *Childe Harold*.
This was because she had not a sufficient knowledge of
the laws which were being broken to see the incongruity
as Byron meant his readers to see it. As much as
Milton, he needed a fit audience ; though the audience
would not as a rule consist of the same people. The
Countess, being Italian, would not be familiar with
the models which Byron was following and at the same
time ridiculing.

It is not without significance that Browning, another
great master of the grotesque, was like Byron an Italian
scholar. ' Open his heart, and you would see, graven in-
side of it, Italy.' Nor is it, I think, fanciful to detect
in his poetry signs of his knowledge of the grotesque
in Italian architecture : there is an extraordinary likeness between his poetry and some of the grotesque
work which Ruskin describes. But there were also

Q

other influences at work. There was medieval music, of which he has given us a characteristic description in *Master Hugues* : music which, whatever it was to its creators, is grotesque to us : and there was the Talmud, which, though containing much of universal value, has much besides that is perverted and fanciful. Browning has borrowed directly from the Talmud in *Doctor* —— and in *Jochanan Hakkadosh*, while his interest in the Jews is visible in *Rabbi Ben Ezra*, in *Holy Cross Day*, and indeed almost everywhere : but the influence exerted on his style by his Rabbinic studies is not to be measured by his direct references. It is said that he had Jewish blood in his veins. If so, the conflict between the Hebrew strain in him and his Nonconformist upbringing is almost enough to account for the incongruities of his style : and if we add his Humanist education and his cosmopolitan life, we need seek no further. At any rate, though I yield to none in my admiration for his genius, I cannot deny the grotesqueness of his style. Nor would I deny that this grotesqueness is in great part the secret of his power, as it is also the secret of the repulsion felt by many to whom it appears as a gratuitous pose. Suffice it to say that if you want to enjoy Browning, you must be prepared for his anfractuosities ; precisely as, in so many medieval cathedrals, you must be prepared for the devil and his angels. But in Browning, more often I think than in Byron, you get the angels as well as the devils : he proves, in the most grotesque of his poems, that if he had so inclined, he could have rivalled Tennyson in direct beauty.

It is true that he often lets his tendencies run away with him, and that incongruities occur where it will be hard to find a justification for them. It is true also that sometimes, as in *Pacchiarotto*, he gives full rein to his comic Pegasus, and disports himself, in elephantine manner, through seventy pages—without the excuse of the elephant in *Paradise Lost*, that he was doing it to make mirth for Adam and Eve. He wreathes his lithe proboscis to make mirth for himself : and his readers share but little in the enjoyment. But in many places—I think in most, at least, of his earlier works—his grotesqueness has a purpose, and attains it.

I remember reading, many years ago, a criticism of Carlyle which said that he was determined at all costs to be natural. The critic did not pause to consider what is the usual result of such a determination. In the ordinary sense of the word, nothing is more unnatural than a naturalness deliberately and obstinately adopted : and certainly, if Carlyle's style was due to such a resolve, it proved exactly what one would expect it to become. It is one of the least natural styles in English.

What the critic meant, I think, was this. Carlyle, thinking that the ordinary style of prose—a style which by long use had become a second nature—had originally been artificial (which perhaps was true), and believing also that in comparison with the style of natural *speech* it failed to some extent through loss of vigour, determined to write as he himself spoke : with ejaculations, parentheses, anacoluthons, and all the other loosenesses which, if not strictly conforming to the rules of grammar, certainly lend force to oral language. He remembered perhaps how much of the tremendous vitality of Shakespeare's style is due to the disregard of formal syntax : and he wished to recapture some of that vitality. He would have agreed with

Abbott that ' there is a liveliness and wakefulness in Shakespearean English which are wanting in the grammatical monotony of the present day ' ; and that if we were to call up the shade of Shakespeare in the words of Antonio, ' Do you not hear us ? ' he would crush us with the reply of Sebastian, ' I do, and surely it is a sleepy language, and you speak out of your sleep.' If Carlyle thought so, he had his reward, for as Lowell says, for vigour of expression we have to go back to Shakespeare to find his parallel.

But this is purchased by an extreme grotesqueness : in fact, if I wanted to give the supreme example of stylistic grotesqueness in English, I should choose Carlyle. He ignored that long history which had created a language for prose purposes, with its own rules and conventions, perhaps, as he imagined, once artificial, but now part and parcel of our traditions. Or rather he did not ignore it—he defied it. At every turn we are reminded of the rules by the systematic fashion in which he breaks them. Nor are we quite convinced, with the critic I mentioned, that the defiance is natural to him. We feel uneasily that it is a pose, adopted to startle, and that his style is really more artificial than the style he is mocking ever was. We know, of course, that he did not always write like this ; we know that his earlier works, such as the *Life of Schiller*, are in the common manner. It is not as if he was *born* to write thus : he *forced* himself to it.

And yet, even with Carlyle, there is a certain pleasure in observing these perversities, as there is in studying the gargoyles—so long as the style is recognised as exceptional, and as a relief from the common. When other authors imitate him, the style nauseates. And there is, also, we feel, a certain special appropriateness in this grotesque manner when it is applied to a subject that is itself grotesque. I do not think we should enjoy *Sartor Resartus*, as I hope we all enjoy it, if it were written in the style of Froude or Matthew Arnold. It is right that Teufelsdröckh, who is a grotesque creation, should express himself grotesquely.

Pose or not when Carlyle adopted it, this style I think became in a sense natural, or at least easy, to him, and certainly suited the message he desired to deliver. He acquired a taste for it : and to some extent tended to dislike styles of a more regular and harmonious kind. But, in my opinion, he never quite succeeded in creating a taste for it in his readers. Even those who accepted his teaching felt uneasy as to the manner in which he proclaimed it ; and there is a note of apology for it among his very devotees. 'This is the way in which the prophet cannot help speaking,' they would say : ' put up with the style for the sake of the substance.' Men felt that he was a Delphian, whose oracles might be uttered in an obscure and contorted fashion, but, being inspired, were worth the trouble of unravelling.

And this, I think, is true, as a rule, of the grotesque artist everywhere. We do not *quite* like him ; and unless we feel that he is a man of genius, whose message is in itself worth hearing, we glance at his work for a moment, taste its peculiar flavour with the short-lived pleasure such things give, and pass on to the artists who conform to rules and standards. For after all, we must remember what is so often forgotten, that the rules and standards would not have been established if they had not expressed something fundamental and ultimate in the general human mind. There may be revolts against them, but they are usually known to be revolts, and the tendency, when passions subside, is always to return to them. Storms are tangible and terrible, but after all they ruffle only the surface of the sea : in the depths all is calm, and when the disturbing influence has worn itself out, the sea falls back into its natural and regulated serenity, moved only by the tides, which obey an eternal law.

XII

THE AUSTERE

WHEN, at forty-two, Macaulay had the task of bringing out the collected edition of his Essays, he hesitated about republishing the essay on Milton. It was, he said, overloaded with gaudy and ungraceful ornament : and, though he did reissue it, he was careful to insist that it had been written when he was hardly more than an undergraduate.

Severe critics have not failed to point out that Macaulay, to the end of his life, never succeeded in entirely escaping the gaudy and ungraceful ; but his case nevertheless remains typical of what happens very often in the literary life. Usually, though not universally—Macaulay has himself recalled the splendid exceptions of Bacon and Burke—the florid style is adopted in the exuberance of youth, and gradually gives way to the sobriety natural to maturity and old age. Keats, as everyone knows, died at twenty-five ; and it was both his theory and his practice to 'load every rift with ore' : in fact, if any serious fault is to be found in him, it is that in such poems as *The Eve of St. Agnes* there is too great lusciousness of imagery, too great profusion of ornament. Yet, in Keats himself, there are signs that, young as he was, he was beginning to see that an occasional bare rift is no unpleasing discovery even for the explorer in the realms of gold. No poet is richer in the tapestries and paintings of his halls than Spenser; he seems absolutely inexhaustible in his stores of flowers : but in his latest verses, the cantos on *Mutability*, one seems to detect the traces of a preference for a sterner and more rugged style. Whether Ruskin was ever really successful in throwing aside the youthful luxuriance of *Modern Painters* may be doubted ; but in his later books he certainly, like Kent, *intended* his ' occupation to be plain.' The most striking example, however, is, of course, Milton. Whereas his earliest poems are full of ' conceits,' his latest, *Samson Agonistes*, achieves its stupendous impressiveness by an austerity like that of a mighty rock on which not a flower, not a patch of herbage, is to be seen. His genius may be likened to an inverted Iliad. In the first book of the Iliad there is not a single simile, hardly a poetic ornament of any kind ; whereas in the later books these crowd upon us in almost too great abundance. In the life of Milton the first stage shows the trappings, the last discards them for naked and rugged sublimity.

But we must notice that as a rule it is not the readers but the writers who feel this growing distaste for ornament. There are, it is true, always men in the reading public who prefer simplicity, however rigid, and suspect the slightest approach to the ornate : who say, ' No flowers by request,' or like John Morley to Stead, ' No dithyrambs, if you please.' These are the House of Lords of literature, who listen with impatience to the glowing periods of the Chathams and attend closely to the calm deliberativeness of the Mansfields. But they are few. The vast majority, I believe, are attracted by the gorgeous, and are not shocked even by a certain measure of Oriental flamboyance. Sound, even if there is not much sense, and

a persuasive accent, please the ear as Belial pleased
Pandemonium. At any rate, it is a significant fact
that the very authors who have despised the gauds
and tricks of style in later years—the Macaulays and
Ruskins—have usually gained their audiences by dithyrambs, and have not ventured to cast the dithyrambs
aside until they are sure of an audience however
quietly they whisper. If Macaulay had not begun as
a rhetorician, he would not, like Byron, have awoke
and found himself famous : and, until he had consoli-
dated his fame he could not have afforded to chasten
his style. If the ' Oxford Graduate ' of twenty-four
had not burst on an astonished world with the Ormuz-
like magnificence and display of *Modern Painters*,
he would have had no hearers ; and it was not till he
had gained a hearing that he could dare to tell his
hearers that they had been admiring the meretricious.
A king, at his coronation, must put on his robes of
state : when the populace has been duly impressed,
he may venture to walk abroad in the ordinary dress
of a citizen. And in real life it is not, as in Andersen's
story, the young who detect the mere man beneath
the imperial vestments.

Of course the word ' young ' must here be understood in a somewhat liberal sense. Who is older than
the undergraduate ? I have seen the almond tree
flourishing on the brow of the freshman, and a mere
boy ostentatiously staggering under the load of a
grasshopper. When I was an undergraduate it was
' the thing ' to smile at the infantile enthusiasm of the
dons, and to censure the aged for their childish love
of rhetoric. At that time the early poems of Bridges
came stealing from the private press of Daniel : and
all my little set—averaging about twenty in years—

felt it incumbent on them to admire the restraint and austerity of *Prometheus the Fire-giver*. We were proud of our superiority to those elders who liked a little show of passion ; and when we were informed that Bridges was perhaps a little cold, we answered, ' It is the coldness of suppressed flame.' For myself, though I never ceased to admire Bridges, I became less fond of restraint and suppressed flame as I grew older in years, and was glad to see that as Bridges himself grew older he put a little more of the divine frenzy into his poems.

Much the same is the case with the youth of nations. Here also I do not mean necessarily a nation's earlier days, but the time at which it becomes conscious of juvenility. A nation is as old as it feels, and is often younger at the age of Methuselah than at the age of Solomon when he received the kingdom. There is no doubt, for instance, that England was more juvenile in the days of Elizabeth than in those of Edward the Confessor ; and that there is much more of the boy in Spenser than in Cynewulf. The sixteenth century threw off the senility of the fifteenth, and roused itself out of sleep like a mighty man that shouteth by reason of wine. Shout, as I have already shown, it certainly did. There is an intoxication in the language of almost all the writers of that time—essayists, romancers, poets, dramatists, narrators—which is scarcely to be paralleled at any other. The sound is not an echo to the sense, but a reverberation as of a roar in the House of Fame. Every phrase seems to multiply the meaning many times over. Kyd, Marlowe, even Shakespeare himself, are in apparent rivalry as to who shall most decisively out-Herod Herod. In a different way Spenser himself shows a similar tendency. His words are less loud, but they are many. The world went on, and

grew a little older. It demanded now, if at a loss of
force and vigour, greater precision, a nearer equality
between sense and phrase : and we find the calmer,
less boisterous Augustan age succeeding to the Elizabethan : the prose of Dryden and Tillotson displacing
that of Milton and Browne : the verse of Denham
and Waller putting that of Shirley out of fashion. It
is true that with the lowering of tone the thought
was lowered also : but the thought, such as it was, was
expressed with closer accuracy than before.

Something like this, amid great and obvious differences, occurred in Athens after the defeat of the
Persian Armada. The city mewed its mighty youth,
and the shop of war had not so many hammers working
on triremes as there were industrious pens competing
for the prizes at the Dionysia. These also, if we may
trust the few remains we possess, produced plays in
which the language strutted like the actor in his
cothurnus. The thought of Æschylus was at once
lofty and profound ; but, by the testimony of his
immediate successors, his words were often too huge
and his phraseology turgid. Both, however, suited
his audiences, to whom they seemed to fit their own
boundless ambitions and the limitless possibilities that
loomed before them. While Æschylus thus uttered his
Delphic oracles on the stage, Pericles ‘ thundered ’ in
the Assembly. But time passed : disasters came,
hopes proved liars ; and a serener drama appeared
with Sophocles, a more ordered oratory, if not more
impressive, with the later speakers.

We find this alternation, as is to be expected, not
merely in societies but in persons. The *magnum loqui*
pleases us in youth ; the quiet style in our riper stage :
and we often note with surprise how the books which

seemed to us magnificent twenty years ago, and
roused our hearts as with the sound of a trumpet, now
seem, like Pharaoh king of Egypt, ' but a noise.'
Either we have become dulled by the repetition, or
there really was some excess of grandiloquence in the
old passages which, at the time we first read them, we
were incapable of perceiving. Or the cause may lie
in a subconscious snobbery. The ' common herd '
unquestionably likes flamboyance : *we* are not to be
classed with the common herd. The ' high-brow,'
to whose company we wish to belong, prefers beauty
unadorned ; and unadorned beauty shall be our
preference also. Be this as it may, if the love of high-
sounding words and ornate phraseology be a mark of
youth, then it is tolerably certain that the mass of
men remain perennially young. And not least youthful,
in this sense, among the peoples of the world is the
British public, to whom you must appeal at once by
a thought not too profound and by a style deliberately
heightened.

There is a curious contrast here between the British
hearer and the British reader which I have never seen
explained. Our people will accept with avidity the
florid book, but they will have nothing to do with the
florid speech. They have an instinctive love of a high-
falutin style in their newspapers, but they instinctively
suspect a highfalutin orator. This has been noticed
from very early times : and none knew it better than
orators themselves. Antony, a first-rate rhetorician,
begins by telling his audience that he has no rhetorical
skill—the most effective of rhetorical devices. So long
as they do not know he is an orator, they will listen to
him ; and as soon as he has convinced them that
Brutus *is* an orator, they will dismiss the arguments

of Brutus from their minds. John Bright always
began his speeches in a faltering voice, and as if he
might break down every minute. He thus deluded
the crowd into fancying he was ' a plain blunt man '
like themselves, who might be trusted not to trick
them with the sleights of rhetoric. Only gradually
did he pass from stammering to fluency, and from
fluency to those soaring flights which carried them off
their feet, and made them, like Wellington's army,
go anywhere and do anything. There is a good touch
in a not too good novel of Lytton's. When Eugene
Aram had finished his astonishing defence—a *tour
de force* which has set him on a pinnacle among mur-
derers—Lytton tells us the judge began by eulogising
the eloquence and art of the speech, thus destroying
its effect. To hint to a British, and still more to a
Yorkshire, jury that they had been carried away by
eloquence was sufficient. ' Ah, we have have been
taken in : he is an orator, and therefore a liar.' They
did not suspect that the judge's deliberately flat and
unadorned summing-up was also a piece of oratory,
all the more effective because so skilfully disguised.

With books and authors the contrary is the case.
A book must open with something startling, or it will
not be read : an author must begin his career with a
splash, or he will not have a career at all. The present
unpopularity of Scott—though I believe his unpopularity is greatly exaggerated—is largely due to the fact
that his novels begin quietly. How can a man have
anything exciting to say who does not excite us at
once ? And an author who wishes to make a name
writes his first book in such a style as to stir the pulses
of the most *blasé* reviewer. He pours out his paradoxes, his epigrams, his purple patches ; and the

reviewer, followed by the reader, says at once, ' This is a fine writer.' There is no suspicion *here ;* no fancy that the brilliancy is a cloak for humbug. No reviewer eulogises the eloquence and art of *a book* in order to destroy its effect on the minds of the impanelled British or Yorkshire *reading* public. This is, as I say, a curious fact, and well worth analysing.

In the first place, I do not think the average reader has enough imagination to perceive that a book is nothing but a man in a binding, or that a newspaper article is nothing but a fellow-creature in the shape of a column of print. He will accept, without question, from such a phantom what would at once arouse suspicion if it came from visible lips. Horace was right, in another sense than he intended, when he said,

> Segnius *irritant* animos demissa per aurem,
> Quam quae sunt oculis subjecta fidelibus.

Even if the name of the writer is subscribed, it produces little impression : his remarks are in print, and that proves their truth. If he writes anonymously, so much the better : he is no fallible mortal, but the Press. Let a man stand up on a platform, and you see he is a man, and therefore, on the authority of the hasty Psalmist, a probable liar. But there is no tendency to guard against the confidence-tricks of a mere parcel of inked paper. This is one reason why authors themselves, though they may practise rhetorical devices for their own purposes, are quick to see through them in other authors. Their own books are bits of themselves ; and they instantly see the face behind the printed mask of another.

Again, the reader, sitting solitary, untouched by the magnetic influence of a surrounding crowd, and

free from the attracting or repelling force of a visible
speaker on the platform, *requires* in the book an
exaggeration in the phraseology, a heightening of the
tone. Let it, for example, be a play that he is reading.
If the words are not extravagant, he has not sufficient
native vigour of mind to receive from them the same
shock which he receives when they are declaimed
with good elocution and play of feature by an actor
on the stage. His dull and sluggish mentality needs
a certain amount of violence before it will respond.
Hence authors who know how to appeal to him will
give him the requisite shocks : the words, instead of
being ' cousins to the deed,' will expend at least twice
the force that is requisite with a keen and quick man,
who is accustomed to translate what he reads into
actuality. Such a man will be disgusted with the
unnecessary turbulence : but the ordinary man, like
a sleeper who cannot be awaked except by a thunderbolt, will think the style—if he thinks about it at all—
exactly adapted to call up the right images.

Once more, the ordinary man, as reader, in proportion to his mental flabbiness, imagines himself astute
and watchful. He fancies that, while reading, he is
reflective and on his guard. No legerdemain can take
him in *now*. He can re-read a passage, he can be on
the look-out for deception or overstatement. He is
thus in the exact mental posture to be the more easily
deceived. He is so proud of his caution that the
conjurer has him absolutely under control. All sorts
of hyperboles, of confusions, of errors pass his scrutiny.
What in a speaker would be laughed at, in a writer goes
without objection. The reader is hopelessly at the
writer's mercy, precisely because he thinks himself the
master of his fate.

But an author of a high order, growing himself more in love with words, and more and more hating to do them violence, accustomed to weighing them more and more accurately in the balance, loth to spend them unnecessarily or to use two where one will do, and also, as I said above, becoming assured that he will be listened to even though he no longer shouts, tends usually to a steadily increasing economy both of words and of ornaments. He becomes, in fact, an *austere* writer : his style is astringent, and causes a dryness of the palate. The same thing is seen in the ' higher ' class of reader. He, too, demands, in increasing measure, as exact a correspondence between the thought and the expression as is possible : he resents over-elaboration, what appears to him excess of ornament, anything that reminds him of Ercles' vein. Plain and direct statement—whatsoever is more than this cometh of evil.

Now it does not follow in the least that because this austere style is usually adopted late in life by the author, and usually pleases the reader who, whether in years or in experience, is older than the average, it is therefore *absolutely* better than another and a more adorned style. *Absolute* goodness in style, I repeat, is a mere abstraction without content. The style is good that reaches its appropriate audience. If you wish a ' fit ' audience, you may have to put up with its being few : but the mere fewness is nothing to boast of. If you claim that it is ' fit,' that also is nothing to boast of. You have found people who fit you, and nothing more. It may be you are so select that you have yourself for your only reader. Be content : your style is adapted to its audience.

The reader, like the writer, is made by nature and

nurture, being gradually moulded by his profession
and environment and by the manifold impacts of life
upon his mind. A lawyer generally tends to disregard
rhetoric, though he will use it unscrupulously in endeavouring to sway a jury. The more it succeeds in
swaying the juries, the more, as a rule, he will despise
it. A common citizen of a certain amount of intelligence, learning how often he has been misled in his
life by rhetorical devices, will usually come to distrust
them, like the lawyer but usually later. An author,
keen to note in other authors the too lavish use of such
devices, may sometimes be inclined to fear that his own
works are too full of them, and be led to prune his
own luxuriance, lest he be confounded with So-and-
so. Above all, perhaps, he may fear the parodist,
who finds his richest field in the florid writer and scanty
scope in the severe one. But, alike in author and in
reader, the whole thing is relative : and ' goodness '
can no more be predicated of any style without
qualification than of a pair of boots. What is an excellent pair for David would scarcely suit Goliath. All
that the wearer can say is that the boots fit *him*.

No author, however, is of so universal a mind that
he can, like a bootmaker, undertake to fit everybody.
His wares will, as received by different customers,
arouse every feeling from disgust and revulsion to
comfort and even exquisite pleasure. And, being
susceptible to the same influences as his readers, he
will, more or less consciously, tend to give his limited
public what pleases them ; while they, in their turn,
are gradually moved to like him now more now less.
A reciprocal influence is constantly at work, less patent
than that which is seen when an orator is stirring a
crowd and being stirred by it, but no less powerful,

R

and in the long run often more so. If the audience he reaches shows him, in the imponderable but unmistakable way in which these things happen, that it is beginning to weary of a certain style and wishes a change, he will usually tend to give it that change. Should he be of a stubborn and impervious nature, he may refuse to change : in that case he will soon find himself to be a voice crying in the wilderness.

As to everything there is a season, and a time for every purpose under heaven, there occur, though rarely, periods when a whole literary community, for reasons which it is very hard to discover, seems to show a preference for the austere style of which I have spoken. Thus we have good reason to be sure that the Athenian dicasteries, though very large and made up of very ordinary men, for a long time preferred the even and unemotional style of Lysias to more boisterous rhetoric. What the public asks for it receives. And then, as the eternal pendulum swings back, the community, finding the old style flat and unstimulating, demands something stronger. The man who now plies the dicasteries with doses of Lysias will lose his cases : and the style which yesterday was good, will, in the only sense of the word that has any discoverable meaning, prove bad. It fails to move the audience : and that is enough. Similarly we have noticed, even in the ' young ' and energetic country of America, the mildest styles, like that of Howells, becoming popular and holding their ground for years, and then the country demanding something—to use the vigorous slang of the vernacular—' with more pep in it.' The time will assuredly come when the ' pep ' will pall, and when a certain meekness will be tried by those who wish to inherit the earth. Nay, we may confidently

expect that the very advertisments, in order to attain
their end more certainly, will cease to be startling
and become gently and quietly persuasive.

As a rule, however, the community does not show
this monotony of taste. It is made up of innumerable
smaller communities, whose tastes shade off by imperceptible gradations, passing from the most frenzied
Asiatic to the chilliest that ever satisfied the arid taste
of a Brutus. Here the author has to make his choice
—if he can. He must appeal to that portion of the
public whose taste is most in harmony with his own.
If he tries to force his style into one not natural to him,
the public, which has a remarkable if untutored
shrewdness, will assuredly in time detect the falsetto,
and refuse its patronage. But if he sticks to what is his
inborn style, varying it but within due limits, his ' fit
audience ' will generally find him out, and say of his
works that they are ' good.'

XIII

THE DIACTIC IN POETRY

WE have already noticed how much earlier poetry is than prose. A kind of verse, as we saw in our preceding chapters, seems the natural way of talking, and ' loose speech' the artificial. Men learnt to crawl in metre before they learnt to walk, like M. Jourdain, in prose. And even when a rudimentary prose was discovered, such as we see on monuments—lists of battles, names of gods and kings, enumerations of towns conquered—it was still felt that verse was more easily remembered, and attracted attention more strongly. It was therefore retained when what we may perhaps regard as a more potent instrument was ready to hand.

Hence we find tales, histories, praises of chiefs, maxims of conduct, proverbs, all in verse. Rude assonances, like Samson's jeer at the Philistines, or some primitive Agnes Douglas's warning to Montagu, were flung out more or less accidentally, and stuck in people's minds, to keep alive the memory of great deeds for scores or hundreds of years. That almost irresistible tendency, which still works in proverbs like ' Can't be cured, must be endured,' in tiny legendary epics like ' Jack Sprat could eat no fat,' in mythical epics like ' Jack and Jill,' in miniature dramas like ' Mary, Mary,' must have been even more powerful in primitive times. Oral epitaphs in uncouth rhymes may well have implored *lasting* tributes of sighs or indignation, for centuries before men learnt to transfer them to the lesser permanence of stone. We do not hear that Joshua inscribed the boulders he set up in Gilgal. He trusted, rightly, to men's memories.

As literary skill improved, we had long narrative poems, like the *Wrath of Achilles*, elaborate panegyrics of princes, carefully constructed riddles, elegies—but all in verse : and gradually a fixed form of verse was evolved, such as was instinctively felt to suit the ' genius ' of the language. In the Teutonic languages a strong beat was marked by alliteration : in Greek, where stress, as far as we can see, was weak, and quantity more important, two short lines were joined into one, known as the hexameter ; and this, so far as we know, was for long the only measure employed by professional bards, though the religious dance may have discovered others. In Hebrew, it is said, the stress was very strong, and the number of unaccented syllables might therefore, as with us, be considerable : but here, too, the form of verse, for all themes, appears to have been, at one time, tolerably uniform. We find, then, at this stage, gnomes, didactics, political propaganda all in verse, and usually, though not always, in the same kind of verse. There was no prose into which it could fall, and there were very few verse-types. Thus the Proverbs of ' Solomon ' are more or less in the same metre as *Job :* our own old gnomic verses are metrically indistinguishable from *Beowulf;* the half-autobiographical, half-didactic poems ascribed to Hesiod are, whatever their subject, in Homeric measure. The political manifestos of Solon are, it is true, in three or four different metres, iambic, trochaic, or epic : but they are all in *some* metre, and of necessity so. Had prose been invented, it is hard to believe that he would not have used it, and he certainly went pretty near it. The most famous of the Greek gnomic poets, Theognis, also, couched his excellent remarks, not exactly in hexameters, but in a metre only slightly varied from them, and well-established before his time.

But, as so often happens, a fashion originally adopted from necessity was kept up from choice. Certain men, venerable for their antiquity, had written gnomic or didactic ' poetry ' ; it was therefore thought that poetry was the proper vehicle for instruction. Solon and Theognis had used verse because they had nothing else to use : later writers, taking their cue from these famous names, used verse for the same ends when there was no longer any necessity to do so. A far more precise and powerful weapon for their purpose was at their disposal ; but they could not break with tradition, and poured out reams of hexameters when plain prose would have been both simpler for the writer and plainer for the reader. Thus, in Greece, Empedocles threw his explanation of his philosophy into verse which, despite the eulogy of Lucretius, we have the authority of Aristotle for refusing to call poetry. ' There is nothing,' says Aristotle, ' that Homer and Empedocles have in common but the metre : the one is justly termed a poet, the other a physicist ' : and he hints that he knows of so-called poems on medicine or on natural science on which he would have passed the same sentence. But there is something in Aristotle's tone which seems to show that he was arguing against a common error of the time. Apparently there were many under the delusion that verse and poetry are the same : and even to-day there are some who harbour that idea.

Most good judges, however, would agree with

Aristotle. It is hard to deny that, somehow and for some reason, direct didactics are the ruin of poetry. This is proved by the one test which can almost be called infallible—the all but unanimous verdict of the readers of poetry. Even those who, deluded by the verse-form, may *call* a set of propositions poetry, do not *feel* it as such. If there is one mark of true poetry, as of true eloquence, it is this, that it must keep its hearers awake : and it is certain that Empedocles and his like send their readers to sleep. Whatever doctors may think, there are few soporifics more reliable than doses of the *Excursion*. It ought then, one would think, to be quite clear that poets ought to avoid teaching. Why then have some of the greatest, like Lucretius and Coleridge, imagined that the highest form of poetry is the philosophical ?

One reason I have already indicated—the force of tradition. Lucretius—a great poet if there ever was a great poet in the history of the world—being also a philosopher, sees that Empedocles has conveyed some profound doctrines by means of verse : and these doctrines move his generous mind, not unnaturally, to a feeling of emulous admiration. Filled with the desire to convey to the world doctrines which he believes to be still sounder than those of Empedocles, he adopts the form that Empedocles had employed, hoping that thus he may exert an even stronger influence on others than Empedocles has exerted upon *him*. But the only result is that even his poetic power is stifled. He is truly poetical only when he ceases to preach philosophy : fortunately he ceases pretty often, and we have thus in his poem many passages of sublimity and pathos scarcely surpassed in all literature.

But there is another motive. The line dividing poetry from philosophy is very indistinct, though very important. Every reader of poetry knows that *mere* poetry is hardly ever true poetry at all. A poem must not be thin or empty : it *must* teach, though it must not be didactic. It must have content. When we grasp it, it must not, like Anchises in the shades, elude our hands. There is not, I believe, a single passage in the whole of Greek criticism which does not assume that a poet must be a schoolmaster after all : and poets like Homer, Simonides, Pindar, Æschylus, are constantly quoted as if they were authorities on philosophy. Even when Plato demurs to this idolatry, it is with a certain reverent hesitation : he admits that the poets are inspired like the Pythia, even while he denies the consistency of the oracle. And there can be no doubt that all the greatest poets, on their side, agree in this with their readers. Dante, Milton, Goethe, would never for a moment have admitted that they were but idle singers of empty days[1] : every one of them felt he had a message, and must be free to utter it or die. Nor, when we read the inspired parts of Wordsworth, do we feel that, in a certain sense, they are less philosophical than the uninspired : they teach us, in another fashion, but they teach us none

[1] Similarly Virgil leaves us in no doubt as to his conception of the ideal poet. At the court of Dido that ideal bard is set before us, singing to Æneas, who represents the ideal Rome. Iopas, ' docuit quem maximus Atlas,' is no mere artist : he is as much of a teacher as Orbilius himself, though less disagreeable :

> Hic canit errantem lunam solisque labores,
> Unde hominum genus et pecudes, unde imber et ignes,
> Arcturum pluviasque Hyadas, geminosque Triones,
> Quid tantum Oceano properent se tinguere soles
> Hiberni, vel quae tardis mora noctibus obstet.

This is not Art for Art's sake.

the less. Shakespeare himself we recognise as a great
poet largely because he is almost infinitely *wise :*
and the author of Job moves us, even through the veil
of translation, because of his unfathomable depth of
thought. Imagine, in these poets, the same amount
of purely *poetic* power, vast as that is, without the
thought, and how immense the loss !

No one, I think, has yet succeeded in marking exactly
at what point the philosophy which thus penetrates
all great poetry becomes a hindrance instead of a help
to our poetic enjoyment. We all feel the change,
but none of us can precisely explain why we feel it.
Everybody knows when Dante's theology begins to
weary, and experiences the relief when, without forgetting his theology, he soars into poetry : but it seems
impossible to *analyse* the difference. We all tire when,
in Milton, ' God the Father turns a school divine ' ;
but precisely *where* lies the difference between the
first two books of *Paradise Lost* and the third, one cannot tell. The magnificent lines on death in Lucretius
are not less full of thought than those on atoms and
void : and yet the *exact* reason why the former move
you like the voice of an archangel and the latter are
no more interesting than an ordinary science-lecture,
can scarcely be stated in words. The utmost that the
most competent critics have been able to say is that,
in order not to cease to be poetry, the teaching in
poetry must be ' indirect ' : a statement true enough,
but, as we all feel, inadequate. I have, I think, seen
somewhere a comparison drawn, obviously by some
schoolmaster, between this ' indirect ' teaching and
the preparation for life given by the old classical
curriculum: a preparation certainly indirect enough. As,
in the view of this pedagogue, the study of Latin and

Greek might be of little immediate value as a training for a trade or a profession, but yet had an immense worth in enlarging the capacities of the mind, so that special knowledge might be easily acquired, in the same way, it was held, the study of poetry ought to give no overt philosophical instruction, but ought so to elevate the soul that it becomes more enlarged, more receptive, and more noble. Here again there is an element of truth. But we are left without a precise and accurate definition of the reason why a poem without any philosophical substratum remains, as a rule, unsatisfying, while a poem that undertakes to expound a philosophy with philosophical discrimination is usually more unsatisfying still. Criticism, here, seems to be less critical than mere taste. If you reply with the dogmatic canon that poetry, to please, must be vague, not only do we wonder why poetry should differ in this particular fashion from pleasing narrative, sculpture, or painting, but we wonder why you should rule out half the poetry that the world has consented to call the best. There is not much that is vague in the *Iliad* or the *Odyssey*. If you say that it must not put too severe a strain on our mental powers, you make, if not a larger, yet a more serious, subtraction from our poetic treasure-house. It would be a poor praise of poetry to claim that it cannot give us that highest pleasure which springs from strenuous mental exertion. Who can deny, if he has once made the effort, that a large part of his enjoyment of the *Paradiso* or of *Faust* has sprung from difficulties overcome? Poetry appeals to the emotions, it is true : but, at its highest, to emotion founded on the intellect. The poet sees the 'everlasting universe of things,' but, as Shelley says, it flows through the *mind :* 'lending splendour where from secret springs the source of human *thought* its tribute brings.'

If then the utmost powers of reflective criticism fail to explain how and where the intellect may rightly be called an intruder in poetry, no wonder that the poets have often failed. Many of the very best have fancied themselves *primarily* teachers, and only secondarily givers of pleasure. There is no need to travel far in the search for examples. Coleridge, whose wonderful mind was divided into watertight compartments, has given us half a dozen specimens of almost perfectly ' pure poesy ' : but in his capacity of critic he not only wrote much verse in which the alien element of pedagogy is painfully visible, but constantly urged Wordsworth on to the composition of a philosophical poem : and Wordsworth, not, it is true, a very good critic where his own works were concerned, needed little urging. The great poem ' on man, on Nature, and on human life ' was begun, and a small fragment of it was completed—small, but too large for most readers. Dante flung the whole theology of his time into his *Comedy*. Milton would have been heavily sarcastic if he had been asked to leave the ' scheme of salvation ' out of *Paradise Lost*. Virgil put *some* practical directions as to farming into the *Georgics :* and even Spenser, in whom the love of pure beauty was as strong as in any poet that ever lived, preaches the Puritan doctrine, every now and then, as plainly as Cartwright or Udall. There is a good deal of science in Goethe's *Faust*. All these poets want us not merely to feel a certain emotional elevation in reading their poems, but to *know* more at the end of the perusal than at the beginning. It is no answer to say that a farmer would get some very disappointing harvests if he followed the advice of the *Georgics* without discrimination, or that the philosophy one learns from the sixth book of the *Æneid* will not hold water : the fact remains that Virgil intended us to learn both agriculture and philosophy, and that Dante, a fairly good judge, regarded him not merely as a teacher of style but as a doctor of thought. The *cacoethes scribendi* is also, even in the greatest, a *cacoethes docendi*.

But where Hesiod, Lucretius, Virgil, led the way, others were bound to follow : and many, unfortunately, had not the poetic gifts of Lucretius and Virgil. Long before the great Latin poets, Greeks had begun. 'Alexandrine' poetry is full of such poems, as instructive, doubtless, as schoolbooks, and not much more artistic. The *Phaenomena* of Aratus will be remembered for ever, as one of its lines was quoted at Athens by St. Paul : but it is otherwise as little of a true poem as the works of Empedocles. The *Theriaca* of Nicander tells about the bites of serpents ; and the same writer actually versified some of the medical observations of Hippocrates. So popular was he that the *Theriaca* was paraphrased in another metre by Marianus, probably the very same epigrammatist one of whose poems had the honour of receiving two translations from the hand of Shakespeare himself. There must be some force in the impulse to crush science into metre. Among the multitude of Roman versifiers who crowded the Augustan age, several chose Aratus and Nicander as their models. Of these, Æmilius Macer is known solely by the fact that as an elderly man, so we learn from Ovid, he read to his youthful admirer his poem on Birds :

Saepe suas volucres legit mihi grandior aevo,
   Quaeque necet serpens, quae iuvet herba, Macer :

a passage which seems to show that the poem was a tolerably close imitation, if not a mere paraphrase, of Nicander. More famous than Macer, though strangely enough never mentioned by any contemporary writer, is Manilius, the author of a poem on Astronomy, which no less a man than Richard Bentley thought worth editing, and no less a poet and scholar than Housman has recently edited. A specimen of this work is given by Mr. Garrod in the book to which I have already referred : it is probably the best that could have been chosen, and shows clearly that a pedagogue is not necessarily a poet. I need do no more than quote an excellent paragraph from Professor Jebb's little biography of Bentley. 'Scaliger pronounced Manilius equal in sweetness to Ovid, and superior in majesty ; a verdict which Bentley cites with approval. To most readers it will be scarcely intelligible. Where Manilius deals with the technical parts of astronomy he displays, indeed, excellent ingenuity ; but, in the frequent passages where he imitates Lucretius, the contrast between a poet and a rhetorician is made only more glaring by archaic diction. The episode of Andromeda and Perseus in the fifth book, and a passage on human reason in the second, were once greatly admired. To show him at his best, however, I should rather take one of those places where he expresses more simply a feeling of wonder and awe common to every age.' Jebb then quotes a few lines of which it is sufficient to say that their substance is far more powerfully expressed by Cicero in the *prose* of his dialogue *De Natura Deorum*. As a work of science, then, the poem would have been better if written without the trammels of verse ; as a work of poetry it is no great matter. And yet such is the glamour of antiquity, and such the strength of the tradition that poetry should teach, this work, from the day when it was unearthed by Poggio Bracciolini in the fifteenth-century down, as we have seen, to the time of Bentley in the eighteenth, was regarded as of transcendent merit ; and even when perceived to be dead it yet spoke. It was, I doubt not, the memory of Macer and the repute of Manilius that led Cowley, a man of genius within limits, to waste his own time and some of the time of a few readers, over his interminable books ' Of Plants.'

Whether Ovid's *Art of Love* is exactly a didactic poem or not—it would certainly be as well if it found but few to obey its teachings—I do not know : but it is assuredly of the *genre ;* and it is probably Ovid's best, as it is his most characteristic, piece. None, at any rate, can deny its amazing cleverness, or its enormous vogue : its influence is to be seen in all sorts of places and in the most varied times. It is possible that Ovid would not have written it if he had known that it would banish him to Tomi ; and I am pretty sure he would have cancelled it if he could have foreseen that it would be imitated by so contemptible a writer as Dr. William King. In any case, astonishingly brilliant as it is, it is no more poetry, in the strict sense of the word, than Butler's *Hudibras.*

I pass to another didactic poem, which, with hardly the exception even of the *Georgics,* has made a profounder impression on subsequent literature than any other in this kind. Horace's *Art of Poetry* it is almost impossible to discuss in cold blood, for nearly every line of it is so familiar, much of it is so sagacious, and its author has such a knack of making his reader a personal friend, that it seems a kind of sacrilege to dissect his writings. But the attempt shall be made. *The Art of Poetry* is certainly not itself an example of the art it describes. It is a versified letter, and nothing more : and it is less of a poem than a dozen others of Horace's versified letters that might be chosen. Nor is it a good *treatise*. Whether founding or not on the essay of the Greek critic Neoptolemus, Horace keeps no order, no proportion ; he avails himself to the full of the letter-writer's privilege of digression, and he omits whole subjects that ought to come under his theme, including the most important of all, that imagination which the world is unanimous in holding the one necessary ingredient of poetry. The epistle, then, falls between two stools. It pleases, because Horace's good sense saves him from indulging in lofty flights, and because under it all we feel the character of the man, but it does not please as poetry : and it fails to satisfy as a dissertation. I have no doubt that the work of Neoptolemus, if we could recover it, would be found far more thorough and, within the limits possible to the Alexandrian school, more comprehensive.

To pass over certain medieval performances that might be named, it was in the Renaissance time that the full tide of didactics swept over poetry ; and it was then that the example set by Horace began to be most strenuously followed. We may perhaps call Fracastoro's famous medical pastoral a mimicry, at some removes, of Nicander ; but Vida's *Art of Poetry* is Horace all over. This work, which gained for its author posthumous praise from the youthful Pope, and during life the more substantial reward of a wealthy bishopric, is, with possibly a single exception, the best known of all sixteenth-century Latin poems ; and, if by ' elegance ' is meant ingenuity and skill in the Latin language, it deserves the epithet ' elegant ' which has been so often given to it. But the *Game of Chess* is perhaps still more famous, as it is more original and still more ingenious. It is one of the first in a whole *genre* of literature : that in which the forms and phraseology of the poetry are applied, in semi-serious fashion, to a comparatively trivial subject. It differs from deliberate burlesque in that it is didactic after the style of the *Georgics :* a careful student will learn from it, if not how to defeat Capablanca, yet a very fair acquaintance with the game as it was played in Vida's time. It has a considerable value to lovers of English literature ; for there is no doubt that Pope, who imitated the *Art of Poetry* in the *Essay on Criticism*, had an eye on the *Game of Chess* when he described, in the *Rape of the Lock*, that game of ombre which has been actually played over since, and found correct at every turn.

That Vida was a very clever man is obvious enough ; and even those who cannot judge his cleverness at first hand may be willing to admit it on the authority of Pope. What Pope did not know about cleverness is not worth knowing. But cleverness does not make poetry : it is often antithetic to it : and, in these writings, the didactic spirit is saved from wearisomeness only by an ingenuity which is a bar to our *poetic* enjoyment. We shall see, ere long, what happens when the ingenuity gives place to mere pedantry, and when the attempt to be poetical leads but to a frigid mimicry of poetical devices and mannerisms. It is, as a rule, only when the author abandons the pretence to be a poet, and gives himself up to ingenuity pure and simple, that the reader can find pleasure in him : a pleasure like that which one receives from a skilfully-contrived puzzle or parody, but far removed from that given by the least ambitious of true lyrics or the least sublime of true odes.

With the *Art Poétique* of Boileau we have a new outburst of this kind of didactic verse. By an important coincidence this work appeared at a moment when France, under her great monarch, dominated the world of politics and the world of fashion. Boileau was to give her the domination in the world of literature also ; and his reign was to survive the catastrophe of Blenheim by at least eighty years. His poem rapidly crossed the Channel, and very soon asserted as strong a supremacy in England as in its native land : indeed, Charles and James were less decidedly vassals of Louis than Dryden and his followers were vassals of Boileau. It had, of course, long been known that this influence was wide, deep, and lasting : Boileau's subjects themselves made no secret of their allegiance : but its full depth and width were not understood till the remarkable book of Professor Clark appeared in 1925. I must refer my readers to that book for a complete survey of the Boileau cult in England : but a few details it may be worth while to give here.

Boileau's *Art* came out in 1674. In 1680 it was translated, or rather paraphrased, by Sir William Soame, who had the invaluable assistance of Dryden as reviser. The method adopted was to keep closely to the original in theoretic passages, but to substitute English names for French where Boileau had given concrete illustrations. Thus for Villon, Desportes, Malherbe we read Fairfax, Davenant, Waller. Nothing, by the way, could show more clearly that this ' poetry ' is but versified prose than a comparison

s

between the lines on Waller which Dryden contributed
to Soame and his words in the Epistle Dedicatory to
the *Rival Ladies* :

> Waller came last, but was the first whose art
> Just weight and measure did to verse impart :
> That of a well-placed word could teach the force,
> And showed for poetry a nobler course.
> His happy genius did our tongue refine,
> And easy words with pleasing numbers join.

The Epistle has : ' But the excellence and dignity of
rhyme were never fully known till Mr. Waller taught it:
he first made writing easily an art ; first showed us
to conclude the sense most commonly in distichs,
which, in the verse of those before him, runs on for
so many lines together, that the reader is out of
breath to overtake it.'

Soame was immensely influential.   Dr. Clark has
pointed out innumerable passages in which Pope and
Young have not merely followed his general maxims,
but borrowed his very words.   The famous lines in the
Essay on Criticism,

> You then whose judgment the right course would steer,
> Know well each ancient's proper character ;
> His fable, subject, scope in every page,
> Religion, country, genius of his age,

are but Soame made more lively :

> Keep to each man his proper character ;
> Of countries and of times the humours know ;
> From different climates different customs grow :

while the still more famous

> True wit is Nature to advantage dressed,
> What oft was thought, but ne'er so well expressed,

is, significantly enough, stolen from the *prose* of Boileau, to which Pope had been led by the study of Soame : ' Qu'est-ce qu'une pensée neuve, brillante, extraordinaire ? Ce n'est point, comme se le persuadent les ignorants, une pensée que personne n'a jamais sue, et que quelqu'un s'avise le premier d'exprimer. Un bon mot n'est bon mot qu'en ce qu'il dit une chose que chacun pensait, et qu'il la dit d'une manière vive, fine, et nouvelle.'

The Second Epistle of Young, again, is well described by Clark as a sort of little ' Art of Poetry ' modelled on Boileau's more comprehensive treatise.

But this form of didactic verse was in the air, and might have flourished even if Boileau had never written. At the very moment at which Soame's work appeared, Roscommon and Oldham were bringing out versified paraphrases of Horace ; and Oldham had, apparently, anticipated Dryden in using English characters to illustrate the Horatian maxims. For the ' mediocribus esse poetis ' he gives us

> Whoe'er will please, must please us to the height :
> He must a Cowley or a Flecknoe be,
> For there's no second-rate in poetry :

and his doctors, lawyers, and preachers are Willis, Selden, Sprat, Tillotson.

Such versified treatises as these, running back as they do to Horace and perhaps to Neoptolemus, dealt in ' poetry ' with poetry : but they naturally led to treatises on other subjects. There is a close alliance between letters like Horace's epistles and the ' hodgepodge ' which the Romans called satire, in which any subject that happened to turn up was discussed. In Horace's satires are, every now and then, small

informal essays which remind us of Addison's. When
once the *Ars Poetica* had been imitated, it was inevitable that the satires should fall under review; and
when the satires were imitated, essays on any subject
that happened to be interesting would be undertaken.
The Satires of Oldham, from which I have just quoted,
contain many of these miniature discourses. In the
hands of Dryden, Pope, and others, these became more
ambitious and far-reaching. Of them all, in my
opinion, the best is the *Religio Laici*, which, as Dryden
himself tells us in his preface, is really a letter. It
was, in fact, addressed to Henry Dickinson, 'an ingenious young gentleman' who had translated Father
Simon's *Critical History of the Old Testament*: and
Dryden's words are well worthy of quotation:

'The verses are addressed to the translatour of that
work, and the style of them is, what it ought to be,
epistolary. If any one be so lamentable a critic as to
require the smoothness, the numbers, and the turn of
heroic poetry in this poem, I must tell him that, if he
has not read Horace, I have studied him, and hope the
style of his epistles is not ill imitated here. The expressions of a poem designed purely for instruction
ought to be plain and natural, and yet majestic: for
here the poet is presumed to be a kind of lawgiver;
and those three qualities which I have named are
proper to the legislative style. The florid, elevated,
and figurative way is for the passions; for love and
hatred, fear and anger, are begotten in the soul by
showing their objects out of their true proportion,
either greater than the life or less; but instruction
is to be given by showing them what they naturally
are. A man is to be cheated into passion, but to be
reasoned into truth.'

In accordance with these principles, Dryden has in this poem given us an astonishing example of skill in the art of reasoning in rhyme ; and it was with a true conception of his own powers that he undertook and carried through his task. That his success was at once perceived to be great is shown, if by nothing else, by the number of attempts in the same kind which were afterwards made. When Dryden himself became a Papist, his masters called on him to do the same service to his new church as he had done to the old. The result was the *Hind and the Panther*, which, though in form a somewhat clumsy allegory, is really a theological dissertation, crossed here and there with some political allusions. From these two poems sprang the *Essay on Man* and one or two of Young's disquisitions, some of which are even more brilliant than Dryden's, and inferior to his only in their less skilful reasoning and mastery of their subject. The *Essay on Man*, in particular, though deplorable as a piece of consecutive thinking, and well deserving both to be explained away by Warburton and to be ridiculed by Lessing, still lives by its epigrammatic force, and has probably supplied more material to the makers of dictionaries of quotations than any other work of similar size. How strong has been its hold on the literary mind is shown by the numberless attempts made to achieve a similar success. I need mention only Gray's fragment on the *Alliance of Education and Government* and Mrs. Browning's *Essay on Mind*. Gray, of course, never completed the task—how many of his plans did he complete ?—but even as it stands it is worthy of comparison with *Religio Laici* itself, and far superior in ordered thought to its Popian model. ' Instead of compiling tables of chronology and natural history,' says Gibbon, 'why did not Mr. Gray apply the powers of his genius to finish the philosophic poem of which he has left such an exquisite specimen ? ' The reason is twofold. Not only was Gray a student first and a poet afterwards—more truly interested in ' chronology and natural history ' than in creative work—but he was, in taste, a romantic. He was reaching out beyond prose-poetry to what was to come later, and saw in the untutored work of Welsh and Norse bards a more genuine inspiration than in all the work of the classicists put together. He did not actually receive the promises, but he greeted them from afar. Similar reasons, as we have already seen, prevented him from finishing his Latin poem, *De Principiis Cogitandi*, in which he found plenty of exercise for his philosophic and trained intellect, but little scope for the struggling poetic impulses of his soul. As for Mrs. Browning's performance, it was a youthful effort ; but it is a curious example of the survival of the Popian influence into an age that might be imagined to have got rid of it altogether. It is the child dressing up in the fashion of its grandmother.

But theology and poetry itself are far from being the only themes with which ' poetry ' can deal ; and the *servum pecus*, those who shout with the crowd, were quick to seize their chance. Every little coterie was, at that time, like Pembroke College in Johnson's undergraduate days, a nest, if not of singing-birds, yet of parrots.   Time would fail to enumerate the number of themes, dragged from all corners, which these writers chose to handle in pedagogic style, but usually without the expert knowledge of the pedagogue. Some of their verses have little more merit than the *Propria quae maribus* which they had learnt at school. Nearly all show what a dreadful result can be attained when a vocabulary, consecrated by the use of a great man, is taken up by little men. Philips's *Cider* we know on the authority of Johnson to have satisfied a practical expert. ' I was told by Miller, the great gardener and botanist,' says Johnson, ' that there were many books written on the same subject in prose, which do not contain so much truth as that poem.' Philips certainly knew his subject, and he knew his Milton; but he did not know how to transfer the style of his idol from the Garden of Eden to the West-country orchards. The opening lines might be taken as a continuation of his Miltonic parody, the *Splendid Shilling* :

> What soil the Apple loves, what care is due
> To orchats, timeliest when to press the fruits,
> Thy gift, Pomona ! In Miltonian verse
> Advent'rous I presume to sing, of verse
> Nor skill'd nor studious ; but my native soil
> Invites me, and the theme, as yet unsung.

He was urged, then, to this task by the sense that no previous poets had thought the subject fit for poetry—and they were right.

There is good advice in Armstrong's *Art of Preserving Health*, which was first published in the year of Pope's death :

> But other ills the ambiguous feast pursue,
> Besides provoking the lascivious taste.
> Such various foods, though harmless each alone,
> Each other violate, and oft we see
> What strife is brew'd, and what pernicious bane
> From combinations of innoxious things.
> Th' unbounded taste I mean not to confine
> To hermit's Diet needlessly severe ;
> But would you long the sweets of Health enjoy
> Or husband pleasure, at one impious meal
> Exhaust not half the bounties of the year.

Whether the Thomsonian diction of this poem was entirely approved by the world is doubtful; for Armstrong assures us that the works he had lost or destroyed would probably have been better received by the public than anything he had published. I do not, therefore, choose the *Art of Preserving Health* as a type of popular taste ; and the less so as Armstrong has himself written an epistle on the subject, in which he expresses a sound contempt for the opinion of the ' Mobility ' :

> Have you not seen the angel of salvation
> Appear sublime, with wise and solemn tap
> To teach the doubtful rabble when to clap ?
> The rabble knows not where our dramas shine,
> But where the cane goes pat—" By G—, that's fine! " . . .
> Zounds, shall a pert or bluff important wight,
> Whose brain is fanciless, whose blood is white,
> A mumbling ape of Taste, prescribe us laws
> To judge us poets for no better cause
> Than that he boasts *per ann.* ten thousand clear,
> Yelps in the House, or barely sits a peer ?

No lover of nature would speak harshly of John Dyer, a true poet, and an estimable man, who is remarkable as one of the few who in the Popian age resisted the Popian influence. Even after *L'Allegro, Grongar Hill* can charm : and I confess to finding sublimity in the *Ruins of Rome*. But, despite the praise of Wordsworth, I could wish that Dyer had left the *Fleece* alone. ' How,' said Johnson, ' can a man write poetically of serges and druggets ? ' The poem is long : it pursues the fleece all the way from the sheep's back, through all the processes of Bradford manufacture, to the farthest wilds of America and Asia : and, as if it were not long enough already, indulges in digressions on countries whose only connection with

the subject is that they do *not* produce the fleece.
One is reminded of the schoolboy, who, being asked
for an account of Thomas Cromwell, and knowing
nothing of him, produced a life of the Protector,
ending up with the statement, ' But, as Thomas Cromwell was not the same as Oliver, some of my remarks
may seem irrelevant.' Dyer was buried in woollen
before he was dead. Yet there can be little doubt that
there were not a few to whom his work appealed :
Johnson tells us, ' You will hear many people who will
talk to you gravely of that *excellent* poem *The Fleece.*'
There was obviously a taste for didacticism in 1750.

Both the poems and the critical judgments of William
Somerville illustrate that uncertainty of the standard
which warns us all against dogmatism. He was unquestionably an able man ; yet he had the lowest
opinion of Chaucer, and held that Addison had as
much genius as Shakespeare with more art. As for his
own works, they were for long very popular. One of
his couplets received from Johnson the tribute of
unqualified admiration—a rare thing indeed from the
unenthusiastic sage. Allan Ramsay compares his Muse
to Pindar's, and vows that if Pope had written the
Bowling Green he would have won more fame than
by the *Rape of the Lock*.

> Sir, I have read and much admire
>   Your Muse's gay and easy flow ;
> Warm'd with that true Idalian fire
>   That gives the bright and cheerful glow.
> I conn'd each line with joyous care,
>   As I can such from sun to sun,
> And, like the glutton o'er his fare,
>   Delicious, thought them too soon done.

There were other admirers besides Ramsay. Edition
after edition of the poems was called for, and for at

least seventy years Somerville was never omitted from a collection of the ' Poets.' Yet what would be thought to-day of a man who could improve David's lament over Jonathan into eighty lines of Popian couplets, of which this is a specimen ?

> How wonderful his love ! the kindest dame
> Lov'd not like him, nor felt so warm a flame.

Somerville's chief claim to immortality is the *Chase*, in four books and two thousand lines of blank verse ; which has been illustrated by Stothard and Hugh Thomson, and is still known to the curious. It is in places vigorously descriptive, and has the merit of being inspired by a true love of its subject. But it is, of course, didactic : the times demanded that verse should instruct. We are told how to breed hounds, how many to keep and how many to destroy ; how to choose ' the dog of great moment ' ; how to set traps ; how the tiger was once hunted with a mirror, and how the Arabs hunt the boar : all this variegated with praises of Frederick Prince of Wales, and eulogies of mercy, which Gray honoured by imitating them in his *Inaugural Ode*. But Somerville, on the whole, sticks to his subject. When he thinks he has digressed long enough, he cries, ' Hence to the kennel, Muse,' and learnedly informs us what to do if a hound gets rabies. A comparison between this poem and Masefield's *Reynard the Fox* would be a good theme for a doctorate-dissertation : which would cover the whole distance between the eighteenth and the twentieth centuries, and would mark the irresistible force exerted upon a man by the time in which he lives. He would be a bold man who, taking a comprehensive survey of periods, environments, and changes of taste,

would give the palm of genius to the writer of to-day.
To judge fairly, however, would demand an almost
superhuman detachment : for if the poet is under the
influence of his own surroundings, so, and probably in
an even greater degree, is the critic. Suffice it to say
that there is no reason to think ourselves in any way
superior to the man who, representing the ideas of his
own time, addressed Somerville in the lines :

> Thy genius in such colours paints the chase,
> The real to fictitious joys give place.

And now—though there are innumerable other
samples that might be collected, from French, German,
and Italian literature—how can I end better than with
the immortal *Sugar-cane?* Few have read it, but there
are not many who are ignorant of the stupendous line
that once adorned it—' Now, Muse, let's sing of rats.'
Still fewer will to-day hold that the published version
is a real improvement :

> Nor with less waste the whiskered vermin race,
> A countless clan, despoil the lowland cane.

The inevitable reaction came. It is interesting to
note that one of the chief charges brought against
Pope by Thomas Warton, who was a herald of the
coming romantic dawn, was that Pope was almost
invariably didactic. But it was by no means always
the half-romantics who set themselves against *this*
aspect of Popianism. Thomson, Dyer, Akenside—to
take but two or three examples, were as didactic in
their way as Pope in his, nor was Gray less so : and
Wordsworth himself was quite as much of a pedagogue
as Pope, if less lively. The fact is that a classicist need
not be didactic, nor need a romanticist dislike didacticism. We are seeing to-day a reaction in favour of

the classicists, but so far there is little sign we are to expect a *Fleece* or *Chase*. Preaching of all kinds is out of favour—except in the drama. Nevertheless, if the past is any guide to the future, it is probable that ere very long we shall be reading sermons in odes and lessons in ballads, while the theatre will be sought for mere emotional excitement.

XIV

ART FOR ART'S SAKE

DIAMETRICALLY opposed to the theory that poetry, directly or indirectly, should teach, which leads, in its extreme form, to such eccentricities as those I have described, is the theory that poetry should be an end in itself. This is the interpretation, in a new sense, of Plato's well-known dictum that there is ' an ancient antagonism between poetry and philosophy ' ; and it declares that, after the long-continued strife, the two combatants must retire ten kilometres within their respective boundaries. Carried to its logical issue, it implies that form is everything and matter nothing : that to give body to a poem is to degrade it, and that true poetry is to be attained only as, in some religions, salvation is to be attained, by the sheer annihilation of ' sense.' This, more or less consistently and uncompromisingly held, is the theory known as ' Art for Art's Sake,' which has been widely and strenuously defended not only with regard to poetry but also with regard to the other arts. It arises with tolerable regularity as a reaction against the excess of didacticism. Such a poem as *Festus* naturally provokes a reaction of the kind ; for it becomes pretty plain after a time that most of what *Festus* says would be less wearisome in prose. The ' preaching ' of Thackeray, with which Taine found so much fault, engenders a school of mere story-tellers ; the moralising historians are succeeded

by calm and colourless narrators of mere facts, and it is
the pride of an Anglican Bishop that his *History of the
Papacy* is read without repugnance in the Vatican
itself : while, in general, 'tendency-writings' no
sooner reach their zenith than they are displaced in
favour of the fancied impartiality of plain statement.
But in no art is this swing of the pendulum more
clearly marked than in poetry. We find a faint example
of this vibration even in the Attic drama. Æschylus
undoubtedly meant to teach, as openly as a Hebrew
prophet : Sophocles kept his own opinions in the background : Euripides used plays as a means of propaganda : and after an interval came the harmless and
unprovocative art of Menander.

There is unquestionably a certain plausibility in this
theory, even though driven pretty far, when applied to
such arts as sculpture or music, the toughness or
vagueness of the medium employed being an obvious bar
to the attempt to convey a distinct 'message.' It takes
some forcing to see in the 'Dying Gaul' a cry to the
Goths to glut their ire and destroy their oppressor :
and no philosophical lesson can easily be learnt from
the 'Laocoon.' When music tries to pursue a 'programme' it is usually less impressive than when it
confines itself to its natural functions. It is open to
argument, also, that the moralising of such a painter
as Hogarth diminishes the pure worth of his artistry.
Not that even in these cases there is not something
to be said on the other side : and we may be sure that
Hogarth would have said it with vigour and emphasis.
But grant the utmost that can be demanded : admit
that sculpture, music, and painting must elevate the
mind not by direct exhortation, but by the sublimation
of the senses : there remain many arts to which the

theory will not easily apply. There are few, for example, who would for a moment allow it in the art of cookery, or who would accept the doctrine that the eating is no proof of the pudding. Let gastronomy be as ethereal as Brillat-Savarin could wish : the last word is not with the cook. And, though there have been generals who would rather lose artistically than win clumsily, the majority of people, and not least their own armies, dislike an artistry so exquisite that it leads to invariable defeat. An art of logic, it is true, can be and has been constructed without reference to content. Schoolmen have delighted in ' conversions,' ' figures,' and ' moods ' in which mere symbols are manipulated like pieces on a chess-board ; and much ingenuity has been displayed in these manipulations. But the great mass of people, and many logicians, contend for the application of these rules to something other than symbols, and hold the view that unless the art is thus capable of being put into practice, and made to work from ' material ' premisses to ' material ' con-clusions, it is a mere exhibit in an intellectual museum : otherwise most men but cast a glance at it and pass on. Mankind is not interested in x : it begins to care for it only on recognising the something definite which it stands for. ' Formal ' logic, then, always remained a toy of the schools, and not till Mill and others called it down into the market-place did it begin to exert a real influence.

There is no great harm in being a toy of the schools. But poetry is emphatically not for the schools ; it is for the world or it is nothing. The world may be large or small, but it is never a mere coterie of experts. A poem is not a villanelle or virelay written to show a technical skill which can be appreciated only as a chess-game is appreciated by men who themselves play chess : it appeals to emotions which all men may not be experiencing now, but which all men are capable of experiencing. When a prisoner like Charles of Orleans amuses himself with complicated patterns of verse, he is saving himself from ennui, but he is not producing poetry, any more than the fashionable idlers of Martial's time were writing poetry when they worked out their laborious Sotadeans and palindromes. Martial, not himself the most serious of poets, nevertheless knew what to think of men like these :

> Turpe est difficiles habere nugas,
> Et stultus labor est ineptiarum.

I should imagine that no school of versifiers ever carried this pretty trifling further than some of the Provençal troubadours. I cannot here speak from first-hand knowledge. I have not read troubadour poetry. But those who have read it assure me it is unreadable. The poet without an audience is not even a voice crying in the wilderness : he is Aeneas staring at a ghost, stupefied : ' et vox faucibus haesit.'

But again, the medium of poetry is words, and where words are the medium the theory can never be maintained in any but the most limited sense. The slightest consideration will show that though poetry is in part music, it can never, like music, be a ' pure ' art, defecated of all ' matter.' Nor can you work it, as mathematics may at times be worked, with bare tokens, the significance of which is forgotten throughout a long process, and recovered, if at all, only at the end. Words are signs for *something*, and you cannot keep that something out of them : they instantly call up a picture. They have, in fact, meanings, and the

meanings inevitably start up whenever you hear them
spoken or see them written. They are neither mere
sounds nor mere impressions on paper. If I write the
word ' dome,' the reader at once discerns a dome, and
cannot help discerning it : if it is misprinted ' home,'
though the loss in sound may be negligible, he is embarrassed and troubled. To speak in ' form ' without
conveying ' matter ' is impossible : it is to reduce
speech to a meaningless ' Kentish fire.' But more than
this. Meanings are not mere dictionary-significations :
they carry besides whole atmospheres of suggestion
and association, and are a large, if not the chief, element
in the beauty or ugliness of the words. Whether in
' denotation ' or in ' connotation '—to use the familiar
phrases of the logicians—the words, even singly, and
far more when ' bound in the bundle of life ' to form
clauses and sentences, are charged with a power that
is only dimly represented by their sounds or by their
appearances on paper. It is perhaps conceivable that
you may draw a beautiful picture which shall correspond to no known thing, as it is certainly possible to
write a sonata without any content but itself. But
words are winged—they are carrier-pigeons bearing
messages of which they know nothing. Even if you
write sheer nonsense, the individual words call up
pictures ; if they did not, you would not get as far
even as nonsense : it would be utter vacuity. Nonsense itself, to be itself, must arouse at least a momentary idea that it is sense. Should you try to make
a beautiful line by stringing together a set of ' beautiful ' words, you must, first, take the meanings of the
separate words into account, and then consider
whether the associations of the combination are pleasurable : for the same sound may be beautiful in one

T

sense and ugly in another, and the same word may be
beautiful in one setting and repulsive in another.
There is a purposed snarl in Horace's ' rem, facias
rem,' and an exquisite pathos in Virgil's ' sunt lacrimae
rerum.' Nothing, probably, would be uglier than
verses consisting exclusively of ' beautiful ' words thus
combined : we should be annoyed by the disappointed
expectation, and resent the deception : like the
Eastern travellers ; ' we should be ashamed because
we had hoped.' All the beauty that lies in the meaning
would be lost, and the reader's disgust would be pro-
portionate to his disenchantment.

If, by some gigantic jest of the Spirit of Language,
a word now denoting some sublime or beautiful thing
should exchange its denotation with a low or ugly
thing—if, for example, ' scavenger ' should come to
mean ' the right honourable gentleman ' and *vice
versa*—in a short time the noble word would become
ignoble and the ignoble noble : and if words are used
without meaning they become at best indifferent.
The poet of mere ' form,' then, cannot help giving us
' matter ' as well. If, in his endeavour to give us ' pure '
form, he does violence to the ' matter,' he defeats his
own end, for he inevitably arouses in us the disgust
which is the sign that he has produced ugliness instead
of beauty. If, *per impossibile*, he contrives to give us
no-meaning, he has robbed himself of the chief engine
for arousing in us the pleasure which is the proof of
beauty.

I shall be met, of course, with plausible examples to
the contrary. A German might bring forward some
poems of Platen, in which the beauty is undoubted,
but which seem to rely on mere sound. An Englishman will confront me with *Kubla Khan*, the charm of

which is ' pure music,' divorced from palpable content, as spiritual as a dream of Ariel when he sleeps under the hawthorn that hangs on the bough. But even here, if we look closely, we shall find that the beauty is far from being merely born of murmuring sound. Every word conveys a meaning by its power *as* a word, and that meaning is the beauty. Every sentence conveys a meaning *as* a sentence, and that meaning is its beauty. The mere *sound* of ' pleasure-dome ' is little, without the whole fairyland of romance and gramarye which it recalls, without the sense of a vast empire and of an immemorial past which it stirs in our brain. Substitute words with the same scansion, but without the associations, and the poem falls in ruin, the horns of Elf-land cease to blow, and all vanishes like Prospero's cloud-capped towers. It is because we can form a picture corresponding with the poet's vision, which he has expressed to us in his words, that the poem is beautiful : it is, in fact, because the poem is *not* mere art for art's sake.

Nor, even is the case of certain so-called Nonsense-verses, such as those of Edward Lear and some others, really dissimilar. These, as few would deny, give a real artistic pleasure, without making any attempt to justify the ways of God to man or to lift the veil of familiarity from the world and show the one within the manifold. That pleasure springs, in reading Lear, largely from the illusion created by the poet that there *is* a meaning in the words, though somehow we have missed it. The nonsense-words are so skilfully presented, so admirably set in sentences which might be quite rational, that for a moment we accept them as part of our normal vocabulary. For that moment they have a meaning and therefore a beauty. When we discover that we have been deceived, the pleasure is that of a cheated memory. We retain the enjoyment of having, for a transient interval, been admitted into a 'material' world of which we had not suspected the existence. It is a new fairyland ; but a fairyland is not a mere unsubstantial dream: it is our own land with the hedges and notices to trespassers removed. Children, to whom it is as real as the workaday world, therefore continue to enjoy Lear as fully as if there were no make-believe in his poetry.

With Lewis Carroll's nonsense-verses—if I may dwell on this theme for a little—the pleasure we receive is of a totally different kind : and it is possible to maintain that it is not poetic at all. As with his whole method, his nonsense-verses are *constructed* : they consist in pushing some logical or mathematical proposition into a corner. He plays with words as he plays with equations, and teases us with the sort of fallacies which delighted the Eleatics and the schoolmen. Every one of his illusions is Achilles and the Tortoise over again, applied to incidents, to people, to ideas. In his verses he applies it to words. What we have to do with those words is to solve a little ingenious problem. Lear's ' Pobble that has no toes ' raises a momentary *picture* in our minds : ' 'Twas brilling and the slithy toves ' sets us a little sum to do. There is then in Lewis Carroll no example of ' form ' without ' matter ': the matter is the essence of the interest. Neither Lear nor Carroll can be fairly adduced as an example of ' pure ' poetry.

Very few, however, would carry the theory of Art for Art's Sake so far as this, or would reduce poetry to a series of musical sounds or a string of more or less mathematical symbols. The conception, when it gains any vogue, is rather that of a kind of impartiality, an Olympian superiority to creeds, or a still loftier 'highbrow' aloofness. As, in this view, the historian ought to set down the actions of his heroes without passing any sort of moral judgment upon them, or founding any political theory on their success or failure, his business being simply that of an orderly and artistic recorder, so with poetry. Ethics to the philosopher, politics to the publicist: to the poet the actual theme is nothing, the character of his vision of no importance. We have no more right to ask of him that his theme shall be ennobling than we have to ask of the historian that his generals and statesmen shall be Havelocks and Turgots. The *how* is everything, the *what* is indifferent. Let the poet have his vision, and let him but describe it in the most appropriate words he can find: there his duty ceases. To the moralist, the poet's subject may be moral, immoral, or 'amoral'; to the writer and the reader all that is beside the purpose. A clear vision, and an adequate presentation of the vision, that is all he or we need trouble about. When Milton spent years in searching for his 'great argument,' he was wasting his time. A trivial one, dressed in such language, and adorned with such rhythm, as Milton could command, would have been as satisfactory as *Paradise Lost*. It was 'a crushed necessity' for Dante to go thin and pale as he wrestled with the enormous drama he had undertaken. Put the same ornaments, the same metrical harmonies, at the service of a theme like that of the *Romance of the Rose*, and we shall have as good a poem as the *Divine Comedy* at a tenth of the cost. All that learning, Virgilian or Thomist, is not merely no addition to the worth of the poem, but, properly considered, a subtraction from it.

Now art thus chosen for its own sake, and pursued without turning to the right hand or to the left, is capable of raising man to great heights. I am far from denying that some men who have thus followed it, as Merlin followed the Gleam, have reached a kind of ecstasy of holy pleasure to be paralleled only in the visions of the saints. For a description of such ecstasy, given by one who had unquestionably experienced it, I can but refer the reader to the concluding chapter of Pater's *Renaissance :* which to me is the *ne plus ultra* of Pater's writing. It is curious, like all of Pater, and it is enigmatic, like most of him : it rouses strange conjectures in the reader. But it shows how, in the right mind and interpreted in the widest fashion, this doctrine can enlarge the soul and take possession of a man until he is indeed possessed.

The interval between this moment and nonentity is short. 'Some spend that interval in listlessness, some in high passions, the wisest, at least among the children of this world, in art and song. For our one chance lies in expanding that interval, in getting as many pulsations as possible into the given time. Great passions may give us this quickened sense of life, ecstasy and sorrow of love, the various forms of enthusiastic activity, disinterested or otherwise, which come naturally to many of us. Only be sure that it *is* passion—that it *does* yield you this fruit of a quickened, multiplied consciousness. Of such wisdom, the poetic passion, the desire of beauty, the love of art for its own sake, has most. For art comes to you, proposing to give nothing but the highest quality to your moments as they pass, and simply for those moments' sake.'

In the face of such testimony I would scarcely maintain that the doctrine, understood in the widest sense, is wholly false. And when I recall the 'intervals' of astonishing pleasure which I have myself enjoyed in reading such passages as some of De Quincey's prose poems—passages in which it would be hard to find a distinct meaning, but which yet disturb us with the sense of elevated imagination, pages of Blake, Jacob Boehme, or Swedenborg, in which the rapture soars far beyond my comprehension, some paragraphs even of Jeremy Taylor or Wordsworth—when I recall these, I confess that art without any end beyond itself may yet have some great purpose.

And yet, when I return to earth I have my doubts, and I cease to agree with Keats that the world of common sense is one to be fled from. There is something in poetry that teaches after all ; and a life lived for art alone is too selfish to satisfy.

As I have said, this doctrine is by no means a new one. It seems bound to appear and predominate at intervals as men tire of the wisdom of their fathers, and the children rise up and call them cursed. We find it, in a form conditioned by its age, in the Alexandrian era : and it coincides in time, not unnaturally, with the formation of large libraries, when men could see all too easily that a great book was a great evil. Callimachus, himself a librarian, must have been struck with the heaviness of many of the books for which he had to find houseroom. His own works should not sin in that way. He and his school, a powerful band, would certainly have agreed with the young men of the Nineties, and would have found a good deal to say for themselves in very eloquent words. They, too, had their moralising Idylls and their Brownings with *La Saisiaz* and *Christmas Eve*, to be packed away on the upper shelves. They might have said, and truly, that there is nothing to indicate, in a poet as such, the possession of any remarkable power of exact thinking or of any special store of accurate knowledge. For that, you go elsewhere. It was a commonplace that Homer gave a very uncivilised system of theology, and Plato had shown that Simonides was a very unsafe guide in matters of philosophy. On the other hand, when men who *did* know tried their hand at poetry, the result was pitiful. Empedocles, for example, was a trained physicist, but he needed to go to school again if he wished to be a poet. Callimachus and his followers, therefore, declined to mingle poetry with either fact or theory. They made a profound study of the technique of the art, and, if we may believe their own countrymen, attained an unsurpassed skill in the practice of that technique. They were like musicians of superlative executant ability ; and they both wrote and played scales and studies with amazing dexterity. As poets, they were resolved to seek one thing only, beauty of form. They recognised, of course, that poetry is not music, and needs substance to give it not merely coherence but existence ; it must have a theme and express it. But matter should be reduced to its proper place, and stay there ; and didactic should be sent to *its* proper place—across the border. If I write a eulogy of Berenice, said Callimachus, there shall be as much mythology as you like, but there shall never be any doubt that the mythology *is* mythological—machinery, ornament, or what you will, but as removable as the gold on Phidias's image of Athene : and the man will be a fool who takes it seriously. A natural consequence follows. As a vision swims rapidly away, the description must be short. The long poem, in which the intervals are filled up with episodes, or with passages more suitable for prose, is a contradiction in terms. The episode, in fact, *is* the poem, complete in itself and needing no help from surroundings. Here, curiously enough, Callimachus and his school meet the modern school, whose ideas have been fully enough expressed, once for all, by Edgar Allan Poe.

There is no need to say that some very pleasing poems have been written on such a system. Nor need one deny that the insistence on artistry is often a very desirable corrective for poets who, relying on native genius, become careless of the ' rules.' But, considering the whole movement broadly, and allowing for the exceptions that must be made in every generalisation, we shall perhaps not be unfair in saying that such a conception is really a confession of weakness. An art is surely something directed to an end : and to say that the end is to be the art itself seems to be a defiance of its definition. If the advocates of this system desire their poems to please, then their art must be one of the arts for pleasure's sake ; and they must define in what way it differs from other pleasure-giving arts ; that is, they must define poetry, which cannot be simply defined as an art to please itself. If they mean the poet is to write to please *himself*, they are welcome to their definition ; but it is well known that poets, as they are easily annoyed by criticism, are easily pleased with their own works. Hence we usually find this theory arising among those who, not having a wide range of reading or experience, are easily satisfied with performances of their own. It is the theory of irresponsible youth. It is adopted by those who have little power of thought either poetic or prosaic, or in ages which have the youthful quality of disliking hard, cautious, or long-continued reflection. Young writers, revolting against the ideas of their elders, periods in which, for one reason or another, mentality is stagnant—it is among these that the theory obtains sway. You do not find it when thought is making rapid strides, or when reproductive ideas, already formulated, are being classified, corrected, or enlarged. Great poetry never appears but in great and stirring ages : it is the flower on a living and spreading growth.

The theory is not a reaction against any particular school of poetry : it arises as a reaction against any school that happens to have been powerful at any time and to have spent its force. It is in itself neither classical nor anti-classical, neither romantic nor anti-romantic : it is simply the natural result of the prevalence of any poetical doctrine whatever in which the masters have utilised their genius for the purpose of impressing *themselves* upon their contemporaries. Sometimes it is scarcely a reaction : it expresses rather the decadence of the school to which it is itself attached. As theological controversy is often the expression of the decay of sincere belief, so the decline of a school is often shown by the empty continuance of the husk of a style when the kernel has rotted. As Mr. Fausset has acutely observed, ' the cultivation of form for its own sake is equally typical of Romanticism and Classicism when they are mutually exclusive, the Romantic cultivating form in detachment from actuality, the Classicist in subservience to tradition. But because Classicism is by nature merely objective, its descent into formality is often difficult to detect. Common-sense is so near to the commonplace, restraint of force to poverty of impulse, and respect for tradition to slavish imitation, that the change from life to death is, for contemporaries at least, often imperceptible.' In other words, art for art's sake, with the classicist, consists in saying again what has been said before : with the romanticist it consists in saying nothing at all. There can be little doubt that this is sometimes because the poet has nothing to say ; and the sentence to be passed is that of ' death.' The letter without the spirit is dead ; and the abundance of leaves on the barren fig-tree but provokes the just curse, ' No man take fruit of thee for ever.'

The fact remains clear after all argument that if a man has something to say, and if his natural mode of speech is the poetical, he will say it, and say it poetically. He is not going to say it in a speech which he knows is not his natural and more effective medium. As well ask him to write in a foreign tongue as ask him to forgo his native and chosen vehicle of verse. What he has learnt, he ' will teach in song.' He will feel the compelling impulse like the prophet of old—' the Lord God hath spoken, who can but prophesy ? ' and, theory or no theory, he will utter his message. It is useless to tell Wordsworth to write his *Ode to Duty* in the form of his *Convention of Cintra*, or to tell Milton that all the essentials of *Paradise Lost* are in the *Treatise on Christian Doctrine*. The teaching will out, and it will out in poetry. Hence we often find the very apostles of pure form, when they have grown older and reached years of discretion, when they have learnt something from books or from life, throwing the whole doctrine over, and pouring out ideas as fluently as the author of *Festus* himself. What they have seen and heard declare they unto the world. It would be hard to name a single poet of any eminence who, after the years have set their mark on him, has not put some substance into

his poetry, and usually more and more as his experience
has enlarged. This is eminently true of those whom the
world has agreed to consider the greatest. The
Shakespeare who, as the first heir of his mere invention,
wrote *Venus and Adonis*, gave his public art for art's
sake : nor is there an overload of didactics in *Love's
Labour's Lost*. But the author of *Lear* and *Hamlet* was
certainly not gravelled for lack of matter. The later
poems of Goethe are packed with thought as profound
as if it had been written in the crabbed prose of Kant.
Æschylus, Euripides, Dante crowded their mature
works with a very distinct philosophy. The latest
instance is one of the most impressive of all. An aged
poet of our own time, who had told us that he loved,
sought, and adored all beauteous things, and many of
whose earlier works were perhaps in too high a degree
types of pure beauty, gave us in his last poem a summary of his reasoned beliefs, a legacy of all his garnered
thoughts, a testament of his philosophy, in order that
the world might benefit by the experience of one
who had lived long in it and learnt much from it. He
did not, it is true, imitate one of his least famous
predecessors in the Laureateship, and give us a
' didactic ' poem on Tea. But he was didactic none
the less. At the risk even of preaching, this most
artistic of poets, who had spent years on the study of
the minutest technical details of his profession, resolved that his final offering to the world should not
be *mere* poetry, but a *Summa Philosophiae*, a *Religio
Medici*, and a *Confessio Poetae*.

XV

THE SENTIMENTAL

I know nothing which more clearly illustrates the variability of taste than the history of what is called 'sentimentalism'—that is, in two rough and ready words, false pathos. Where the falsehood begins and the pathos ends is a matter for the individual, and individuals will judge differently. One man's tears will be another man's laughter. Most of us will agree that the man described in Boswell, who, to console himself for the absence of his son, proposed to 'write an elegy,' was a good deal of a sentimentalist : but the stages by which such an expression of grief may pass into real pathos are very gradual, and there are points at which few people can be quite sure as to their judgments. I should imagine that there are no more truly pathetic writers than Mrs. Gaskell. Of all her writings Cardinal Newman preferred *Sylvia's Lovers*. This is the very one of her books in which, to me, the pathos appears, for once, overdone and perfunctory : yet I am far from asserting that I am right and Newman wrong.

But there are certainly times at which sentimentalism, and what may with some certainty be called so, flourishes more than at others. The pathos is wasted on trivial griefs, and the expression of it is extravagant. Even when the grief is not trivial—when it is as real as that of Andromache for Hector—there is something about the way in which it is set before us that is peculiarly repulsive to other times and manners. Not even an out-of-date kind of wit has such a capacity for nauseating as an out-of-date kind of pathos. We are specially disgusted because we feel that out best emotions are being played with. 'Had this tragedy been left to speak for itself,' we say, 'we might have wept : but this intolerable presentation of it compels us, against our will, to see the ridiculous side.' It is like the annoyance caused to a reverent man in church when a clumsy preacher forces him to laugh. Few literary pains are worse than this.

No change of taste, then, is more complete or more violent than that which takes place when the themes regarded as appropriate to pathos cease to be so regarded, or when the modes of appealing to our sympathies fall out of fashion. Utter disgust succeeds to absolute satisfaction ; and we find it all but impossible to view our ancestors with anything but contempt. And the change is sometimes remarkably sudden. A single clever sarcasm is, not rarely, sufficient to bring it about. A play sets a whole community weeping. An ingenious satirist laughs at it, and the community at once laughs with him, despising itself for having been deluded, and venting its contempt on the unhappy author. For there is nothing of which we are more ashamed than of having cried over the wrong thing.

Often, again, by virtue of the law of which I have spoken repeatedly, a man who has thus changed his opinion as to what is pathetic or sentimental, changes his opinion as to the *style* of the author concerned. Disliking or admiring what the author is saying, he dislikes or admires the way it is said. Feeling for the substance influences feeling for the manner. It is true that sentimentality cannot be called precisely the substance of the sentimental writer's message; but it is so closely interwoven with that substance, and means so much to the effect which the message tends to produce, that for my present purpose it may be considered as the same thing. What is strong enough to turn a tragedy into a farce, or a farce into a tragedy, is certainly a part of the material of the play, and is certainly distinct from the stylistic merits or defects of the language of the play. The facts which a sentimental writer adduces may be the same as those adduced by a robust or cynical one, but he gives them a turn, and applies them to an end, other than those given by his callous rival. His grouping and his selection are his own, and as contrasted with his style they may be justly called his subject-matter. And it will not seldom be found that those to whom the subject-matter—thus understood—makes a sympathetic appeal, will like the style in which it is conveyed. Conversely, if they dislike the subject-matter, they will dislike the style, or at least find fault with something allied to it.

The heyday of the sentimentalists was the eighteenth century. Unquestionably, though Richardson hardly deserves the stigma of the name, the success of his novels, which was immense both in England and on the Continent, had something to do with the prevalence of the fashion : and there are some passages, not merely in *Pamela* and in *Grandison*, but in *Clarissa* also, which are certainly mawkish and affected. There can be no doubt that it was not only the whole trend of his books, but this characteristic, which revolted the mind of Fielding, and drove him, occasionally, into a cynicism which was really foreign to his nature. At this time, also, the sentimental drama, with its sham pathos and forced tears, began its baleful reign. All know of the popularity of Kelly's *False Delicacy*, and of the difficulty with which the comedy of Goldsmith made its way against the prevailing feeling of the age. The vogue, indeed, lasted, in greater or less vigour, till the end of the century or beyond it, and was not destroyed by the triumphs of Sheridan. The plays of Cumberland reek with it ; and some of Mrs. Inchbald's, excellent in other respects, are in places marred by it. Even her novels, which have merits of a very high order, jar at times as they approach the pathetic. As for the style of the plays of that time, it is quite intolerable to ours. ' O blessed be the torrid zone for ever, whose rapid vegetation kindles nature into such benignity,' is one, and perhaps not the worst, of Cumberland's flowers of rhetoric. Yet, be it noted, this eloquence, even when put into the mouth of a young girl, was far from disgusting the audiences of the day. It was, on the contrary, admired, and these glowing passages were just the ones that brought down the house.

No name among English writers is more closely associated with sentimentalism than that of Sterne. Nor was this without intention on Sterne's part ; he did his utmost to deserve his peculiar fame. The Sentimental Journey was undertaken with the deliberate purpose of seeking occasions for the enjoyment of factitious emotion : and alike in *Tristram Shandy* and in some of the *Sermons* he gives his readers plenty of opportunities of gaining similar pleasure : which, by the way, such being the fashion of the time, they were only too willing to gain. In my opinion, however, Sterne, though thus indulging and stimulating his own and his readers' tendency to 'sentiment,' was also, after his eccentric manner, quietly laughing at it. He was, in a way possible to such minds, at once sincere in his ebullitions of pathos and conscious of a certain underlying insincerity in them. There is nearly always a tone which shows that he was viewing himself, not uncritically, *ab extra*, and scrutinising his own tears as an alienist scrutinises the tears of a hypochondriac. If, in fact, he wept at any mortal thing, it was that he might laugh. Be this as it may, it is noteworthy that some men saw through him. He did not appeal to Goldsmith—the common-sense dramatist who had endeavoured to overthrow the sentiment of Kelly. 'A very dull fellow,' was Goldsmith's verdict on Sterne. And, though Johnson answered, ' Why, no, Sir,' it is pretty certain that Johnson's opinion was not very different from his friend's. Sterne's sermons have many of the qualities of the *Sentimental Journey*. Johnson confessed to having read them. ' But, Madam, I read them in a stage-coach. I should never have deigned to look at them had I been *at large*.' It is difficult, indeed, to believe that the man who thought the Marchioness of Tavistock wept too copiously for the death of her husband would have tolerated the counterfeit tears which besprinkle so many pages of Sterne's works.

Yet the thing *was* popular ; and 'sentiment' remained as a favourite *genre* long after the rise of the Romantic Revival. Even Wordsworth, in classifying his poems, found a place for those of *sentiment* and reflection : though I confess it is hard to detect, from the nature of the poems included under that heading, exactly what he meant by the word. Mackenzie's *Man of Feeling* was, it is true, produced long before the

U

Revival had begun : it came out in the very year of
Scott's birth and when Wordsworth was an infant :
but it was still famous forty years later, and Mackenzie's name, as that of the ' Scottish Addison,' was
still one to conjure with when Scott dedicated *Waverley*
to him. The ' Keepsakes ' and ' Annuals ' of the next
thirty years maintained the sentimental tradition.
Nor did it die out even in the forties. Those parts of
Dickens's novels which are the least effective to-day are
just those in which the ' Tears of Sensibility ' are most
vigorously called forth. They are, I may add, just
those in which, to us, his style is at its worst. We know
also that they were the passages which, whether read
at home or heard from the lips of Dickens himself,
most powerfully moved his audiences. I have met
people who could still recall the passion of sobs which
convulsed whole crowds, while Dickens, such was
his sincerity, could hardly recite for the feelings which
all but overcame him. But one need not stick to prose.
For how many years was not the *May Queen* by far the
most popular of Tennyson's poems, and the one most
sure to draw iron tears down the Plutonian cheek
of the toughest North-country mill-owner ! And, to
take possibly still more familiar examples, I have known
people unable to control their emotions while reading
the final pages of *Eric* or *Misunderstood*—pages which
few of us can read to-day without resentment at the
blatant and obvious attempt to enlist our feelings on
the wrong side. As for *Little Lord Fauntleroy*, on
which a parody has recently been put on the stage with
success, it made the fortune of its author, and secured
a wide circulation not only for itself but for several
others of her writings, some of which had not even prig-
gishness to recommend them. Nothing, in fact, could

exceed the popularity of poems, novels, and music-hall songs of this pathetic class, except perhaps their later popularity when revived as comic turns. And incidentally, the *style* of Farrar and his rivals, once so widely admired, has become unendurable. It suited its subject and its audience in its day ; it has fallen into contempt as his Erics, Daubenys, and Russells have ceased to attract respect.

I have, of course, already remarked that the approval was not unanimous. In another connection, as the reader will remember, I have referred to the fact that Philip Francis cared little for a famous passage of pathos which not all judges would think sentimental. He told Burke that the wonderful paragraph on Marie Antoinette, which Burke wept as he wrote, was overdrawn. He certainly did not care for its ' subject-matter ' : and the passages made still less impression on Paine and Mackintosh, who thought the tears ought to have been shed for the dying bird and not for the plumage. It would be easy to find many, during the whole vogue of this lachrymose literature, who detested every manifestation of it.

Popular, however, it was, even in England ; and if popular here, it was still more popular abroad : though abroad, as here, it had its enemies. Never was any English novel quite so sentimental as some of Sudermann's ; and there appears to be in the German mind a strain of sentimentality more permanent, and more likely to rise into prominence at intervals, than in the minds of most other nations. The amazing popularity of *Werther* is only one example of this characteristic ; anybody only slightly acquainted with German literature could easily supply a hundred others. As might be expected, it is accompanied by a strain of equally conspicuous manliness and even hardness, which often manifests itself at the very same time, and even in the same authors.

But the typical eruption of sentimentality, it need not be said, occurred in a nation very different from the German, and—it is probably safe to say—not usually given to it. The master of all sentimentalists is Rousseau, born and brought up among harsh and matter-of-fact Calvinists, and wielding his influence mainly among a people distinguished, as a rule, by a remarkable combination of logic and practicality. At just the moment when he rose to fame, the god of that people was the very antithesis of sentiment, the most concrete and material-minded of all men of genius. We know what Voltaire thought of the *Nouvelle Héloise*. He predicted for it a life of a few months, and not much of a life while it lived. Regarding Rousseau as the enemy of the human race, he could endure neither the theories of the weeping philosopher, nor the language in which they were couched : the style which captivated so many thousands was to him detestable.

That, whatever Voltaire might think or pretend to think, the style of Rousseau appears to the vast majority of his countrymen a beautiful one, is, I imagine, beyond doubt : but I should also imagine that something of his enormous influence was due to the fact that the very sentimentalism, maudlin as it often is, which characterised him was what the age, or a great number of people in the age, were already prepared to welcome. Whatever the cause, whether the popularity of Sterne and Richardson, a wave of mingled anti-clericalism and humanitarianism, or what not, the moment was ripe for Rousseau. The same beauty of style, the same pathos, the same overt or implied teachings, might have been tried a few years before : assuredly they would have been tried in vain. But the sentimentality, at that time, carried them through ; for sentimentality was in the air that men breathed. It had often been observed that there is a remarkable similarity between the suicide-passages in the *Nouvelle Héloise* and the nauseous glorifications of self-murder which crowd the 'poetical' works of Frederick the Great ; and attempts have been made to show that Frederick was acquainted with Rousseau. The attempts are probably failures ; but the likeness shows how fashionable Rousseauism was even before Rousseau was known. There is indeed no more conclusive proof of the spread of the fever than the crocodile tears of the Great King over the horrors of a war which he had himself provoked, and over the devastations of Saxony which he had himself ordered : or than the ostentatious way in which he exhibited his poison-pills, which he took care never to swallow, to the whole world. The Austrian satirist might well mock at the royal Cato who had killed himself nine times, and yet was still alive.

It was, then, Rousseau's harmony with the tone of the time, rather than the beauty of his style, that started him on the strange career which was to have such portentous results. With us to-day the case is different. The sentimentality we can scarcely bring ourselves to endure ; but the man Rousseau, and the mighty revolutions of which he was in such great measure the cause, dominate our minds, and blind us to the washy and drivelling maunderings of his puppets. The destroyer of empires drowns the mawkish novelist. The same is the case when we read his other works. They may carry little intellectual conviction, and their reckless onesidedness and exaggeration may be always obvious, but the sense that they once *did* carry conviction, and that their hyperboles were taken as an inspired gospel, is ever with us. The books, in fact, as has been said, were not books but deeds ; and Rousseau, being dead, yet *doeth*. This remembrance still makes his weakness strong, and overcomes armies of men alien to his spirit.

It is needless to add here any words as to the tremendous influence of Rousseau on purely literary modes and fashions : an influence hardly less wonderful than that which he has exerted in the social or political world. I have already spoken of *Werther* as the most striking example : but the whole *Sturm und Drang* movement in Germany, superficially so different from Rousseauism, would have taken a different course if Rousseau had never existed : and though the great Germans shook themselves clear of *Sturm und Drang*, they never quite threw off the badge of subservience to Rousseau. Lesser men, all over Europe, inevitably followed him in a slavish herd ; and I am not at all sure that even now, in certain countries, there are not men who write as they do because Rousseau wrote before them.

Now there is nothing essentially literary about sentimentality. It is a tendency, a disposition, or a habit of mind, found in all sorts and conditions of people, and perhaps more notable in those who have never written a line than in those who have covered whole reams of foolscap. But, like other turns of mind or natural trends, it produces a taste. Those who are themselves sentimental will have a relish for sentimental books ; and those who are naturally robust will be nauseated by such books. You cannot dissociate the literary taste from the man's whole composition : it is a part of him, and cannot be studied in isolation from him, any more than you can study a living organism in the dissecting-room. Nor, to speak generally, can you alter this disposition : as the tree is sown, so will it grow, and grapes cannot be gathered of thorns.

Nevertheless, there are times when a gushing sentimentalism runs like wildfire through a community, and people catch it from their neighbours as if it were an infectious disease. At such times all virtue is reduced to an empty compassion, and ' pity, like a naked new-born babe, striding the blast,' calls up everywhere vacuous tears which all but drown the wind. Symptoms are attacked instead of causes, and imaginary ills are bemoaned even more frantically than real ones. Pity, in fact, is cherished for its own sake as a luxury, and, when nothing actual is found to call for pity, the words are pitiful. Plays, poems, novels, waste on phantasmal woes the emotions which ought to be reserved for the real ; and the habit is formed of regarding such factitious feelings as ends in themselves. At such times we often find men and women who will shed tears over Dick Turpin or Eugene Aram, but who will not stir a step to help the genuinely and undeservedly distressed. It is then that the Kellys flourish, and the *Werthers* take the world by storm. A fashion —for such this epidemic is—has once again become the parent of a taste. And then, as ever, the fashion passes away ; a more manly habit of mind resumes its dominion ; people become ashamed of the cultivation and exhibition of their feelings ; the relish passes into disgust, and, not impossibly, a certain cynical repression of all feelings, however noble, takes the place of the old flaunting emotionalism. Which is the worse, it is for the moralist to say. It is enough for the literary critic to note the phenomenon as it affects literature, and to do his best to preserve an even mind amid all the fluctuations of popularity and obloquy to which the fashion is exposed. He will calmly observe how a class of literature once passionately worshipped is, in a few years, rejected with scorn and loathing ; and he will mark the possibility that, in a few more years, as a new wave passes over the world, the hated idol may be again set on its throne, and the temple-courts may once more be thronged with devotees.

XVI

PURITANISM AND ANTIPURITANISM

WHENEVER a wave of religious enthusiasm sweeps over a community, and this world begins to appear of no value in comparison with the next, it is not improbable that there will arise a certain antagonism between religion and art. Against 'art for art's sake' the religious hostility will be deadly; and quite possibly all art will be involved in the same condemnation. When Christianity began to invade the Roman world, that 'world' was the enemy, and its art was a service of demons. Poetry, rhetoric, sculpture, painting were together cast into the outer darkness : they were all to perish in a catastrophe that 'must shortly come to pass'; why cherish them? St. Paul was plainly a most persuasive speaker ; but the tricks of oratory were hateful to him except as means to one urgent end. He could quote Aratus, but only to 'save some' of the Areopagites. He wrote, or dictated, some of the most splendid passages in the Greek language : but it is certain that he thought nothing of their style ; he was using impassioned words because his soul was on fire. In perhaps his very greatest passage, he tells us that to speak with the tongue of men and angels is in itself to be no more than sounding brass and a tinkling cymbal. To him words were weapons : so soon as they became ornaments they were worse than useless.

The same thing, now less now more, is seen whenever religion becomes a compelling power. Moses, leading his people out of Egypt, forbids them to do what the Egyptians did everywhere—make likenesses of what was in heaven above or in the earth beneath or in the water under the earth. Similarly with scores of religious leaders who desire to bring their people out of the house of bondage. St. Peter will have nothing to do with the art of dress : the adornment must be a meek and quiet spirit ; and General Booth here at least agrees with St. Peter. Architecture fares equally badly ; the only beautiful houses must be like that which St. Thomas raised for King Gundafar in India. The saint engages to build a temple, and gives the money to the poor. Meanwhile the temple, invisible on earth, is daily rising in heaven, a building of God, eternal, not made with hands : such architecture alone befits those who have here no continuing city. I doubt not that Ahab's ivory palace was but another of his idolatries in the eyes of Elijah. Music, that handmaid of religious ecstasy, must be a chained slave. ' Is any merry ? Let him sing psalms ' : but let him not go to the play. Dancing—King David may have danced, and behind him may have gone the maidens playing with timbrels ; but the Church is a Michal looking on with stern disapproval. John Wesley is comparatively liberal. ' I have no objection,' said he, ' to dancing, provided it is done by men with men, women with women, by daylight, and out of doors.' Wesley was a Protestant, but the history of Catholicism is full of a ' Puritanism ' which leaves him far behind ; of movements sternly otherworld, and directed to the scorn and destruction of artistic beauty. Nor did intellect escape. The splendid mind of Pascal, one of the keenest and most comprehensive ever given to man, was constantly checked and hampered by the religion which he drank in from the air around him. He was daily fretted by fears that, when he had made one of his great physical or mathematical discoveries, he had been committing some mortal sin, and wasting on ' the pride of life ' time and thought that should have been devoted to saving his soul : until finally, in the very fullness of his powers, he renounced science altogether, and gave himself continually to prayer. Many of the Latin Fathers, over whom the phrases of Cicero exercised too strong a fascination, repented in dust and ashes when they had yielded to the charm ; and thenceforward shunned the magic sentences as St. Antony shunned the lure of women. It needs but small acquaintance with religious history to know that, at sundry times and in divers manners, beauty, like light, is suspected as one of the chosen disguises of Satan.

These examples will be sufficient to show how misleading is the idea conveyed by the unlucky name of ' Puritanism ' so often given to this attitude of mind. It is a great mistake to think that the soldiers of Oliver Cromwell, or even the emissaries of his namesake Thomas, were the first to demolish a beautiful image, to hesitate over grace of style, to enjoin what to others is a gloomy and depressing way of life. The quarrel between religion and art has nothing directly to do with the dispute between Cavalier and Roundhead, or with the controversy between Catholic and Protestant. It is a strife which cuts clean across theological boundaries, and in which the combatants find allies in both camps : nay, it is often a civil war in the mind of an individual man, dragging him in different directions ;

a war in which the victor is the vanquished. You can see such a civil war in the stern Dissenter Milton and in the equally stern Conformist Dante. You can trace it in countries where Christianity itself is utterly unknown, and in ages before Protestantism can be conceived of. It arises in Mohammedanism and in Judaism. Something like it is seen in the rigid anti-Hellenism of the elder Cato, and in that dislike of rhetorical art which he summed up in the famous maxim, ' Rem tene, verba sequentur '—a maxim which Goethe puts into the mouth of the disillusioned humanist Faust. Something like it is seen among the Greeks, and not in Sparta only, but in Athens. It is visible in Xenophanes, himself a poet, who condemned the poems of Homer and Hesiod for their immoral stories of the gods ; and it is visible in the most artistic of philosophers, whose soul was like a star and dwelt with the very idea of beauty ; whose prose was the Greek that Zeus himself would have written had he written in Attic ; yet what reader does not know how ruthlessly he excluded whole modes of music from his commonwealth, and ordained that Homer, if ever he ventured into the city, should be honourably crowned with flowers, but firmly conducted beyond its bounds? No one, in the most frenzied days of the Fifth Monarchy, ever desired to crib and cabin Art more fanatically than did Plato. There are people who think the attempt to suppress stage-plays a mark of exclusively Protestant narrowness. A whole association, in Catholic France, smiled upon by Catholic bishops, and supported by hundreds of devout laymen, endeavoured on religious grounds to silence Molière, and would have succeeded but for the favour of the King, who had not yet become sanctimonious. Two nuns, close relatives of the poet, set aside one day in every year to pray for his soul, which was in deadlier danger with each succeeding play. Yet Molière's dramas are innocent and moral in comparison with the ' school of abuse ' which excited the prophet-like animosity of Gosson and Prynne. It was the play itself, and not the kind of play, that the pious hated. And even when, under the influence of Madame de Maintenon, the King himself became religious, and the Court put aside the *Misanthrope* for the missal, even then the religious themes of Racine could hardly reconcile some people to the fact that they were clothed in a dramatic form.

There is then, I repeat, no necessary connection between the ' Protestantism of the Protestant religion ' and what is known, so inaccurately, as ' Puritanism.' Puritanism, properly so called, is neither artistic nor inartistic, neither prudish nor outspoken, nor is it priggish unless every sincerely religious man is a prig. Those who think Milton a prude have never read him ; and those who think Spenser a prig know nothing about him. Such fancies are part and parcel of the crass blindness which imagines that the Puritan beliefs of these two great poets, and of scores of others who could be named, were incompatible with a love of beauty, or which fancies that Cromwell, whose taste in painting equalled that of Charles I himself, was an enemy of the fine arts. So far as historic Puritanism was indeed hostile to those arts, its hostility was due to accidental causes, and was largely justifiable. If Plato and Xenophanes were right in objecting to the stories of Hesiod and to the lay of Demodocus, the Puritans were tenfold right in objecting to many of the plays which held the stage in their time ; and if they ' stretched a point too far ' in their war upon the theatre, they went no further than the wisest of the Greek philosophers in ' refusing a chorus ' to Æschylus. And who was the ' Puritan ' who led the decisive assault on the immorality of the stage? The determined enemy of all Puritans, the Nonjuror Jeremy Collier.

None the less, it happened that, at a time when theological zeal and religious earnestness were at their height, certain forms of art, which also were at their height, incurred, partly justly and partly unjustly, the censure of the religious. It happened that the majority, though by no means all, of the censors belonged to the Puritan party. Hence, by a natural but unfortunate confusion, the name Puritanism has become associated with an enmity to art with which, in the strict sense, it has nothing to do ; and it is probably hopeless to attempt to correct the misconception. Regrettable as it is, the word Puritanism will long continue to be the opposite of Humanism, and that though, in any strict sense of the terms, some of the most humanistic of poets have been the most religious, and though, as was long since observed, poetry and religion have largely the same field. Both deal with that which eye hath not seen nor ear heard : the poet's dream is of the light that never was on sea or land.

But my present task is to show that if you are of the ' Puritan ' spirit, your taste will be ' Puritan.' It is all but impossible to approve a style when you disapprove the substance : and as the style takes colour from the substance you will often find it impossible to separate the two. A man who, like Richardson's grandson, disapproves of novels, will be unable to endure Clarissa, not merely because it is a novel but because of the style in which it is written, which he

has come to associate with the disliked form of literature.   If the man does actually find himself being
captivated by the form, he resists the fascination as
a device of Satan : but as a rule the fascination is not
there.   Gladstone, detesting Disraeli's politics, detested also the way in which they were set forth : and
it may be remembered that during the Education
controversy, Balfour, when attacked by Dr. Clifford,
said with truth that he did not like the Doctor's *style*.
But it was unquestionably the matter that really
annoyed him.   And so everywhere and at all times.
When Byron was proclaiming, in the thin and vapid
early cantos of *Childe Harold,* ideas that just suited
the times, Moore said by way of compliment that he
feared the poetry was too good for the age.   When,
in the full maturity of his powers, Byron gave the world
what to us is his masterpiece, *Don Juan,* the substance
was too bad for the age, and the manner also was
thought too bad for it.   The style of Tennyson is what
it always was ; but because his King Arthur is no longer
the ideal gentleman, the style is blamed along with the
too ' blameless ' King.   Those who have read ' Victorian ' criticisms of Burns, will have noticed how a
certain moral disapproval of the subjects of some of his
poems has prevented the critic from seeing the vigour
and directness of their style.   It is safe to say that, if
you know the critic to hold strongly ' Puritan ' views,
you will find that he sets the *Cotter's Saturday Night*
above *Holy Willie's Prayer* or the *Holy Fair,* and cries
O si sic omnia.   Something of this feeling is obvious
even in the comparatively wide-minded judgments of
Principal Shairp : and the perception of it roused the
wrath of Stevenson, who had been brought up in a
Puritan household and had revolted against its in-

fluence. Similarly, to take an instance from a very different theological school, you will observe, as I have already said, in the incidental critical judgments scattered through the writings of Newman, a tendency to appraise writings less by their mere style than by their moral and religious tone.

But when we turn to the other side, and look at those who, with all their individual peculiarities, are one in their hostility to Puritanism, we meet, as a rule, with a narrowness ' in its opposite as great ' as that of their opponents, unrestrained and ' sans bound.' It is natural enough that the reticences of ' Victorianism ' should arouse resentment, and that the suppression of facts known to everybody should nauseate like the official denials of politicians at question-time. When a poet or a novelist draws near to a certain subject, and then turns aside with a grimace, we all feel as we feel towards the priest and the Levite who passed the wounded man on the other side. Again, many a man who had been through the filth and horror of the war may well have been sickened by the euphemisms under which those horrors were too often disguised. It is natural enough that in all such cases the lover of truth should endeavour to redress the balance ; and he is more than excusable if, in his hatred of sentimentality and falsehood, he tends to emphasise, even unduly, the aspect which has been kept out of sight. One may imagine that Mr. Siegfried Sassoon's divine frenzy was heightened by reading or remembering some of Kipling's or Campbell's poems in glorification of war, or some of the communiqués in which a hideous disaster was called a strategic retreat, or a more hideous success idealised into beauty. But it is also to be noticed how different Mr. Sassoon's *style* is from

Campbell's or Kipling's : and the same difference is
to be noticed in taste and criticism. Men of to-day,
disliking the matter, or rather the conspicuous absence
of certain matters, in the work of their predecessors,
tend to dislike their manner ; and a new school of
taste arises through the rise of a new way of looking at
life in general. The new school, whether of writers or
of critics, may have many names and include many
classes : it may be Humanist, Naturalist, Impressionist,
Realist, or even, strangely enough, Romanticist : but
all these, uniting in their hatred of Puritanism,
resemble their enemy in disliking the style associated
with a substance which annoys them.

Such a phenomenon, being an almost necessary
characteristic of humanity, is, of course, not really new.
It has not often been seen more plainly than to-day ;
but it appears regularly whenever the conditions are
favourable. The reaction against Puritan religion and
politics was very strong when Puritanism, after ruling
the country for twenty years, suddenly fell with a crash :
and all know with what violence the religious and
political pendulum swung to the opposite extreme.
But there can be little doubt that the marked change
in phraseology and style that followed the Restoration
was a part of the wider reaction, and due to it. Detesting the restrictions imposed by the Saints on religion
and manners, the new era broke the fetters both of
morals and of diction, and asserted the right to be free
and easy both in life and in letters. The Sabbath
should be a day of sport—' in it thou shalt do all manner
of play '—and the long sentence should be abolished
with the long sermon. The license of Dryden's plays
was a reaction against the suppression of the drama :
the lightness and brevity of his sentences, both in

x

prose and in verse, were a reaction against the long-winded periods of the earlier writers—who, be it remembered, whether Cavalier or Roundhead, were equally ' Puritan.' The periods of Clarendon are as involved as those of Milton ; those of Jeremy Taylor as intricate as those of Owen or Baxter : and all alike were in morals too precise for the loose-living Court and the coarse-tongued stage of the ' golden days.' The writers of Charles's reign must be free or die : but they would not speak the tongue that Milton spake.

There is thus nothing surprising in the recent re-action against Victorian Puritanism. We see a natural dislike of the rigid conventional morals of the last century, leading, after the manner of reactions, to an excess which defeats its own end ; but also we see a dislike of the Victorian manner of expressing itself, and an attempt to evolve a new style. We find adverse judgments, sometimes amazingly crude and violent, on writers who, if their themes and their opinions had been different, would have been admired and imitated. And we find also, as always at such times, clumsy mimicries of authors who, though choosing unpleasant subjects, have contrived to deal with them in a manner which has, like chivalry, all but redeemed their gross-ness. Nothing is more ludicrous than to see a German or English setting of a French theme, which the original author has adorned with grace and charm, but which the awkward plagiarist has deformed as Wycher-ley deformed the characters of Molière. The lightness has vanished ; the repulsiveness remains, or rather forces itself into notice.

Some of these writers, with a grotesque violation of exactness, have chosen to dub themselves Realists. Neither the pleasant nor the unpleasant, if we may believe the philosophers, has a real existence : they are both ' subjective ' and are given to the object by the percipient.   But these writers, for some reason or other, claim to be more real than others because they dwell almost exclusively on the unpleasant side of life. To attain the whole, they think it sufficient to ignore at least the half, and hope to delude their readers by giving their performances a name involving universality.   But realism, in the strict sense, as Mr. Herbert Read has pointed out, is nothing more or less than definiteness.   There is realism when Dante describes *exactly* on which foot he leaned more heavily when ascending the mountain ; and there is realism when Henry James tells us *exactly* the thoughts of a man between his knocking at a door and the opening.   The so-called realism of so many novels of to-day is distinguished just by the way in which it misses this precision.   It solves its quadratic equation, and omits to give the *plus* answer—imagining that the evil *minus* alone satisfies the conditions.   All life is not revolting ; all virtue is not hypocrisy ; there are many more things in earth than are apparently dreamt of in the ' psychology ' of these Horatios.   But the secret of this strange taste for the distasteful lies in the revulsion against the too-obvious ignoring of one side of life of which our Victorian grandfathers were guilty ; and we may expect, ere long, a corresponding revulsion in our children against our own still more wilful ignoring of the other side.

There is no need for me to multiply examples : the reader can, only too easily, take thought for himself.   School-stories which, in reaction from *Eric*, become sentimental through very detestation of sentimentality—but sentimental on behalf of evil : war-novels which, like boring descriptions of a bore, become almost as terrible as what they describe, and, through hatred of falsehood become false; ' Freudian ' biographies and character-studies in which the crudest and most superficial psycho-analysis is applied, in journalistic fashion, to popular ends; iconoclastic histories in which the authors seek the praise of profundity by the shallow method of imputing evil motives; these are a few types which may stand as representative of the rest. A general confounding of good and ill, of right and wrong, is the mark of most : and a scepticism which is—here alone wisely—sceptical of itself seems to inform nearly all these writers. The future historian of manners, if he relies on these as his authorities, will gain a very extraordinary idea of our times. Fortunately there are a few authors, even in our Sardis, who have not defiled their pens ; and the historian, if he consults these also, will be able, in some degree, to correct his impressions. If he is wise, he will remember besides that even a popular writer is not always approved, and that there is a mighty body of opinion and feeling which is not represented even by writers who try to produce ' what the public wants.' Already there are signs that the movement is exhausting itself, and that the reaction against the reaction is beginning. Should it obey the Newtonian law, and prove ' equal and opposite,' we shall probably see an outburst of ' Puritanism ' which will be equally exaggerated and not much less harmful. But these things are in the lap of the most Puckish and irresponsible of the gods.

XVII

' REALISM '

No one who really knew Englishmen would say that they take their pleasures sadly. This is the superficial view of a foreigner who has seen them only rarely and from a distance. But it is, I think, true that they often find their pleasures in sad things, which they manage to enjoy as some other nations enjoy a carnival. Like Macbeth, they can sup full of horrors ; but unlike Macbeth they can find satisfaction in the meal. Not once nor twice the ' best-seller ' of the year has been a book so gloomy that the *Inferno* is light reading in comparison ; and sometimes the whole country has been for months in the mental condition of Richard II, unable to talk of anything but graves, worms, and epitaphs. It is not so long since a thoroughly British schoolmaster, in order that the boys might get the utmost pleasure out of their occasional holidays, invariably fixed them on a day when there was a hanging in the neighbourhood : and writers, even now, follow his example in their own fashion. It is a commonplace that, if you want to please the British public you must prophesy disaster and tell them unpleasant home-truths. The familiar case of Brown's *Estimate* is typical. When Minorca had been lost, and disaster crowded upon disaster, Brown told his countrymen that they were a race of idle pusillanimous rascals, well deserving their misfortunes ; that their day of glory was over and rightly so ; and they bought his book in thousands : nay, to use Cowper's remarkable words, he *charmed* the town. But the same thing appeared in the Napoleonic wars : the prophets of ruin were eagerly read, the encouragers hardly listened to. In the Great War itself there was a similar phenomenon ; and if—*quod Deus omen avertat*—another war ever comes, doubtless we shall see it again. Native pessimists will be popular, and foreign *Hymns of Hate* will be chanted more vigorously than our own *Tipperarys.* I have known a man who, in order to secure full pleasure from his summer holidays, always took a copy of Schopenhauer with him to the seaside, and refreshed himself with it regularly after his pessimistic bathe.

Statesmen, with their usual fatuity, do not seem to know this. During the war, at any rate, they forgot this national characteristic. To keep people hopeful, they tried to hinder the dissemination of bad news, and, of course, they failed. Had they scattered it broadcast, the country would have ' borne up,' as that typical Englishwoman Mrs. Gamp bore up on the death of her husband—with a fortitude hardly to be distinguished from hilarity. The Government should have pondered the case of Thomas Hardy, who, though by no means unknown, was never really popular till he had produced two of the gloomiest books since the highly-successful *Voyage to the Houyhnhnms*—books that would make some nations turn to *Rasselas* for comfort.

The name of Hardy is sufficient to dispel the illusion that, like antagonism to art in general, such a taste is a ' Puritan ' monopoly—an illusion which, though widespread, is unpardonable. Voltaire was certainly no

Puritan, nor is *Candide* a homily ; but no Puritan sermoniser ever attacked optimism more vigorously than Voltaire in that book. As a matter of fact, Puritanism, though it often took strange ways of showing it, was a cheerful creed. The constant and often boisterous joviality of Cromwell would have made the liveliness of Charles II seem like the compounded melancholy of Jaques : nor is it easy to find a man who has borne disappointment and physical privation with less despondency than Milton, whose mirth, though it 'after no repenting drew,' was genuine and hearty. John Wesley, at the end of his career, declared that he had not known a quarter of an hour's depression in his life : and many a Quaker showed his own happiness, though he may have diminished that of others, by singing in prison.

The taste for gloomy books can be observed from time to time at all periods of our literary history, and perhaps most clearly in the Catholic period, before the Church had been split to pieces, and before the dissentients had themselves been sundered into Arminians and Calvinists. The most popular book in the Middle Ages was the *Consolations of Philosophy*, which is certainly not exclusively consolatory. This work was translated by Alfred, by Chaucer, by Walton, by Queen Elizabeth, and read by thousands either in the original or in translation. The most exhilarating passages in it are certainly those which speak of the happiness of people who lived long before the author, as contrasted with the misery of his contemporaries. But whatever we may think of Boethius, there can be no hesitation as to Innocent III, whose *De Miseria Conditionis Humanae* enjoyed a vogue only second to that of the so-called *Consolations*. The Pope is probably the most thoroughgoing and uncompromising painter of woe that ever put pessimism on paper ; and one who can rise from the perusal of that book without feeling that man is the most wretched, filthy, contemptible, and odious of creatures that ever swarmed on earth, must have a pericardium of triple brass. We are left with not a rag to excuse the slightest vestige, I do not say of self-conceit, but even of decent humility. From birth to death we are shown the utter degradation of our state, and taught to despise ourselves and the world that endures our presence. But this book, the work of one of the greatest of the Popes, was read with avidity, and certainly not merely because of its authorship. Such sentences as ' Formatus est homo de spurcissimo spermate ' or ' Semper mundanae laetitiae tristitia repentina succedit ' struck an answering chord in the minds of men. Nay, as everyone knows, the genial and healthy-minded Chaucer, most English of poets, not only pillaged passages from *De Miseria* to heighten the attraction of the *Canterbury Tales*, but actually translated the whole treatise under the title ' The Wretched Engendring of Mankinde.' None of Chaucer's hundreds of borrowed sayings are rendered with more zest than those in which Innocent gloats over the unhappiness of his fellow-creatures.

But what shall I say of Richard Rolle, whose *Pricke of Conscience* is also liberally larded with scraps from Innocent ? Richard's poem finds inspiration in the thought of horror, and never rises to such heights as when he discourses on fever, dropsy, jaundice, gout, angers, and all the evils that can ' appayre ' us : unless it be when he comes to write on the four terrors that make death even worse than life—the painful parting of soul and body, the fiends that haunt the death-bed, the dread account that has to be given, and the awful doubt as to whether the soul shall wend to joy or bliss. But there is no doubt that Richard, as he was one of the best, was also one of the most popular writers of the fourteenth century.

I do not deny—indeed it is part of my thesis—that there were always many who disliked this style, and that even those who liked it for a while often wearied of it. Even Henryson, who dealt much in tragedy, seems to have thought it not appropriate to all times and moods. 'Ane dooly sesoun to ane cairfull dite,' he says in the first verse of his *Testament of Criseyde*, 'suld correspond and be equivalent'; and he excuses the 'dolefulness of his ditty' by the terrible weather which prevailed when he began to write it. But Chaucer himself is an unimpeachable witness. The Monk is in the full flood of his tales of catastrophe, those 'tragedies' of the fall of great men from prosperity to ruin, when the Knight, representing culture, checks him, and the Host, voicing popular opinion, tells him plainly that the whole collection is not worth a butterfly. 'The tale anoyeth al this companye, for therin is ther no disport ne game.' None the less, we need not be surprised that both writers and readers continued to find pleasure in this species of pain. Much of Chaucer's own *Parson's Tale* will probably seem to most moderns more melancholy than the Monk's; Lydgate imitated the Monk in his *Falls of Princes*; and it would take a good arithmetician to count up all the *Complaints* and dirges of the succeeding century. When the great revival of poetry came under Elizabeth, it was ushered in by the *Mirror for Magistrates*, a series of stories very similar in subject to those of the Monk, and prefaced by Sackville in the *Induction* with a poem whose extraordinary power is rivalled only by its sombreness of tone. Winter is there at its most wrathful :

> Hawthorne had lost his motley lyverye,
> The naked twigges were shivering all for colde :
> And dropping down the teares abundantly,
> Each thing (me thought) with wiping eye me tolde
> The cruell season, bidding me withholde
> Myself within, for I was gotten out
> Into the feldes, where as I walkte about :

and the whole poem ' corresponds and is equivalent ' to the dreary chill of the landscape which it describes.

I leave to the psychologist the analysis of the peculiar pleasure which in certain circumstances is undoubtedly to be derived from the description of pain, and which, when excited by true genius, is perhaps the highest form of literary pleasure attainable. We all feel that *Othello* is a work of loftier order than the *Comedy of Errors* or even than *Henry IV;* the woes of Lear move us more than the scapes of Falstaff : yet we feel also that there are some tragedies in which the pain caused to the hearer is possibly beyond the legitimate limits of art. Aristotle admitted that Euripides was the most heartrending of poets ; but he may well have thought, as some think to-day, that the piteous pathos of the *Trojan Women* rouses thoughts too deep for tragic tears. The Athenians unquestionably felt that the pain caused by the *Taking of Miletus* was more than the author had a right to inflict : and some modern novels, in my opinion, also transgress the due bounds. I have known many men, of good cultivation, who rule out tragedy entirely from the true domain of the novel, regarding life as sufficiently sombre without the addition of imaginary griefs : and who refuse, for

instance, to read the end of *Clarissa* on the ground that
the sorrows are piled on too heavily. Whether these
men are right or wrong, there is undoubtedly something
to be said for them ; and I think that there have been
many highly popular books which, as they deal too
much in the gloomy, should be excluded from ' pure '
literature. The instinct in favour of a ' happy ending '
is not, in my opinion, so contemptible as some think
it : and the substitution of Tate's version of *Lear* for
Shakespeare's, which had the weighty approval of a
whole century, and the implied approval of so sound
a judge as Johnson, is not to be stigmatised off-hand as
absurd. It is at any rate noteworthy as an indication
of the change of taste which inevitably follows when
a certain style has predominated for any length of time.
As with the famous Mr. Oliver Edwards, the public
may endeavour for a while to bear tragedy in philosophic fashion, but ' cheerfulness will always break
in.' ' Heaviness may endure for a night, but joy
cometh in the morning.'

Curiously enough, while plays were thus being doc-
tored into serenity, other kinds of literature, if such
they can be called, were providing the world with
a compensating melancholy. While *Lear* was being
turned into something not far off a comedy, and
Cordelia was walking off the stage arm in arm with
Edgar, a whole library of books was teaching the
country the lessons of Pope Innocent. Drelincourt
on *Death*, Blair's *Grave*, Hervey's *Meditations among
the Tombs*, Young's *Night Thoughts*, were all financial
successes. The *Grave* was indeed rejected by two
publishers as too serious for the age ; but it well
remunerated a third : Hervey's *Meditations* captured
one public as the *Beggar's Opera* captured another ;

and the popularity of the *Night Thoughts* was certainly not exhausted after a hundred years and twenty editions. Young was unquestionably a man of genius and a master of rhetoric: but if the success of the *Thoughts* was largely due to the epigrammatic force of the style, that of Hervey was certainly in part due to the subject, of which it is true Dr. Johnson did not disapprove, though he made great fun of the way in which it was treated. It is true that the youthful, among whom was Boswell, seem to have approved of the very style which Johnson ridiculed ; but even they, with all their juvenile vitality, were not repelled by its gloomy theme. There are times when even boys do not mind imitating Prospero, and dedicating every third thought to the grave. And when they do so, they seem to acquire a taste which does not revolt at vapidity and pomposity, provided the author is vapid and pompous about misery.

If religious authors have thus aimed at harrowing the feelings of their readers, and have found numerous readers who delight in being harrowed, secular writers have not been behindhand. Young's *Last Day* itself, and all his midnight complaints, are less terrific than many Elizabethan plays, which had not Young's excuse that his cruelties were meant in kindness. Whether *Titus Andronicus* is Shakespeare's or not, it was popular enough to be thought worthy of inclusion among his plays, and it is, I think, probable that Shakespeare added a few touches to it. There is no reason to believe that its horrors would have disgusted him, and they certainly did not disgust the audiences. And, like the skipper of the *Hesperus*, it had plenty of little daughters to bear it company : plays by Kyd, by Wilkins, by Webster, by Ford, by Tourneur, nearly all of which, so far as we can judge, hit the popular fancy. Some of them might appeal to the gentry on the stage by their splendour of thought and diction, but the horrors did not repel the gentry ; and they captivated the groundlings. It might almost appear as if the playwrights had made up their minds that, an they would, they could outdo the most terrific of the preachers. It is one of the merits of the Restora-tion period that, though the means it adopted to give pleasure were not always creditable, it usually aimed *directly* at pleasure, and rarely sought it through its opposite.

When we come to recent times, we find that books of a sombre cast attain their audience in consequence of a reaction against a too easygoing optimism. It is perhaps true, for example, that ' Victorianism ' blinked unpleasant facts : it was natural, therefore, that Georgianism should dwell upon them, and dwell upon them even with an excess of emphasis. But it is prob-ably also true that much of the sombreness is due, like the naturalism of which I have already spoken, to the false but flattering idea that the gloomy is more ' real ' than the cheerful. As many writers seem to think that to probe the depths of vice shows a greater penetration than to explore the recesses of virtue, so there are many who seem to think that pessimism is the mark of a greater profundity than optimism or meliorism. Such an outlook on life as that of Chaucer or Words-worth is to them a proof of shallowness of mind ; and Heraclitus is to them the only sound philosopher. Whatever the cause, we have had lately, especially in our novelists, small evidence of a desire to study life with serene detachment, to see it steadily and to see it whole. And this attitude specially characterises those who most vigorously repudiate 'Puritanism' and all its works ; who habitually speak of it as Gibbon is said to speak of Christianity—as if it had done them a personal injury. There is an ' indignatio ' about their books which is incompatible with sane judgment ; and we understand a fury in their words, but the words not always. Strangely enough, this fury leads them to attack most savagely the cheerful side of Puritan philosophy. A man who sees in the conception of an overruling Providence a compensation for the ills of this life is to them a red rag to a bull. That anyone should think there is somewhere a state in which the broken arcs will make the perfect round, however harmless such an opinion may be, is precisely what stirs in them a frenzy of exasperation, and drives them to present the world in the worst light conceivable. There is excuse for the gloom of Gissing in the poverty and unhappiness of Gissing's own life : one can hardly expect a bright picture of Grub Street from one who, knowing himself worthy of a better domicile, is compelled to live for years in that thoroughfare. But there are others without this excuse, and some whose melancholy seems deliberate and wanton. I know how passionately Hardy repudiated the charge of exaggerating the darkness of life ; he seems to have been genuinely surprised when pessimism was imputed to him, and protested that his sportive 'President of the Immortals' was really a benevolent and parental Zeus ; but despite his protests I think the imputation not unjustified : and, though it led him to renounce the novel and turn to poetry, his poems are if possible even more pessimistic than his prose. As to some other more recent writers, I do not *think*; I am sure. Mr. Cowper Powys, for example, hardly redeems, by the real force

and beauty of his style, the repellent dreariness of the
themes he chooses, and the sordid ugliness of the
characters he draws. Many of the war-novelists, again,
seem to take an Iago-like pleasure in picturing horror
for its own sake, and in dwelling on the stupidities,
the wickednesses, and the loathsomenesses brought
out by the conflict while passing by all the compensating virtues. Such writers, though they may not know
it, are harking back, from sheer modernity, to medieval-
ism, and giving us the notions of Pope Innocent from
motives the opposite of his. The Pope aimed at so
painting the miseries of men in this life as to induce
them to fix their gaze on the next : these authors
neither allure to brighter worlds nor lead the way.
They appear to be literary anarchists, denouncing the
evils of the present régime but offering no substitute,
and contenting themselves merely with stirring up a
useless rebellion against the inevitable. It is apparently
their object to stimulate the mad frenzy of a rat in
a corner, or to urge the bird in the cage to beat its
wings eternally against the bars. What good such beat-
ing can do is hard to see : but the relentless author
goes on with his Cade-like harangues, and finds a
strange satisfaction in torturing both himself and
others. He is Byron's Cain once more : exasperated
by the presence of evil, but still more keenly exasperated by the sight of a humility which takes it as
it comes or of a philosophy which seeks compensations
for it. He hates the Ruler who allows the evil, and
hates still more the men who will not murmur at the
rule. His excuse is always the assumed necessity of
telling the ' truth.' Je n'en vois pas la nécessité : but
were the obligation never so great, did it come with
the force of Kant's categorical imperative, I have yet

to learn that this truth is more than half the reality, and therefore any better than falsehood. It may be true that we shall all die : but we owe no gratitude to those who are always dinning our mortality into our ears. And these writers do worse : they tell us we are already dead.

As one surveys the world, one sees, or thinks one sees, a good deal of happiness ; crossed, it is true, with a good deal of misery ; but still happiness. It is strange, then, that authors of the kind I have described should try to persuade the happy that their happiness is but imaginary : first, because they ought to see that imaginary happiness *is* happiness, and secondly, because one would think the aim of intelligent men would naturally be to increase the sum of enjoyment rather than to diminish it. It is still more strange that the readers should find pleasure in this very diminution of their pleasure. But so it is ; and so it will always be at certain intervals, and in certain people. And then, as they discover that this way of pursuing the great end is still more futile than others, they will once again turn to the cheerful writers, who try the more rational method of encouraging men *in order to* encourage them.

XVIII

THE TASTE FOR THE EXOTIC

No nation liveth to itself, and none dieth to itself. As plagues laugh at boundaries, so do more beneficent influences. Civilisation affects neighbouring barbarism, and ideas pass stealthily from country to country. Fairy-stories, like that of Jason, have been tracked all round the world, as the dust of Krakatoa glorified sunsets twenty thousand miles to westward. Adventurers brought to England words, as well as wealth, from Lithuania, and Crusaders, returning, enlarged our vocabulary. Literary fashions, also, have passed, more slowly perhaps but equally surely, from nation to nation, have been imposed by conquest upon the weaker, or have been insinuated by the vanquished into the victor. After the crushing Peace of 1763, the French indulged in Anglomania ; and after the Armada there were still Englishmen who imitated the Spaniards.

Even the Jews, though always a proud, and at least latterly an exclusive race, assimilated foreign culture on a vast scale. Very early in their career they ' spoiled the Egyptians ' ; and for a long time afterwards they adopted foreign gods. To judge by the denunciations of the prophets, they were very quick to mimic foreign extravagances of apparel, and alien modes of life and speech. Their religion was permanently modified by their contact with Babylon, Persia, and Greece ; and at times the love of alien ways became an absolute infatuation. Hebrew Joshua posed as Jason, and High-Priest Eliakim changed his name to Alcimus. Nothing but the heroism of the Maccabees saved Judaism from becoming a variety of Hellenism. This example is enough to show that a taste for the exotic may be both good and bad.

Extant Hebrew literature is so small in amount that we cannot make an accurate calculation as to how far it was influenced by these foreign forces. But the first chapter of Genesis is certainly of Babylonian origin ; the story of Joseph may have come from Egypt, and that of the Flood from the Euphrates. It is more than probable that many individual Psalms, and possibly the very habit of Psalm-making, sprang from Babylon : the likeness in style, tone, and metre between many of those addressed to Yahweh and those addressed to Bel or Marduk is astonishing, and cannot be explained as a mere accident. Is the following, for example, which I take from Cheyne's Translation of the Psalms, by David or by a Chaldean priest ?

> The anger of my Lord's heart,
>   May it be appeased !
> I am cast down,
>   And none reacheth forth his hand to me.
> I utter my prayer,
>   And none heareth me ;
> I am enfeebled and overwhelmed,
>   But no man delivereth me.
> O my God, my sins are seven times seven,
>   Forgive my sins ;
> Absolve my faults ;
>   Guide thou him who submitteth himself
>   to thee.

As a matter of fact, this Psalm, which might well be chanted in our churches, dates from the seventeenth

century before Christ : and the following, addressed
to the Moon-god Sin, is perhaps even earlier :

> Thy will, thine, who knoweth it ?
> And who can change it ?
> O Lord, thou rulest in heaven,
> And thy dominion is in the earth ;
> Among the gods there is none like thee.

At times we find even literal translations. In the Book
of Ecclesiastes there are one or two passages taken
directly from the famous Gilgamesh epic. The familiar
' Let thy garments be white, nor let oil be lacking on
thy head ' is from the ' Descent of Ishtar ' : and this
is the more remarkable as Ecclesiastes is so Greek in
tone that some scholars have thought its author to
have been acquainted with Cynic or Stoic philosophers.

Later Jewish writings, of course, are impregnated
with foreign influences. The Talmud, in spite of its
native appearance, is full of anecdotes, stories, and
philosophisings which must at one time or other have
been borrowed. It is only just to say that, whatever
the debt of Judaism to other nations, it has been
generously repaid : for what European literature and
science owe to Jewish writers and thinkers is beyond
reckoning.

It may seem that the case of Greece is different. For
it is a curious fact that while the Athenians, not only
in St. Luke's time but long before, spent their time
in nothing else but either to hear or to tell some new
thing, neither they nor the rest of the Greeks, as a
general rule, manifested a keen desire to learn a
foreign language or to adopt any intellectual or
æsthetic fashion from abroad. They were quite
satisfied with their own ways and their own science.
They met the Persians, but borrowed from them

neither the habit of telling the truth nor anything else : and it must have struck them as an eccentricity in Xenophon that, when writing a romance picturing the ideal king, he should have chosen the Persian Cyrus as his hero. They had much to do with the Italians and the Sicels, but it would be hard to say what they learnt from them. The curiosity of Herodotus, it is true, was unbounded, and he shows none of that contempt for the barbarian which was so common among his countrymen ; but Herodotus was an Ionian and an Asiatic. Aristotle actually condescends, when investigating forms of polity, to discuss the Carthaginian constitution, and to compare it not unfavourably with that of Lacedæmon ; but Aristotle was a Stagirite, and had been brought up under Macedonian influences. Even he suffered somewhat from patriotic narrowness. It has often been observed that certain of the weak points in his philosophy may be explained by his neglect of foreign languages. Had he, for instance, known Hebrew or Persian, he would have perceived that not a few logical conceptions which he took for universal laws of thought were really but peculiarities of Greek diction and grammar. Other Greeks, as might be expected, were far more restricted in outlook than the traveller of Halicarnassus or the thinker of Stageira. With an arrogance more excusable in their case than in that of most other nations, they were content with their own achievements, and thought them more their own than they really were. They ' forgot the rock whence they were hewn, and the hole of the pit whence they were digged,' fancying themselves of unadulterated stock, and sufficient for their own needs. It is probable, on the contrary, that the beginnings of Greek art were Egyptian or Oriental ;

their alphabet, by the confession of their own legends, certainly came from Phœnicia ; much of the general culture must have been derived from some other foreign source : but once started it went on without much external assistance. It is fortunate for the world that the Greek mind was sufficiently powerful to make immense advances even under these self-imposed restrictions.

Not, of course, that this protective system kept out all imports. After, and before, the conquests of Alexander had Hellenised the East and at the same time Orientalised Hellas, many foreign ideas overleaped the barriers. Much in Pythagoras bears traces of eastern origin, and it is not without reason that Plato is said to have spent some time in Egypt. The vastly influential Stoic philosophy unquestionably owes much to the Syrian strain of its founder ; and there can be little doubt that the mathematical discoveries of the Alexandrians were largely based on the arithmetical achievements of the native Egyptians. Barbarians, Aristotle held, were by nature slaves ; but even when enslaved they surreptitiously contributed much to their masters. Nevertheless, in comparison with most other nations, the Greeks may be considered as intellectually isolated and independent. Their civilisation was not stagnant like the Chinese, but it was thoroughly Chinese in its exclusiveness.

Very different has it been with the rest of Europe, and especially with the Romans, who annexed not only the lands of other peoples but their gods and their culture, and made a complete conquest of everything Greek. With some exaggeration it may be affirmed that Roman literature is Greek literature translated, and Roman art Greek art transplanted and vulgarised

in the process. And this the Romans did with a deliberate and continuous purpose, to improve and enlarge
their own possessions. Seeing the vast superiority of
the Greeks, they set to work to make themselves, as
far as possible, the equals of their captives. For two
or three hundred years they spent their energies in
Latinising Greek metres, Greek styles, Greek classes
of literature ; in trying to be Roman Homers, Roman
Alcæuses, Roman Theocrituses, Roman Callimachuses.
To introduce into their coteries an as yet unknown
Greek lyric measure was, in their view, to be original ;
and to walk on a Greek road was to be an explorer of
yet untrodden paths. To imitate another was to find
yourself.

What Rome did to Greece other nations did to her.
The people she conquered annexed her civilisation in
their turn. It was at second-hand, through Rome, that
the Western world received a diluted Hellenic culture ;
and the history of the West is that of the willing or
compulsory acceptance of this civilisation. When
Rome was imperial, her arts were spread by her armies ;
when she became Papal, they accompanied the march
of her missionary legions.

In Britain the first invasion, though it ended in
a conquest, and though its effect lasted through four
hundred years, was nevertheless ephemeral : it came
by the sword and it perished by the sword. The
traces it has left are scarcely more than relics for the
museums, a few hundred miles of road, a few ruined
fortresses, a few thousand pieces of pottery. The
traces of the second inroad are everywhere and in
everything ; they stare at us in our language, in our
religion, in our ways of thought.

Yet, vast as was this influence, and rapidly as it made

its way, it would be a mistake to imagine that the
reception given by our early English ancestors to
Roman literature, and their adoption of Latin models,
sprang from a mere *taste* for the exotic. It was due
to a stern necessity ; indeed to several stern necessities.
Wise men, while, of course, recognising that their own
state was not uncivilised—in fact *because* they had this
recognition—recognised also how much they had to
learn from the newcomers. If they wished to rise
to the level of the invaders, they must learn Latin,
and study Latin books. How they felt may be gathered
from what Alfred has told us of his feelings when a
barbarian invasion swept the Latin culture temporarily
away : it was a terrible loss ; and therefore its first
acquisition must have been felt as an immense gain.
But further, the invasion came as a religious crusade,
and the religion (I am speaking broadly and loosely)
was an exclusive religion. The old cults, and the old
literature, were to be rooted out. Fortunately the
attempt completely to root them out failed : but it was
made, and partially succeeded. Poets and reciters,
once converted, had, like Cynewulf, to renounce the
old epics and stories, and give instead metrical lives
of saints. Some liberal-minded men might retain such
a poem as *Beowulf*, but only at the price of lending
to certain passages a Christian colouring. As a rule,
the poets (or those whose works remain) wrote epics
based on the Old Testament, keeping the ancient
forms, but introducing a new substance. You had to
accept Latin not merely to improve this world but to
make sure of the next. We do not find the men of
letters studying Roman writers in order to enlarge and
vivify their own style : they kept the one-half of their
minds, so to speak, closed to the other. When adopting

a foreign subject they treated it in the native way ; the story of Helena or the voyage of St. Andrew is in the exact manner of an English epic, metre, alliteration, ' kennings,' all unchanged : but the point is this, that the English epic has not been remodelled by the study of Virgil ; it is *Beowulf* with a saint instead of a Viking for a hero. Andrew is a ' gesith ' of Christ ; Constantine is a Hygelac or Hrothgar ; there is no sign that the poets ever tried to turn a Hengest or a Walter of Aquitaine into an Æneas : and the *arrangement* of the story remained as before. Even when a ' riddle ' of Eusebius or Aldhelm was brought over, it became English in the transit. It would, in fact, be very difficult to find, in all old English poetry, more than a few lines which show even *imitation* of classical poems. There is *one* description of a storm which is supposed by some to contain reminiscences of the first book of Virgil, and there are lines here and there, perhaps sometimes monkish interpolations, which remind one of this or that Latin passage ; but the whole tone is native. Even rhyme, so familiar in Christian Latin verse, makes but a sporadic appearance in early English. A ' Cædmon ' took his subject from the Vulgate Genesis, but he made no *Æneid* or *Thebaid* out of it. Conscious effort to transfer classical method and arrangement, or to adopt classical forms, is conspicuous by its absence.

When, however, we pass to later, post-conquest times, we do find precisely that ' taste for the exotic ' which we have hitherto missed : we discern an almost exact repetition of what happened in Italy at the end of the Republican period. Bilingual writers, familiar with French style, reproduced it in the English tongue : the old alliterative system tended gradually to dis-

appear, and rhyme, with more regular accent, took
its place.   Lyrics appear, not, as before, blended with
epic, but isolated and distinct : a change that could
not have happened but for French influence : and
romances are written in French fashion, often, indeed,
being mere translations from the French.   Later still,
we note a more deliberate imitation.   Really great
writers, feeling at once the strength and the weakness
of their own language, and casting about for every
possible means of widening its range and improving
its quality, look abroad first to continental France and
then to Italy to find what they desire.   In the case of
the two chief poets of the fourteenth century, Chaucer
and the author of *Pearl*, we can see this impulse very
clearly.   The latter, though writing in a more than
English dialect, and retaining all the native devices of
alliteration and stock phrase, openly owns his dependence on ' Clopingel ' and his *Romance of the Rose :* nay,
he has been suspected of borrowing from the *Divine
Comedy* itself.   Chaucer's whole literary life is the
story of a search abroad for mediums of expression
which he might regard as worthy of the genius stirring
within him.   He tries the French octosyllabic, and
perceives that, while powerful up to a point, it is not
equal to his deeper and wider ideas.   He experiments
here, and investigates there : he finds his subjects in
Latin literature, and from Ovid or Virgil gains hints
as to the balance of a story.   He lights on Italian, and
at last descries what he has been seeking.   At first he
tests himself in almost literal translation, but gradually
he acquires freedom, until in *Troilus* and the later
Canterbury Tales he is no longer the mere pupil, but
the original who has learnt how to make his own that
which he has borrowed, and to plagiarise without steal-

ing. Nothing more English than Chaucer's best works
has ever been written ; and yet nothing shows more
plainly the influence of Latin, French, and Italian
models. He is like the Venice that Shakespeare describes—a city with a marked and distinctive native
character, and yet one ' whose trade and profit con-
sisteth of all nations.' Chaucer is made up of Machault,
de Guileville, Boccaccio, Petrarch, Dante ; and yet
he is Chaucer and nobody else.

We can dimly see, however, that as in Rome there
were Catos who resisted the Greek invasion, so there
were in England some who, consciously or unconsciously, clave to their ancestral style. The ' rum, ram,
ruf ' of the ancient alliterative poetry Chaucer utterly
rejected, as, to judge by *Sir Thopas*, he probably
despised the romantic ballads. Yet there were plainly
some who would have none of the foreign style, and
deliberately kept the native, nay, revived it where it
had fallen into oblivion. Even the author of *Pearl*,
though as we have seen he certainly knew the French
poets, in *Gawayne*, his longest and in some respects his
best work, deliberately followed the old fashion, and
produced a poem in which scarcely a trace of foreign
style is to be found. Similarly, the author of the
Vision concerning Piers the Plowman, whose appeal was
not to the court but to the people, addressed his
audience in a dialect and a metre which were meant, if
they did not wholly contrive, to recall the pre-Conquest
poems. He was resolved to have as little as possible to
do with importations from abroad : for him purely
English goods were best. This dispute is typical of
what always happens when there is a great expansion of
literary interest : nor is it to be regretted that such
disputes arise. There is room for all schools ; and the

rivalry is beneficial to all. The native school, in its attempt to show it can do without assistance, is moved to ' do wel, do bet, and do best ' : and the same force acts upon its antagonists.

We have but little direct information as to this rivalry in Chaucer's time : but when we come to the Elizabethans there is no such lack. Rather we have a plethora of criticisms, essays, discourses, showing the liveliness of the warfare and the zeal of the combatants. In the Elizabethan Age the ' taste for the exotic ' was an absolute mania ; and the opposition was equally fanatical.

Critics have laboured to discover the secret of the sudden and enormous outpouring of the Elizabethan Age, and, of course, have discovered no single cause. If, among the multitude of causes that might be adduced, I were to select the chief, I should answer, without hesitation : the Elizabethan Age was great because it was an age of borrowing, an age in which men spoiled the Egyptians without scruple, and seized avariciously every hint from other lands. Drake and Hawkins did not help themselves more rapaciously to the wealth of the Spaniards than Spenser and Shakespeare helped themselves to the intellectual treasures of France and Italy. They made England great because they refused to consider England only, but cast their net over the whole of Europe. If they heard that French poets were trying experiments with the French language, they tried similar experiments with English. If they heard of an Italian novel, they procured it, translated it, adapted it for the stage. Whatever was done in any corner of their world by men, they made the ' farrago ' of their books. Like Chaucer they remained Englishmen, but they enlarged the Englishman into the European. Nay more, they put the whole known past under tribute : they ransacked Greek and Latin literature for themes, for guidance, for warnings, for suggestions. No one has yet counted the number of versions of ancient and foreign books which indefatigable workers turned into the vernacular, and on to which the authors pounced eagerly for ' copy.'

It is no part of my business to draw out into detail the story of this enormous and ceaseless pillage : those who wish to realise merely the robberies by which Spenser built up his *Faerie Queene* may read it in Professor Renwick's admirable book. They will learn there what a vast amount of foreign wealth went to the making of those seventy cantos. But the rest were like him. Marlowe, Greene, Fletcher, Ford, Webster, all alike stole, and made what they stole their own. Timon might have been speaking allegorically of the writers of the time when he burst out into his famous declamation :

> The sun's a thief, and with his great attraction
> Robs the vast sea : the moon's an arrant thief,
> And her pale fire she snatches from the sun :
> The sea's a thief, whose liquid surge resolves
> The moon into salt tears ; the earth's a thief,
> That feeds and breeds by a composture stolen
> From general excrement : each thing's a thief.

And, in the whole Elizabethan firmament, the sun was the greatest of the thieves. Not Autolycus stole more indiscriminately and shamelessly than Shakespeare.

The immense scale of this borrowing would take a volume to illustrate : but a yet fuller idea of it may be gained by anyone who will read Sidney Lee's essay, entitled ' Shakespeare and the Italian Renaissance,' in which we catch a view of the incessant travels of

Englishmen to Italy, and of the intellectual spoils which they brought back with them; of the rarer and more far-between visits of Italians to England, and of the wealth they left behind for those who were capable of picking it up. Sidney, Bacon, Daniel, Spenser, Harvey, Hoby—every worker in every field, owned his obligations to the foreigner, and did his best to share his gains with his countrymen. Even ' home-keeping youths ' enlarged their ' homely wits ' by studying the foreign languages or poring over the translations which scholars poured out almost daily for their use. Whether Shakespeare himself knew Italian, French, or Spanish may be doubted : but the influence reached him directly or indirectly, and its effects are visible in almost every play he wrote.

We never, in fact, see any great advance in English literature, but we find, if we look closely, that it was either founded on or intimately associated with a new discovery of some foreign country. An age of transition has usually been an age of translation. Men suddenly find out that another country has something to give them of which they have subconsciously felt the need ; they have ideas waiting for expression, but no medium for expressing them, or means of expression without the appropriate thought. Foreign thoughts, foreign styles, approach the shore ; and, like the dark Iberians, the natives go down to welcome them— becoming richer by the traffic, not for a few months, but for generations. So, emphatically, it was in the Restoration Era, when everything French was sure of a welcome across the Channel. This Gallic influence has been exaggerated, but only because it is possible for men to exaggerate anything, however vast. It was certainly immense. The criticism, and the example, of

Boileau, the theories of Bossu, which were a development of Boileau's, the plays of Corneille, Molière
and Racine, and a host of minor forces, came over to
give direction and strength to tendencies already
existing : and they continued to work for a hundred
years. The number of actual translations of French
works is prodigious ; the number of imitations still
greater.

When, in turn, the reaction came to ' Romanticism,'
once again foreign importations played their part.
The new criticism, of which Lessing is the representative name, is associated with the migration of Shakespeare to Germany : the romantic movement in England is closely associated with the migration of German
writers to England. Scott's versions of *Götz von Ber-
lichingen* and of Bürger's ballads (themselves inspired
by Percy's *Reliques*) are but straws pointing the way
in which a mighty wind was blowing : the whole school
of novelists of the ' Terror ' school is German in origin ;
Coleridge's criticism, whether actually borrowed from
Schlegel or not, bears marked traces of its Teutonic
sources, as does the whole work of De Quincey and
Carlyle. The mania, indeed, like the *Anglomania* of
Voltaire and his followers half a century before, was
almost too violent, and needed repression rather than
encouragement : some Germans were accepted simply
because they were Germans : the plays of Kotzebue
and the criticisms of Schlosser would have been seen
through much sooner had they been English. But on
the whole the conquest was a great benefit to the conquered. How great, we have only recently begun to
realise with approximate exactness.

The whole Romantic movement, indeed, might be
defined as the peaceful penetration of England by

her neighbours, and of the neighbours by her. It was a happy pestilence, sweeping from Germany to America, and back again, silently but irresistibly, all alike being affected and affecting. The part played in it by the French Revolution has been described a hundred times ; but the French Revolution had its English causes. Shakespeare crosses the Rhine, and the result is Goethe and Schiller, who in their turn pass back to us. But the movement was still more wide-spread than even this description might indicate. If we had gained so much from one or two countries, what might we not gain from many ? Searchers went forth into more distant countries, and returned to endeavour, more or less successfully, to naturalise their plunder. As Coleridge had brought so much from Germany, Southey would see what Spain and Portugal could bring, either of their own or of their colonial annexations : nay, he went further, to Persia and to India. Whether from a want of genius, or from a certain incompatibility between his themes and the English mind, his epics failed to rouse much interest ; and his *History of Brazil*, which he hoped would at least make the fortunes of his grandchildren, did not even pay the publishers ; but the attempt showed the general trend of feeling. A more popular poet, Thomas Moore, achieved a great but short-lived success with *Lalla Rookh*, which, whatever his grand-children may think of it, brought *him* three thousand pounds. And Byron's best poems are all informed with an interest in foreign countries, an interest which foreign countries have fully reciprocated. You can find the same thing even in the smaller poets—and when the smaller poets try a style, it is always because it is the vogue. James Montgomery's *Greenland*, John

Wilson's *Isle of Palms*, would not have been written if their public had limited its gaze to the North Sea and the Channel.

So far as this interest was based on a perception that no nation can be self-sufficing, that every nation has something to contribute to the intellectual advance of every other, it was wholly good : and most people will admit that the increase in range and depth which English literature showed at this period was a real advance on what had preceded it ; that even *Thalaba* is an improvement on the confined ' citizen ' poems of the eighteenth century. One of the chief claims of Gray to the gratitude of posterity is his perception of beauty in Welsh and Icelandic poetry, and in his attempts—too few—to introduce these beauties to English readers : and even Macpherson deserves *some* gratitude for similar though less honest endeavours. But the foreign element, to have its perfect work, must be assimilated : it must become part and parcel of the native literature. It was here that Southey failed, and it was because of a certain lack of sincerity that Moore's success was only temporary. He had made a careful study of his brief, and the mimicry of Oriental style was really wonderful ; but *Lalla Rookh*, after all, is but a *tour de force*.

As with the Elizabethan Age, so with the Victorian : the chief cause of the enormous output, of the increase in width, of the immense *average* advance that the Victorians made as compared with their predecessors, was the receptiveness of their minds, and their willingness to learn from everywhere. This can be seen in small things as in great. *Hiawatha*, for example, is not perhaps the highest poetry, but it shows the desire to understand civilisations, if such they can be called, that are different from ours, and its vast popularity has given it an influence totally out of proportion to its intrinsic worth : nor are the Algonquins by any means the only nation whose legends Longfellow ransacked for inspiration. Tennyson is perhaps the most insular of modern poets of distinction, but he learnt from science and borrowed from the Welsh and the Irish. Browning's themes are almost all foreign : even when he wished to write a patriotic ballad he chose a Breton sailor as his hero ; and he found more to stir him in Italy and France than in England : nay, he was one of the first to pry into the closed cupboards of the Talmud. Swinburne went to France, Morris to the Sagas of Iceland. Whether these men were the equals in genius of the Wordsworths and Shelleys may be disputed ; but that the literature as a whole was taking a wider sweep is beyond doubt. Since then a multitude of influences, among which the growing interest in anthropology is not the least, have strengthened the impulse to gather in everything from abroad that can be gathered. We have seen the star of Ibsen cross our horizon, the novels of Björnson and Knut Hamsun, the work of Tourguenéff, Tolstoi, Dostoieffsky, a host of books from Poland, Hungary, Holland, Italy, and Spain, nay from India, China, and Japan ; fairy-tales from the Malay, from the Polynesian, from South America ; Persian poetry, Czecho-Slovakian, Swedish, Serbian, Roumanian. The effect cannot be seen clearly as yet ; but that it will be great is certain. There will be, ere long, a literature English in language, but world-wide in appeal.

All this springs from some of the simplest and most elemental strains in human nature. Man is an inquisitive animal, and he is an imitative animal : we

z

can trace these characteristics alike in the most primitive tribes of which we have knowledge and in the
children whom we have about us in our own generation.
We want to know and see, and seeing we like to imitate.
The habit decays, too frequently, as we grow old;
but in a people, which is never more than partially
old at any one time, it constantly renews itself; and
we often see an 'old' nation putting itself in pupilage
to a 'young' one, and then, in its turn, instructing
its teacher. All the nations of the world are doing
so at the present moment; imitating and being
imitated, teaching and being taught. I am patriotic
enough to believe that my own country, while
gaining much from others, is giving them more. As
Athens was the schoolmistress of Greece, I like to
fancy that England may become the schoolmistress
of the world. If so, one may put up with a decline
in other respects. It may be that we shall see
on a larger scale what happened to Edinburgh two
hundred years ago. When Edinburgh ceased to be
the political capital of a kingdom, she soon gained a
greater glory, that of intellectual supremacy. Re-
nouncing the position of the Scottish Rome, she became
the Northern Athens. So, perhaps, it may be with
England. The star of physical empire may move
westward: but the dominion of the mind may be ours.

XIX

CATHOLICITY OF TASTE

It does not fall precisely within the limits of my subject, yet it may be desirable, after discussing such a multitude of forms of taste, to consider what ought to be our attitude towards them. I do not mean that we should decide what is the *right* taste—the whole tendency of our studies has been to show that there is no such thing, or—what is in effect the same—that there are innumerable right tastes. What I mean is this—as we contemplate this crowd of competing styles and judgments, what ought to be the wise man's view of them? A parallel may be found in politics. Every nation has its own peculiar point of view, conflicting in some measure with that of others. The narrow-minded patriot assumes without reflection that his own country's ideas are right. But the philosophic publicist, while not losing his own patrotic preference, takes a far wider survey, and endeavours to understand the conceptions and prejudices of all, finally subsuming them under one universal idea. He is cosmopolitan as well as national. Similarly with the true critic, whatever his personal predilections, when he comes to survey the multitudinous predilections of others. He tries to understand and to generalise.

Help may be obtained by returning once more to the original meaning of taste, and by considering its physical aspect. Let me, at the risk of wearying the reader, recall something of what we were saying at the beginning. Few people admire gluttony, and most of us agree that the Church was right to put it among the Seven Deadly Sins. Yet though we should hesitate to ask Apicius to dinner, we should choose as a guest the man with a hearty and even indiscriminate appetite rather than the man with a long list of dislikes. I am not speaking here of the obvious perils involved in asking Carlyle to spend a week with us, or of the terrible results of offering him nothing he could digest. The fastidious man may be as eupeptic as his omnivorous friend, as easy to get on with, and as ' clubbable.' But, so long at least as the meal lasts, the man who can devour a plain rice-pudding with as much zest as the finest creations of Brillat-Savarin, is the better companion both for others and for himself. At any rate, he causes the housewife less anxiety beforehand. It is a pleasant trait in the Epicurean Mæcenas that he could appreciate a Sabine repast with Horace as thoroughly as one served in the Esquiline mansion by his own cook. Horace would have liked him less had the preparations for receiving him involved much trouble and expense.

Something similar may be said of literary enjoyment. It is not desirable that one should live so long and so exclusively on the more exquisite varieties of mental food as to have no palate for the coarser and more robust. There are—or perhaps were—men who can enjoy nothing less ' precious ' than the prose of Walter Pater or the poetry of the French Symbolists : anything less dainty is to them as ' earthy and abhorred ' as the commands of Sycorax to the delicate Ariel. An adjective not at once surprising and yet miraculously appropriate is a mere patch ; the verb must be always unexpected and yet satisfying : and the collocations must be such as have never been seen before. A good, hearty, vigorous style is to them vulgar and rough : what used to be called ' masculine ' or ' nervous ' they regard as boisterous ; and a tone above a whisper is uproarious. They remind us of the women of the early nineteenth century whose business it was to cultivate delicacy of health, and who were vain of their ability to faint on the slightest provocation. This, however, would I confess, I find myself preferring to this excess of niceness the manly receptivity of such a reader as Bishop Thirlwall, who, though nourished on the masterpieces of Greece and Rome, could stomach even the mushy novels of his time—boggling only at the *Wide Wide World*.

Even if the preference is of a less valetudinarian cast,—even if it is for styles which have been recognised as great through almost all ages, it is as well not to contract the preference into exclusiveness. You may admire Homer, but leave room for Apollonius ; you may prefer Demosthenes, but you will miss much if you ignore Lysias : you may, like certain old scholars, confine yourself to the classics of the Golden Age, but the Silver is not to be despised with impunity.

The fact is that catholicity of taste is not incompatible with discrimination : it is, rather, almost indispensable to it. If you have nothing of a lower kind with which to compare the best, the best will seem but ordinary. If all the world were as high as the Himalayas, Everest would not be so imposing ; and if every soprano could sing C, we should think less of our prima donnas. The barrel-organ has its use as providing a contrast to Paderewski. You must know the evil in order the more wisely to choose the good. As sanctity

is not mere innocence, so true taste is not to be attained
by the exclusive knowledge of good books : the critic,
like the Christian, is he who knows the bad and rises
superior to it.

By ' catholicity ' we do not, then, mean the willingness to accept anything whatever. We rather imply
that *discriminating* width of taste which, while never
losing its hold on the truly good, can yet appreciate a
multiplicity of styles. We mean by it a certain lofty
and commanding versatility which, while not rejecting
the new, can retain an attachment to the old, and
which, while loving the native has a welcome for the
exotic. It is at once cosmopolitan and patriotic. Such
a taste, like all tastes, must have its preferences, but it
will not be narrow. ' True love,' whether for mankind
or for letters, ' in this differs from gold or clay, that to
divide is not to take away.' It will recognise that the
goodness of the new wine does not make the old worse :
that a poem which has once been meritorious does not
lose its merit because another style has appeared, and
that a genre which is approved on one side of the
Channel cannot become depraved by crossing over. A
catholic-minded man, in this sense of the word, is not
to be influenced by place or time, and will receive a
good thing from Nazareth as from Jerusalem. Had
he lived in the beginning of the nineteenth century he
would have been able to appreciate the Romantic
poets without depreciating the Classical : he would not
have thrown aside his Pope because he could admire his
Wordsworth. Nor, to-day, would he cast aside Tennyson or Milton, because he can see the beauties of the
moderns. His critical power would save him from
exaggeration on one side or the other : and his catholicity would enable him to think more highly of the

old because he can contrast it with the new. His
mind is capacious enough for both : and, by this capacity, he becomes a better judge of each than the
devotees of either. It is a great mistake to imagine
that width of mind involves tepidity or indifference :
there is no reason why a man should not admire many
things and yet admire them all with enthusiasm :
nay, the more you love one style the more keenly, if
your mind is but broad enough, will you love another.
The danger is rather on the other side. Fastidiousness
tends too easily to that *nil admirari* spirit than which
nothing can be more injurious to true criticism.

A mind of the sort here described, capable at once
of the widest intellectual charity and of the most
delicate perception, is, of course, excessively rare, and
does not exist in full manifestation outside of Utopia.
To prove all things, holding fast that which is good,
and yet to vaunt not oneself and to think no evil, is
a height of perfection as difficult of attainment in the
mental as in the Christian life : and so many extraneous
motives come in to warp the judgment that mere
humanity can scarcely expect to disregard them all.
Those who can admire equally, or rather with equal
justice, two opposing styles are as few as, according to
Coleridge, are those who can sympathise equally with
Aristotle and with Plato. There was in Leigh Hunt an
astonishing insight into the greatness of Shelley and
Keats when hardly anyone else recognised it : but this
insight was purchased at the cost of blindness to a
different kind of excellence, and was probably sharp-
ened by political and personal attachments. He was
predisposed to expect genius in these poets, and therefore found it more easily than those whose predilections were different. No critic, probably, has ever

surpassed Hazlitt in penetration and acuteness ; but we know that, whenever a new book came out, his impulse was to re-read an old one : his taste had been formed early, and he was not over-ready to ' grasp in the comer.' Matthew Arnold, great as in some respects he was, was limited ; his nature was somewhat arrogant, and he had a tendency to oppose the opinions of those—and they were many—whom he despised : nor did his contempt work less strongly because he was quite unconscious of it. His critical judgments were often distorted by baseless prejudices which were none the less real because he could defend them as if they were reasoned opinions. Even Coleridge, who had known the pains of being ignored as an innovator, showed signs in later life of a dislike of innovation ; while Wordsworth, toward the end of his career, approved of hardly any poetry but his own. Ruskin, the devotee of Dante, loses no chance, and indeed makes many chances, of depreciating Milton ; and Landor, the devotee of Milton, did not care for Dante. Goethe himself, the myriad-minded, whose interests were almost universal, also thought Dante overrated. Where we do find wide sympathy, again, it is not always true catholicity—it is sometimes rather an imperceptive-ness, or imperviousness to higher considerations. Dryden, for example, the least jealous of poet-critics, shows a marvellous capacity for admiring talents the most various and the most different from his own. He praises Shakespeare, Milton, Chaucer, Congreve, and a host of poetasters whom his praise, and nothing else, has saved from oblivion : and he would have praised Flecknoe himself if he had not required him as the poetical father of Shadwell. But this, pleasant as it is, seems due rather to a kind of critical good-nature, to a willingness to believe the best of everybody, than to a *discriminating* catholicity, which, recognising faults and limitations, yet sees the compensating greatness. He is perhaps a little too generous, like those men whose charity to their neighbours irritates by its inability to distinguish the bad from the good. Of all English critics, perhaps Gray is the only one who unites the keen and penetrating eye with an absence of prejudice.

And this is because of all English critics, Gray had the most learning and the fullest historic sense. He had nourished his mind on the greatest writers, and thus had a standard. But his erudition, and his imagination, were such that he could enter easily into the minds of different ages and nations, and realise what were the characteristics which made certain poets answer exactly to the demands of their surroundings. The age was so and so : the poet had to be such and such to suit its requirements. While reading the poet, Gray became his countryman and his contemporary, and appreciated him accordingly. On the other hand, he could read his own contemporaries against a background of the past : and hence his criticisms on them have scarcely ever been reversed. I know but two cases, and those doubtful ones, in which his judgment was distorted by the influences of his own time. He failed, perhaps, to see the metrical skill of Collins, and personal attachment, it would seem, led him to assign to Mason a higher position than anyone is likely to give him again. But it would be hard to find, among the numerous notes scattered in Gray's letters, any other failure in due appreciation : he is very nearly the type of the man who, from whatever school a poem may proceed, can feel its merits without omitting to mark its defects.

He knew too much to be taken in ; and he felt too keenly himself not to recognise true feeling in whatever guise it might present itself. He saw the greatness of Dante ; and he saw also the tiny talent of Gresset.

I dwell on Gray because his example shows the wide range of qualities which are involved in real catholicity of taste. If Gray, ' the most learned man in Europe,' a poet himself, and one whose taste had been trained by long study of the best literature of many languages, hardly attained it, how can others hope even to come near it ? None the less, though like virtue unattainable, it is an ideal worth aiming at. For the range of pure pleasure open to the wide-minded is obviously far greater than that possible to the confined : and, on the other hand, the man of wide taste is far less likely (if I may mix my metaphors) to be deluded by false lights. And everyone who misses a pleasure through ignorance or prejudice earns the appropriate penalty. He misses it.

Ignorance, indeed, is the main cause of narrowness. Those who unthinkingly rejected the whole eighteenth century because of the Hayleys and the Pyes, did so because they had not sufficient knowledge of the real merits of the greater men ; because they did not take the pains to understand the age to which the eighteenth-century poets appealed ; because they looked for faults only and would not search for virtues. The same has been the case with those who have rejected the 'Victorian' Age. Inquire into what they know about that age, and you will find an almost universal blank. As Dr. Andrew Bradley has shown in detail, and as anyone who takes trouble can see, the popular censures on Tennyson proceed, and can only proceed, from total ignorance of a large part of Tennyson's work. A few poems—perhaps his worst, perhaps not —are selected from the large mass, and—in defiance of the fact that Tennyson was writing for sixty years, and that no poet is more various—are held up to ridicule as samples of the whole. This is the old story of the traveller who, asked what Babylon was like, presented a brick as a specimen. Here again the punishment is just. The censor, in his wilful ignorance, misses some of the purest and most unique pleasures to be found in English literature. That the sinner does not feel his loss is no mitigation of the chastisement.

The mention of Tennyson suggests another point, which is of almost universal application. Turenne remarked that the man who had made no mistakes in war had not made war long. Similarly, an author who has written nothing bad has written very little. All great authors, Homer, Dante, Shakespeare, Goethe, have written what better judges than George III might well call very poor stuff, which we are often inclined to wish away. It is the price at which they gain their greatness. But there is also in most writers, even in the highest, an intermediate region, certainly not bad, and yet not quite worthy of them. Thus Tennyson, who published very little, in proportion to the mass of his work, that was actually contemptible, published a good deal that was not quite on a level with his best. It is the fashion to wish *this* also away. Edward FitzGerald, as is well known, cared for hardly anything of his friend's that appeared after the volume of 1842, and wished that practically none of it had been written. There are many others who would like to rule out most, if not all, of the *Idylls of the King*, because of a certain inadequacy, or perhaps falsity, in the treatment of the romantic material. The *Idylls*,

they say, are neither Malory nor Spenser, they are
neither medieval nor modern, but a hopeless blend of
both : Arthur is now a sort of Prince Albert, now a
myth of sense at war with soul, and now a pillage from
Geoffrey of Monmouth. Away, therefore, with the
whole farrago !

This, I conceive, is an error. Assume, for the sake
of argument, that the charges are true. None can
deny that in the *Idylls* are innumerable scattered
beauties, both of natural description and of melody,
which we could ill afford to lose. Take, as one example
out of hundreds that might be chosen :

> They sat
> Beneath a world-old yew-tree, darkening half
> The cloisters, on a gustful April morn
> That puff'd the swaying branches into smoke.

Here is a piece of observation, translated into perfect
verse : and who would throw it from him as worthless,
even though he may think the poem in which it appears
is, as a whole, an error ?

But more than this. Though the *Idylls* were in fact
all that their detractors call them, and if the multitudinous small beauties were entirely absent, true
catholicity of taste would yet welcome them with
open arms as indispensable if a fair and complete view
of the greatness of their author is to be attained. Part
of the greatness of a great man is his very littleness,
and the *abundance* of his littleness. Let any admirer,
however enthusiastic, of the volume of 1842, even
though he agrees with FitzGerald that the fifty years
afterwards were a disappointment, say whether his
idea of Tennyson would not be lowered if he had
published nothing more ? Do we not feel that the

magnitude of his production is a main element in our
conception of him ?   Do we not feel that the width and
sweep of his mind is revealed even by these comparative
failures?   Nay, do we really wish even *Queen Mary* to be
burnt like Cranmer?   I doubt if many, even of Tennyson's wildest enemies, would not retain every single
thing he wrote, except the *Promise of May* and perhaps
forty more of his nine hundred pages.   The rest may
not have *deepened* his reputation (though I am far from
admitting so much as this) but they have *enlarged* it.

It was in this sense that Dr. Johnson censured Gray,
in his strong colloquial language, as ' a barren rascal.'
He felt, perhaps without clearly realising the feeling,
that Gray, by the smallness of his production, had
prevented men from seeing the true width and
strength of his mind.   All Gray's poems will go into
sixty pages.   Another three hundred, though of imperfect work, would have deepened our sense of his true
position in literature : but it was left for his letters to
show what he really was.   Had he written more verse
—and, be it remembered, he could have written nothing really bad—the catholic reader would, while discriminating between it and the best, have taken it into
consideration and *added* it to his opinion of Gray.   It
is not the first inferior, but the actually worthless,
that compels us to *subtract* from the merit of a writer.
While it is unfair to a writer to collect and publish the
bad or unfinished work which he himself rejected, it
is only less unfair not to take into account the work
which he, in the maturity of his judgment, thought
fit to give to the world.   So to do is not merely to set
up our judgment against his—which, of all *individual*
competent judgments is probably the best—but to
make the great error of taking part for the whole.

Many other illustrations could be given. There are more plausible cases than that of Tennyson. Some would like to burn all but half a dozen poems of Coleridge, all but a hundred pages of Wordsworth, all of Byron but Matthew Arnold's selections, or perhaps even a selection from *them*. It is a huge assumption that either we, or Matthew Arnold and his like, know what is *really* the best work of these authors, or of any author. Time alone can decide, and Time, which consists of many very various times, probably never will. But even if the selection is impeccable, and has achieved the impossible task of picking out the *absolutely* good, catholic taste will nevertheless demand a sight of the rejected. Ninety and nine sheep may be lost : it will go forth and search for them. More especially will it do so if it cares for the poet as well as for the poems, and wishes to know him as, to judge by his own choice of poems, he himself wished to be known. Still oftener will it desire to have the *chance* of so knowing him.

If this is true with regard to writers, it is still truer with regard to their individual works, in which they have made a special attempt to offer a whole for our judgment. Those who would cut down *Paradise Lost* to the first three or four books, would, for the sake of banishing a few weaknesses, destroy the architectonic perfection of the scheme, and lose, besides, that sense of magnitude which, in an epic poem as in the Pyramids, is a chief element in the sublimity of the conception. The catholic taste here, once more, welcomes the less good along with the better, and finds the imperfect whole greater than the perfect part. So vast a design, even if not completely answering the ' idea ' of the designer, must, if justice is to be done, be surveyed in full. We must begin at the beginning, study

the middle, and go through to the end, from the statement of the plan through the crises, to the ' purifica-
tion of the hero.' Similarly with the *Divine Comedy*,
which, despite its completeness, and despite the
magnificence of many of its episodes, probably contains
a larger proportion not only of slightly inferior work
but of actually flat, dreary, and unprofitable passages
than any other poem of anything like comparable
greatness : theology which nothing but the style
renders tolerable, and would-be humour which we
endure only because we know sublimity is shortly to
come ; allegory which misses fire, and narrative which,
terse as it is, drags heavily. Here again the ' catholic '
reader faces his task cheerfully. Considered in themselves, these passages are nothing. But they are
part of the plan, and without them the symmetry
would be destroyed. A just criticism will accept them,
and—while refusing to call them great merely because
they are Dante's—will read them with that tempered
pleasure which their *position* permits them to arouse.

A catholic taste, then, will never allow the best to
be the enemy of the good. Exactly as, in the sense I
have indicated, a single author's place is decided not
so much by his few supreme passages as by the mass
of moderately good work, so with a whole national
literature. The merit of such a literature is to be
appraised not by the dozen greatest names, but by the
average height attained by a multitude of respectable
writers. If that average is high, the literature is great.
The rank of the Elizabethans is to be measured not by
Shakespeare, but by a mean struck through Marlowe,
Ford, Webster, Ben Jonson, and all the rest. We lose
much by not knowing the work of the minor Attic
dramatists—if indeed Eupolis, Ion, Cratinus, and the

others who so often defeated the four great poets, were minor at all. And to-day, the capability of our novel-writers is not to be summed up in a few first-rate names (which they are I leave my readers to decide) any more than the British Navy is to be weighed by Dreadnoughts only. While, of course, the decayed and obsolete vessels are to be ' scrapped,' the sound, if less powerful, crafts must be reckoned in ; and similarly the ' parity ' of British novels must be reckoned by including scores, if not hundreds, of lesser importance, which, though ' not attaining to the first three,' are portion of the total strength of the host. Supreme genius is largely a matter of accident, though it has a habit of appearing at times when a number of more or less talented people have prepared the world for it. If the normal intelligence of a nation is fairly high, it will inevitably produce a large number of literary works of more than normal distinction. Should the great accident happen, and the genius appear, he will find the path made straight for him by these lesser men, and his work— for he, like others is the creature of his time—will be much greater than it would have been but for their help and example.

Considerations like these show the danger of anthologies, which often are as inadequate representations alike of individuals and of schools, as so many quotations, torn from their context, are of books. The life of a man cannot be appreciated by a few hours of heroism or of pusillanimity ; and the author, *as* author, cannot be appreciated by a few lines, bad or good. A dozen passages of Tennyson, skilfully selected by Lockhart, made him ridiculous : another dozen might have made him appear a Shakespeare. If an anthology is to present even a feeble image of the author, it must give an *average* sample of his work : and this is practically impossible. As a rule, it tries to catch him in his Sunday suit, and looking his best. To give a *portrait* of him requires not the skill of a photographer, but the genius of a Velazquez or a Sargent : and the Velazquez who can sum up literary power in a single canvas does not exist.

The sole use of anthologies is to allure to further study. They give the best of a man in order that even his weaker work may be read with humility and patience : in order that, perceiving of what he was capable, we may be slow to despise what seems inferior.

Let us then endeavour to cultivate a catholic and generous taste ; to read widely if not voraciously, and to welcome works of all kinds and of almost every rank : to find room in our sympathies not merely for the great but for the little, not merely for the exquisite but for the rough—nay, not merely for the good but for an occasional experience of the bad. I am not sure, indeed, that if we too punctiliously reject the bad we shall not run the risk of losing some good that ought not to be missed. In every good writer there is something bad ; in most bad writers there is a little good. It is as in the parable—tares are in every field, and we cannot root them up without danger. Let both grow together until the harvest.

2 A

XX

CONCLUSION

I HAVE by no means reached the end of my subject. Every reader will be able to add titles for many chapters I have not written. He will meet a neighbour with a taste for the melodramatic, and will seek in vain in these pages for an argument with which to confute him : or he may wish to study certain remarkable changes of taste in the Elizabethan period, and find I have left them unnoticed. He may well, also, consider that several of the subjects on which I *have* written are treated inadequately, and that I have, in individual chapters as in the whole book, stopped before I have finished. But I do not know that it ought to be the aim of a writer to do his readers' thinking for them ; nor do I believe that the addition of any number of chapters would make things clearer, or convince those who belong to a different school of thought from my own—which, like a French school of poetry or painting, may all too probably turn out to consist of but a single member. I may be like the man in Horace, content with my own unshared opinions— 'populus me sibilat, at mihi plaudo.' There are times, indeed, when even this modicum of applause is denied me ; for I have difficulty in convincing myself. I repeatedly catch myself admiring one kind of writing and disliking another, with far more confidence than, on my own theory, I ought to allow. I cannot help thinking parts of Dante, two or three books of Milton, the *Epipsychidion*, or certain plays of Shakespeare, among the *absolutely* great achievements of human genius ; achievements which *everybody*, in all places and at all times, is bound to admire : and if any man does not admire them, I am all but irresistibly compelled to think his taste *absolutely* bad. So firm is my opinion, that if that of the whole world were against me, it would find me *impavidum* and *tenacem propositi.* Nor does my confidence always rest on knowledge. I profess to no deep acquaintance with painting or music ; but no expert, however superior in technical skill I may confess him to be, will ever convince me that Rembrandt is not one of the greatest of painters, or that Beethoven is not one of the greatest of musicians. I am pleased, but not greatly strengthened in my belief, when I do find experts agreeing with me. My conviction is based on something quite other than reasoning : it is an instantaneous perception that certain things respond to me. That others hear the same response, gives me the sense of companionship, but does not strengthen the perception of the beauty.

Similarly, I am sure, in this same intuitive fashion, that certain of the ' tastes ' I have discussed in these chapters are bad, and not relatively bad only : I feel that no one *ought* to have them, almost precisely as I feel that no one ought to be miserly, gluttonous, or uncharitable. There are some very popular novels, for instance, which I am certain deserve total oblivion rather than popularity ; and nothing will shake that conviction. Yet at the same time I am quite conscious that it is a personal conviction, due to my personal idiosyncrasies, and that it is very probably without weight for anyone else. I have certain very strong physical dislikes, which few of my friends share : and these intellectual dislikes are of a similar kind. If other people enjoy these novels, let them have their enjoyment. No reasoning will convince them, for it is not a matter of reasoning at all : it depends on character, surroundings, heredity, and many other things which reasoning cannot touch. Time, indeed, may and does alter these likings ; but over time I have no control. If a man's tastes ever appear to be changed by argument, it will be found, I think, that the change is due not to reasoning, but to authority—that is, to a tendency to submissiveness or hero-worship *in the man himself*. Somebody whom he admires declares a preference or a dislike : the man, being by nature a follower, follows his leader like a clansman taking up the cause of his chief. His not to reason why ; though he often provides himself with plausibilities that look like reasons. Here I am in full agreement with one of the most dogmatic of critics, and one who never hesitated to fling accusations of stupidity against any who happened to cross him. ' In all criticism,' says Swinburne, ' the merely personal element of the critic, the natural atmosphere in which his mind or his insight works and uses its faculties of appreciation is the first and last thing to be taken into account.' Let me, in fact, thoroughly know a man, and I will tell you how he will react to a book. If the man's disposition, up-bringing, and way of life are somewhat like my own, he will think of the book somewhat as I do. Conversely, if you can get at a man's *permanent* and fixed opinion of a book (a very difficult achievement, I confess) you can form a very fair conjecture as to his life and character. It has been often said that no man can appreciate poetry unless he is something of a poet himself. If then I discover that he appreciates Milton or Shelley, I gather with confidence that there is something of Milton or Shelley in him. Give me, said Fletcher of Saltoun, a man to make a people's songs, and I care not who makes its laws. Tell me, I add, the songs a person or a nation likes, and I will make a good guess as to the character of the nation or the person. But if a man has not already his point in common with Milton or Shelley, you cannot put it there : and wise experience will save itself the vain labour of trying to insert it.

Beauty, like colour and other qualities—the old philosophers used to limit the statement to the so-called ' secondary ' qualities, but the same thing is true of the ' primaries '—is not something inherent in the thing, but is conferred on it by the percipient. It depends, as has often been shown, and by no one more clearly than by that sound thinker Payne Knight, in his argument against Burke and Alison, on a law which has nothing to do with the thing, but everything to do with ourselves, the Law of Association of Ideas. Even Alison assigns a large part in it to Imagination, which, even if it be not reduced to Association, is yet in us, and not in the thing. If this be so, it is obviously idle to expect any approach to unanimity of opinion as to beauty or ugliness. Ruskin's attempt to identify æsthetics with ethics carries us but little further ; for men's ethical ideas vary as much as their æsthetics. There are, it is true, cases where a whole community may be more or less in agreement as to the beauty or ugliness of an action, a picture, a statue, or a poem. This is because the whole community has, by its contemporaneousness and similarity of circumstance, formed similar associations, pleasurable or the reverse, with the actions, sights, forms, or sounds. But change the community and the place, while retaining the thing ; and the sounds, sights, thoughts, may from agreeable become unpleasant, or *vice versa*, because the associations have unaltered : where then is the beauty or the ugliness ? Time acts like place : lines once pleasing to Englishmen cease to please their English descendants, and the change may be due to the greatest or to the most trivial causes. Beauty is like riches : it has wings and flies away. It is—to alter the figure—skin-deep in words as in faces ; and time too often writes wrinkles on its brow.

In all this there may, at first sight, seem to be the grossest inconsistency. Asserting the relativity of beauty, how can I retain any confidence in my own conviction that certain poems are beautiful when other men find no beauty in them ? Can a mere evanescent entity, a phantom as various as Virgil's Fame, be that divine essence which inspired a Shelley to his endless search, and which a Bridges loved, sought, and adored ? If you could have convinced Keats that John Doe's or Richard Roe's idea of beauty was as sound as his own, would he have called it a joy for ever ? And how can I, to whom beauty *is* this evanescent and changeful something or other, yet feel, when I light on a line of Milton or Chaucer, that I have found a reality, presented to me as it were from without ? I seem, when such visions are vouchsafed to me, as if I had for the moment penetrated into Plato's absolute world of real Being, and received from it a direct and infallible message : as if I had gone hand in hand with Spenser to the ' quick forge ' of the world's great work-master, who fashioned things ' as comely as he could.' We can hardly help fancying, at such moments, that we have discovered a treasure actually existing, independent of ourselves, which was there before we saw it, and will remain there when we have departed. We fancy that the poet or the painter has *created* the beautiful thing, and that all we have done is to perceive and appreciate it. How is it possible, after such an experience, to maintain that John Doe, making *his* discovery, has as much right to rejoice in it as we in ours?

The inconsistency, however, is rather apparent than real. If we ourselves did not make beauty, the instantaneous recognition of it would be impossible; and it is our own share in its creation that causes our assured reliance on our impressions. When Keats recognises beauty, and thinks he is responding to it, how can he respond to it unless there is an idea of beauty already present in his mind, and in fact part and parcel of himself? He is certain, and instantaneously certain, that he has made a discovery, because by descent, by training, and by circumstances, he has this idea there, waiting, expectant. A long course of pleasurable associations has made him receptive to this particular impression. Another course of associations would have made him reject this impression, and welcome another: and another man, whose associations are different, inevitably receives the impression in a different manner. Even if he uses the same word to describe it, and calls it 'beauty,' he must receive it in his own *degree*, which may well be lower, weaker, or even entirely other than that in which Keats receives it. And, if Keats is a reasoner as well as a poet, he will admit this, and will not expect all other men to share his feelings when presented with this particular object.

None the less he cannot doubt his own impressions, for they are his own. As well tell him, in ultra-Stoic fashion, that he does not feel pain when his hand touches the fire, as tell him that he does not feel pleasure, and feel it instantaneously, when he is brought into contact with 'beauty.' Yet there is nothing painful in the fire itself : the feeling is entirely ours : it is, in the common phrase, subjective. And Keats will allow this. He will allow, as he must allow, that men are sensitive to the pain of heat in very different degrees, and that any man can accustom himself to enduring a temperature which at first seemed intolerable ; that a Belial, after centuries of hell, may 'inured, not feel' the torments. But Keats knows his own pain, and cannot help knowing it. He knows also his own ecstasy when he lights on a Grecian urn or hears the song of the nightingale. 'Pleasure *ever* is at home' ; and nothing will persuade him either that he has it not or that he ought not to have it. But this is far from proving that beauty, any more than pain, has an 'objective' existence, or that the same thing 'ought' to produce in all men a sense of beauty or of ugliness. It does not even prove that men ought to be affected by beauty or ugliness as Keats was, but in measures proportioned to their less powerful sensibilities. Men may be affected by the same object in diametrically *opposite* ways, and one man may quite sincerely detest what another enthusiastically admires. We see this even in the moral world, in which what strikes one man as a beautiful trait of character often arouses repulsion in another. It is pretty certain, for instance, that to the ancient Greeks the Christian virtue of humility would have appeared as a vice—and incidentally, in accordance with their general ideas,

as therefore ' ugly.' It would be interesting to see
what Aristotle would have thought of many of the self-
suppressing saints of the Middle Ages, or what St.
Francis would have thought of Aristotle's high-
souled man, ' who thinks himself worthy of great things,
being indeed worthy.'

It will thus be seen that I desire to avoid dogmatising
even in opposing dogmatism. It is of extreme importance to recognise not merely the relativity of taste,
but what one may call its absoluteness in reference to
a particular individual at a particular time. The
taste, *as* taste, is a very real thing in everybody. Here
I may refer back to the original physical associations
of the word. As there must be causes, though they
are so obscure that no one has yet analysed them, why
one man receives delight from a food which nauseates
another, so there must be causes why the same poem,
the same painting, the same type of character, attract
me and repel my neighbour. These, however, also
defy analysis : we must be content to accept the emotions as we find them. And yet we shall endeavour
not to reduce one whole mentality to chaos. We shall
trust ourselves, as we trust our own eyes and ears :
while on the other hand, unless we wish to reduce our
whole social life to chaos, we shall be willing to allow
others to trust themselves. Any form of compulsion,
moral or physical, is useless and ridiculous. Men
ordered to admire would but despise the more vigorously. They would feel, like Mammon, that hell
itself is no worse than a heaven in which they had
against their will to celebrate the deity with warbled
hymns, and sing to the godhead forced hallelujahs.
' How wearisome eternity so spent, and worship paid
to whom we hate ! ' Nor indeed is it easy to believe

2 A *

that the Divinity himself would sincerely welcome an adoration of this kind. Worship must be spontaneous or it is nothing. It is better to bow down in the house of a false god sincerely than hypocritically and slavishly to prostrate oneself to the true.

Again, there is no reason to think that the enormous variety of tastes, exhibited even in a single community, and much more on the great stage of the world, is undesirable. There may be spheres in which it is well to secure unity ; but that of æsthetics is not one of them. It is not even, perhaps, always undesirable that the little kingdom of the individual mind should entertain a host of jostling and almost mutually exclusive tastes at the same time. A little anarchy *there* may not be altogether out of place, as it certainly always exists. There are critics, apparently, who, to judge by the energy of their anathemas and the vigour of their propagandism, would constrain everybody to agree with them ; teachers who wish children often to admire *Lycidas ;* æsthetes who want all others to shudder at the wallpaper that frets *them ;* 'high-brows' who, like the Puritans of old, would hedge the pleasures of all within the narrow bounds of their own. The attempt is vain. They do not succeed in imposing uniformity even on themselves : we do not study them long before we discover inconsistencies and contradictions in their own views : with others their success is still less, and probably it is fortunate that it is so. Their opinions may be right—or some of them— but we do not wish them to be universally held : and universally held they never will be. Until you can educate all people in exactly the same way, provide them, as the House of Hapsburg was provided, with monotonously similar ancestors, and give them pre-

cisely the same surroundings from youth up—nor even
then—will anything like uniformity of taste be attained.
Even in the Hapsburg family a freak archduke occasionally arose, with views of his own. He was generally
assassinated, either by himself or by others : but the
freaks reappeared from time to time. And a drab
world it would be if uniformity *was* attained—a world
with etiquette instead of thought, and with convention instead of principle. It is conceivable that by
mechanical contrivance we may largely get rid of the
human services which are now a necessity, that Robots
may dress us as Marie Antoinette was dressed by her
ladies-in-waiting, according to rigid rule and in fixed
order, and that the classes of society may be brought
to a level which will be rightly called dead : but few
can devoutly wish for a consummation in which a
Socialism gone mad shall, like Love and Death, make
all distinctions void, and turn the world into one immense ant-hill. As things are, and as they must for
long continue to be, classes will remain, and the
members of the various strata will on the whole
enjoy different intellectual entertainments. What one
stratum enjoys will be good for that stratum ; what
another, for that other. Nor is this the only way in
which what is inferior, or even ' bad,' may have its
use. Some of those tastes which I have unhesitatingly
dubbed bad, and bad, when considered alone, I still
think they are, may form an interesting variation in
the huge pattern of universal opinion, and may not
unjustly be regarded as good in their time and place.

Eternally changeless perfection becomes imperfec-
tion. There are human beings whom it is little
pleasure to see ; but their plainness adds to the pleasure
with which we scan the next ' beautiful ' face that

catches our glance : and I for one have no desire that everybody should be handsome : if indeed a world in which everybody was handsome would not be *ipso facto* denuded of handsomeness. Comparison may be odious, but it is a necessary factor in our sense of beauty. Similarly, I have no desire that every book I read should be one I can call good : my enjoyment of good books would be so much the less keen. I trust also that the general public feels in the same way : for it is the object of this work to assist the public to enjoy good literature, and if that object can be attained only by a comparison between this work and good ones, let it be thus attained. But let not all books be ' good.' Let there be some for inferior minds. A travelled man, who has seen the cities and known the manners of many people, is often fretted by the relative monotony of his countrymen's characters and opinions when he returns to his native land. Much more should we be fretted if we found our neighbours admiring, with correct and regulated taste, exactly what we admire. Variety is itself a good, but it can be gained only by admitting some specimens of the less good or even of the actually bad.

Literary taste, then, is found to be like all other kinds of taste, a matter for the individual, conditioned by the personality of the percipient. There are, of course, some points in a book which may be marked as, so to speak, more or less absolute. Inaccuracy of any sort—poverty of description, failure to give an approximately full account, mistakes as to facts and dates, want of balance and proportion, inconsistency in the characters, improbability in a work purporting to be realistic—all these defects, and a score of others, may contribute to an unfavourable judgment—though here again there is an extraordinary difference in the way they react on various minds. On some men, for instance, grammatical errors produce a much stronger effect of revulsion than on others; and a want of historical perspective will inevitably annoy a man with the requisite knowledge and picturesque power more than a man without them. Some will disregard a want of proportion in the whole if there is a liveliness and vigour in the parts; others will demand construction as the first essential. Roughly, however, it may be laid down that all competent critics will reject books in which obvious faults like these are prominent. But, as a rule, the critic will react to a work according to his own peculiar personality : if he is such, by nature and nurture, as to sympathise with the work, sympathise he must, and instantaneously. He will then proceed to disguise, from his readers and from himself, that his judgment is thus conditioned; and will find ' reasons ' for his decisions. But the reader must endeavour not to be deceived. He in his turn must remember that the critic is a single human being, with a definite and formed character which must inevitably accept books of a certain kind in a certain manner. He must be ever discounting, and allowing for the personal equation. If the critic is wise, he will confine himself, in the main, to a description of what the book is, and if he ventures on a verdict, will honestly confess that it is after all only his own. He may, like an historian summing up the character of one of his heroes, present his personal view; but enough facts must be given to enable the reader to criticise the criticism. ' This,' he will say by implication, ' is the way the book strikes *me* ; but you will see, by the description of it which I have provided, that it may well strike *you* very differently.'

As to the general public, it must never be forgotten that a sound taste is like happiness, and cannot be gained by a direct search. To parody a line of Pope's, it was a demon, wishing to ruin Sir Visto, that whispered to him, ' Visto, *have* a taste.' Happiness is to be reached solely by the steady pursuit of virtue ; and true taste cannot be reached but in the same manner. Being a function of the whole man, it grows with the man's growth and improves with his improvement. Enlarge his mind by travel, by education, by intercourse with his superiors in knowledge or ability, and you enlarge his taste. But it is useless to take him through a course of æsthetics—except so far as this, being itself a means of mental training, tends to enlarge his *general* powers. It is useless to take a painting or a poem and bid him admire this or despise that. The poem or the painting must be set before him and *explained* with perfect detachment, that it may make its own impression on the man. The contemplation of it will insensibly fall in with the rest of his mental experiences, and contribute its share to his total personality. A man thinks and feels not with one portion of himself, but with his *all :* and to make him think and feel aright, you must make *him* right. As was perceived very early in the study of philosophy, ' the mind is all in the whole, and all in every part ' : and what a man's whole mind is, that it will be when brought to bear on the smallest object. When a child reads a poem, it comes to it with the tiny accumulations of seven or eight years : when a man reads the poem, he comes to it with the accumulations of forty or fifty. If those accumulations have been of the right kind, the poem will be rightly received ; and not otherwise.

To ' improve ' public taste, then, the teachers of the public must put into practice, to a different end, the maxims of Polonius, and, ' with windlasses and with assays of bias, by indirections find directions out.' They must see to it that education proceeds gradually, continuously, and in the true path, to its end, the development of character. And I am inclined to think that, though we are still far from perfection, we are nearer to the right path now than we have ever been before. If I were writing an essay in the ' To-Day and To-Morrow ' series—to be entitled *Sir Visto, or the Future of Taste*—I think I should take on the whole a hopeful view. Taste, I repeat, being nothing but the application of the whole man to a certain object that has form, size, proportion, and content, must alter when the man finds alteration, and bend with the remover to remove : and these changes or removes seem to me to show at present signs of being in the right direction. The slow elevation of the general standard of culture has, despite many lapses, already improved literary and artistic taste. More books are now published, in proportion to population, than ever before ; and it is pretty certain they would not be published if they did not sell. Many of them are poor enough, but a book must be poor indeed, if it does not teach something. The testimony of public librarians is, I think, in the main, to the effect that the number of sound books taken out has increased, is increasing, and gives no sign of being diminished. As better books are asked for, better will be provided : and every good book read has its influence in improving the taste of its reader. It is likely, therefore, that the upward movement will go on with accelerating force. Mechanical inventions have not always been an æsthetic advantage ; but there are some recent ones which I need not specify that have unquestionably been used well. Here we must beware of the historical illusion. In studying accounts of earlier times, one is often led to fancy that their culture was higher than our own. Such a work as Boswell's *Life of Johnson*, for example, makes one imagine that everybody read, and read well. This, however, is simply because it is a book about a reader, and about a man, therefore, whose friends were readers. We fancy everybody was cultured because it is a story of culture. This is the old fallacy, long ago pointed out and illustrated by Bacon. It is as if we were to think, because the Roman or Greek buildings which have survived are so much better than most of ours, that the cottage of Philemon and Baucis was better than our cottages. If there is a Boswell to-day taking notes on a Johnson, he will not perhaps find a Burke or a Reynolds among his subjects, but he will have a more cultivated *set* to write about than even that which gathered at Mr. Thrale's table ; and still greater will the advance appear if an artisan company of to-day be compared with an artisan company of 1830. Greater still will be the advance from 1930 to 2030.

Such hesitation as I feel in making this sanguine prophecy arises from the very multitude of opportunities for improvement, and from the ease with which books may be obtained. To make things easy is too often to lead to their neglect, while difficulties not only sometimes act as a spur, but make the end, when attained, more valued. All my readers can provide examples of this truth. I will give one founded on my own knowledge. In the 1850's, before the Act for compulsory education, in a lonely part of Durham, far removed from libraries and with the public-house as the only club-room, a band of determined students gathered regularly together to read Watts on the Mind, Locke on the Understanding, and Dugald Stewart. Copies were bought by continued and combined effort, and perused and discussed with a vigour proportioned to the trouble it had taken to get them. Finally, no fewer than ten copies of so abstruse a book as Mansel's *Limits of Religious Thought* were purchased, and the Dean's arguments were dissected as freely, if not as profoundly, as by John Stuart Mill himself. I have my doubts as to whether such a club could easily be found to-day—and partly for the very reason that books can be obtained without the expense and trouble that these men had to face. ' Too light winning,' in the words of Prospero, ' has made the prize light.'

Yet I shall continue to hope. Eager and resolute men will not be deterred from a quest because it is an easy one. Nor indeed will it ever be easy. When you have obtained your book, whether with little labour and expense or with much, you have still to master it ; and that is never a light task if the book be worthy. To quote again a saying that can never be quoted too often, ' all things excellent are as difficult as they are rare.' And I have still sufficient faith in my countrymen to believe that the way to gain their most enthusiastic co-operation is to tell them that the toil of achievement will be great, but that the end is worthy of it.